ALLIED FIGHTER ACES

The Air Combat Tactics and Techniques of World War II

MIKE SPICK

GREENHILL BOOKS, LONDON
STACKPOLE BOOKS, PENNSYLVANIA

Allied Fighter Aces
First published 1997 by Greenhill Books
Lionel Leventhal Limited, Park House, 1 Russell Gardens
London NW11 9NN
and
Stackpole Books, 5067 Ritter Road, Mechanicsburg
PA 17055, USA

British Library Cataloguing in Publication Data
Spick, Mike
Allied fighter aces: the air combat tactics and techniques of World War II
1. World War, 1939-1945 – Aerial operations
I. Title
940.5'44

ISBN 1-85367-282-3

Library of Congress Cataloging-in-Publication Data
Spick, Mike
Allied fighter aces: the air combat tactics and techniques of
World War II/by Mike Spick
p.   cm.
ISBN 1-85367-282-3
1. World War, 1939-1945 – Aerial operations. 2. Strategy
I. Title
D785.S69 1997
940.54'4--dc21   97-19006
CIP

Typeset by Ronset, Blackburn, Lancashire
Printed and bound in Great Britain
by Creative Print and Design (Wales), Ebbw Vale

CONTENTS

ILLUSTRATIONS

Figures		*Page*

PREFACE

In 1939, world democracy was in a pitiable state. The Geneva-based League of Nations had signally failed to impose any restraint on the emergent Fascist states. A bloody civil war had left Franco in control of a shattered Spain. Mussolini's Italy had conquered Abyssinia, notwithstanding widespread international condemnation, while Hitler's Germany had annexed first Austria, and then the Sudetenland area of Czechoslovakia. Stretching across the vast land-mass from Poland to the Pacific, the Soviet Union was suffering horrendous purges under Stalin, who also harboured territorial ambitions towards Finland. In the far east, Japanese armies occupied Korea and ravaged China. To the west, the United States of America, the sleeping giant, pursued a policy of non-intervention at best, isolationism at worst. A world war was inevitable; the charge was set, the powder train laid. All that was needed was a spark. This was duly provided on 1 September 1939 when Germany, having first signed a non-aggression pact with the Soviet Union, invaded Poland.

Pre-war, it was widely accepted that air power would assume a greater importance than it had in the 1914–18 conflict, but to what degree was not known for certain. In the event air power was critical to ultimate victory. It hamstrung armies in the field; reduced war-making capacity at home; and reduced naval forces to near impotence. But before any of this could be done, air superiority had to be gained. Without air superiority, air forces were ineffective in the close air support role; with it, armies were disadvantaged, production was curtailed, and naval units became vulnerable.

Air superiority was the task of the fighter, and fighters determined the eventual outcome of the entire war. In Western Europe, North Africa, the Mediterranean, the Far East and the Pacific, Allied fighters held the ring when all seemed lost on the ground. Having stemmed the tide, they then led the way back to eventual victory.

9

'Allied' is defined as those air forces which fought against the Axis powers (Germany, Italy, and Japan), but not for or in alliance with them. This eliminates the Russians, who became allied to the West by default after Operation *Barbarossa* in June 1941; those Italians who switched sides after the capitulation in 1943; the many Eastern European nations which changed sides when it became obvious that Germany was losing the war; and most important of all, the French, many of whom elected to go to Russia to fly with the Normandie–Niemen Regiment rather than serve with the British and Americans. This hardly qualifies them (or the Russians) as *bona fide* Allies. Top-scoring French pilot Marcel Albert (23 victories) flew with this unit. The Vichy French served to muddy the waters still more. The classic example was Pierre LeGloan, who, flying a Dewoitine D.520, was credited with three Italian BR.20 bombers and four CR.42 fighters in the summer of 1940. Transferred to Syria, he claimed seven victories over British aircraft for the Vichy regime before returning to Algeria, where he flew against British and American forces in 1942. He was killed during the following year flying an Airacobra. He was far from being the only pilot to fight on both sides.

Many thousands of fighter pilots, of many nations, flew and fought and died in aircraft bearing the roundel of the British and Commonwealth air forces, or the white star of the USAAF and USN. Of these, a mere handful became famous. About five percent of fighter pilots accounted for roughly forty percent of all aerial victories. These were the aces.

The value of the fighter aces was incalculable. Throughout recorded history, mankind has needed heroes as an inspiration and an example, and this, together with leadership and tuition, the aces provided in full measure. Their effect on morale and capability was out of all proportion to their purely material achievements. And this was only within their units. At home too, the population was greatly heartened and encouraged by their deeds. This is their story.

The question of what singles out the fighter ace from any other successful fighting man of the same period is largely a matter of visibility. Firstly, air fighting has many of the attributes of gladiatorial combat. Rarely is it really a one versus one encounter, but it often seems that way, giving the fighter pilot the mantle of the old-time single-combat champion. Secondly, not only can the deeds be seen, often by watchers on the ground as well as actual participants, but they can be counted. Even as a batsman in cricket is acclaimed for the number of runs he scores, or a baseball player for his home runs, so a fighter pilot is judged by his victory score.

It mattered little that the humble machine-gunner on the ground may have accounted for far more of the enemy than the average fighter ace; his deeds were comparatively invisible. There was less kudos—perhaps rightly so—for hiding in a trench and spraying anonymous death across the battlefield than there was for leaping into the sky in a fighting machine to tackle the enemy face to face. In a nutshell, the name of the game was glamour.

The term ace was first adopted by the French in the First World War, using a five-victory qualification. By contrast, the British decried the ace system as bad for morale. It was never officially adopted by the British, although this did not prevent successful pilots being decorated, and lionised while on home leave. Consequently, when in 1939 the world was once again plunged into war the ace tradition was already there, with records waiting to be broken.

Mike Spick

PROLOGUE

Easing gently out of my dive, watching my graceful target flying backwards towards me, larger and larger in my gun-sight. Quick search in all directions: lots of (Ju) 88s but no enemy fighters. Target's wings overlapping my windscreen—I fire. A flash and a burst of flame from his port engine. He rears up in front of me, steep turning left. Dash the man! Deflection inside his turn. Can only just do it. Fire again. He's swerving to the right. Try for his starboard engine. Fire and fire again.

Black smoke puffs on my left wing; balls of orange fire flashing past my cockpit, crackling in my ears. I plunge left, looking back over my left shoulder, for who the hell's hitting me? Nothing there—just an 88 hanging behind my tail. Can't be him. Swerve back again. My own 88 has drawn away a bit; a pretty thing splaying two plumes of smoke that widen as they sweep back towards me, very pale machine and very close to the water. I wonder if it's going to crash?

109s! Two, head-on views, diving from my left, blinking with light. Curling blue tracers strand about me as I turn towards them. A third—got my sight on him for an instant before he went under my nose. Still turning hard left... Two more 109s, from the right this time. Turn in towards them. Curl down on the last one. Can't turn sharply enough. Damn the helmet! Another 109 below me. Drop onto his tail. I'll get him all right. A gigantic shape, all rivets and oil streaks, the underside of a Messerschmitt, blots out the sky! Gone. But I'm still on a 109's tail, it's right there in front of me, pointing very slightly downwards. My aircraft shudders and shudders and shudders and shudders as I pour bullets and shells into it. It bursts with black smoke and topples over sideways.

More 109s from the right. Turn. My Spitfire vibrates violently and the sea changes places with the sky. I'm spinning. Opposite rudder and stick forwards—I'm level again. Two more from the right... Explosion from my engine—smoke bursting back into the cockpit. Upside down, spinning again... Controls don't answer. All gone slack. Can't stop spinning—Spitfire burning... out of control! Too low to bale out? Might just make it.

Flight Lieutenant Denis Barnham, No 601 Squadron

For this action over Malta on 21 April 1942, Barnham was awarded a Junkers Ju 88 probably destroyed and a Messerschmitt Bf 109 damaged. He recovered control of his damaged Spitfire Vc, and, with a dead engine, made a successful if heavy wheels-up landing on Halfar airfield.

12

There are many points of interest about this particular combat. Firstly, Barnham was flying without a wingman to guard his tail and give warning of attacking enemy fighters. While this was hardly recommended, in the desperate days of Malta's greatest peril it was frequently unavoidable.

Secondly, Barnham was heavily outnumbered—also a frequent occurrence over Malta at this time—but survived, albeit by the skin of his teeth, while giving rather more than he received. Orders at this time made bombers the priority target, avoiding combat with enemy fighters where possible. But it very rarely was. And once embroiled with them, it became a desperate defensive battle for survival.

Prior to his arrival on Malta the day before, Barnham had gained considerable combat experience, flying fighter sweeps and escorts over Occupied Europe. Whilst he had only rarely fired his guns on these missions, and his total score was a single FW 190A confirmed destroyed, he had learned to see other aircraft in the air. This last may sound terribly obvious, but in fact it was extremely difficult, and demanded constant practice. A distant dot could become an enemy fighter in an attacking position in a twinkling of the eye. Seeing enemy aircraft at a distance was a skill that many young fighter pilots did not live long enough to learn.

Another lesson that Barnham already knew was to get in close before shooting. His initial attack, on a Junkers Ju 88, clearly demonstrated this. Not only did its wings overlap the gunsight ring, but his windscreen also, while he was able, and cool enough, to hit each engine in turn; something that could only be done at short range.

Shooting at a manoeuvring target takes 100 percent concentration, and while doing so, it is impossible to keep any sort of lookout. That Barnham had earlier checked the area for enemy fighters and seen none, merely emphasises the rapidity with which an attacking fighter could close the range to a firing position. The fact that he was flying alone did nothing to help matters.

To defeat the fighter attacks, Barnham turned into them. This was standard procedure. Turning away (the instinctive reaction) reduced deflection, giving an opponent an easier shot. Turning into an attack increased deflection rapidly, compounding the assailant's aiming problems. In fact, if the turn was begun early enough, it could be converted into a head-on firing pass. The final consideration was that turning into an attack was a fairly aggressive move which just might deter a half-hearted opponent, whereas turning away looked like an attempt to

13

disengage without a fight, thereby encouraging a less determined enemy.

The final, less obvious point in this combat, is that hard manoeuvring increases aerodynamic drag, frequently to the point where it exceeds the power output of the engine. In consequence, the fighter bleeds off energy. While this can be minimised by trading altitude for speed, there are limits to what can be achieved, leading to the time-honoured saying 'out of airspeed, altitude, and ideas!' As energy decreases, manoeuvre capability is lost.

After several hard defensive breaks, this happened to Denis Barnham's Spitfire, and three times he pushed it over the edge into the realms of lost control. His description of the controls having gone slack probably indicates that he was in an inverted flat spin. But as height was lost, speed was regained, and the movement of air over the flying surfaces restored control once more. It was also a wonderful demonstration of the forgiving nature of the Spitfire; few if any other of the fighters of the era could have recovered so easily.

Denis Barnham survived the war. His final score was five confirmed destroyed; one shared; one probable; and one damaged. He was one of the many unsung heroes of the air war, who did so much to win it by giving just that bit better than they got.

The Fighter Ace

By definition, a fighter ace is a pilot who has destroyed at least five enemy aircraft in air combat. Barely one in every 20 reached this seemingly modest total, while of these, less than half went on to reach double figures. Of the rest, roughly 50 percent failed to score.

As the saying goes: success has many fathers, failure is an orphan. Success in any field of human endeavour is commonly ascribed to a combination of hard work, natural ability, and luck. Fighter combat differs from other activities only in that the penalty for failure tends to be more severe, which puts a premium on courage, or, more correctly, self-control. Let us take each attribute in turn.

Hard work is essential. As fighter combat is an extremely competitive activity, the pilot must master his trade if he wishes to survive. This involves far more than mastery of his aircraft in the air. A sound knowledge of tactics is essential, backed by intensive practice, preferably under peacetime conditions. This in turn helps to build up judgement of space and time and the ability to know what will work most of the time in most situations—and mental preparation is as important as physical.

Natural ability is next, and this takes two forms: part physical, part mental. On the physical side, good co-ordination, fast reflexes, and, above all, first-class vision are needed. The first pilot to sight the enemy gains an immeasurable advantage, whether in an attacking or defending position, although there have been rare exceptions. Both Mannock in the First World War and Galland in the Second had defective vision in one eye, but this does not seem to have handicapped them. Each of them probably saw more with his single good eye than most men did with two.

Mental ability covers the field of alertness, self-control, and aggression. The author has yet to meet a wartime fighter pilot who lacks alertness, but it must be remembered that by definition, the author has only met survivors. Self-control covers the mastery of fear and the tempering of aggression. All pilots felt fear, but what really counted was the ability to control it, and channel it into positive action. Aggression too had to be channelled.

The 'fangs out, hair on fire' pilot often ran up a score quite quickly before eventually succumbing. It was all too easy to reach the point of no return; a situation from which there was no escape. What was needed was a balance between an attacking mind-set, and the ability to recognise when a situation was getting beyond control—'He who fights and runs away', etc. But what really set aces apart from their fellows was a certain instinctive flair.

In fighter versus fighter combat, the dominant element was surprise. Statistically, in four out of every five air combat victories the victor achieved a position of advantage before the victim became aware that he was under attack. This statement has often been misunderstood. It does not mean that the victim was shot down or even fired at, before he became aware of his assailant, although this did happen in many cases. It is simply that the attacker had reached unseen a position of advantage that was difficult, although not necessarily impossible, to counter.

The aces had a particular quality of alertness which made them difficult to surprise, known in modern times as situational awareness, or SA. It was often coupled with an awareness of time and space; how long it would take an adversary to reach a particular position, and precisely what countermoves could be made in that time. We shall be seeing examples of this in later chapters. But the main value of SA was in enabling a pilot to survive an initial onslaught.

Survival was critical. A fighter pilot had to survive long enough to build up a score, and against determined opposition this was easier said

15

than done. Firstly, he had to learn to see what was going on around him in the air. Secondly, he had to be able to react correctly to counter the threat, then turn the tables by converting a defensive position into a neutral or attacking one. This had to be automatic, as there was little time to think, to weigh, to assess.

Finally an element of chance was involved, both in survival and in building a score. In the former, it was impossible for even the most gifted pilot to keep track of events in a really large multi-bogey dogfight, and this left him vulnerable, unable to guard against a lucky shot. Ideally he tried to keep the situation under control, but often the tactical needs of the moment prevented this.

Chance also played a considerable part in building a score. To begin with, the pilot had to operate in a scenario which provided him with an adequate number of opportunities. This was not always the case. In some theatres at certain times, it was not unknown for RAF and USAAF fighter pilots to fly a complete tour of operations without once seeing an enemy aeroplane in the air. Others flew a full tour without ever managing to bring their sights to bear.

In the Second World War, opportunities were far greater in some theatres than others, notably in defensive actions such as the Battle of Britain and the defence of Malta, in which the majority of RAF aces built up impressive scores, while achieving little in the later, offensive stages of the war, in which the heavily outnumbered Axis forces offered far fewer targets.

By comparison, the scores of the *Luftwaffe 'Experten'* far exceeded those of the Allied aces, but this was a question of far greater opportunity, rather than superior aircraft or flying skills. The *Experten* tended to fly far more missions than their Allied counterparts—they were kept in action continuously, whereas the Allied pilots were frequently rested. In addition, during the period when the Allies greatly outnumbered their opponents, many fighter units flew attack missions almost exclusively, with little chance of air combat. Many Allied air aces flew a second, or even a third tour of operations with attack squadrons, without adding to their scores.

Flying and Marksmanship

The ability to fly a fighter to its absolute limits was important for survival, but less so when attacking, when marksmanship became far more important. As Battle of Britain ace Al Deere (17 confirmed destroyed) commented long after the war: 'In the end, it comes down to being able to shoot. I was an above average pilot, but not a good shot, so the only way I could succeed was to get closer than the next chap. Johnnie Johnson (the RAF top-scorer, 34 confirmed destroyed) was a pretty good, average pilot, but an excellent shot.'

Deere fought mainly on the defensive, with the majority of his victories over Dunkirk and during the Battle of Britain. When on the offensive in 1941/2, he did less well. By contrast, all Johnnie Johnson's victories were scored on the offensive. While Deere was noted for a series of hair's-breadth escapes, Johnson's aircraft was hit only once in combat.

Top American ace Dick Bong flew mainly on the offensive. In two years, he opened fire at 88 Japanese aircraft, scored hits on 58 of them, and was credited with 40 victories. His record is comparable with that of Johnson, who scored hits on 59 German aircraft, of which 41 went down. Seven of these were shared victories.

PRE-WAR ALLIED AIR POWER

The Royal Air Force

The widely-held belief that the First World War had been 'a war to end all wars' saw the mighty Royal Air Force reduced to a rump within a year of hostilities ending. From 22,647 aircraft of all types, it was reduced to barely 1,000 machines; and from 188 operational squadrons to a mere 25. Of these, many front-line units were deployed overseas in the 'flying policeman' role, leaving few for the defence of the realm. In fact, at one point in 1920 British air defence consisted of a single squadron of Sopwith Snipes. Following this, the existence of the RAF as an independent force was threatened, both the army and the navy wanting to resume control of their own air units. Fortunately this trend was successfully resisted, but it was a close run thing.

The source of the trouble was the time-honoured, difficult question, still relevant today following the dissolution of the Soviet Union: 'Where is the threat?' Then as now, a credible threat to British air space did not exist. It therefore became necessary to invent one. Following the end of the Great War, France had maintained *l'Armée de l'Air* at a much higher level of strength than Britain's RAF. Much has since been made of France as the historical enemy, and Germany as a traditional ally, but it

17

is doubtful whether anyone took a French threat seriously. It was simply the only one in sight. To this end, early documents illustrating the 'Fighting Area Attacks' (for which see below) showed recognisably French aircraft as targets, while most of the RAF fighter airfields established during this period covered southern England, and were placed to repel an attack from across the English Channel.

In 1923, the 'Ten Year Rule' was introduced, which in effect laid down that any major threat would be detectable ten years beforehand, and that this would give adequate time to rearm. Like all political theories, it was arrant rubbish, but it seriously hampered the build-up of British fighter defences. Financial constraints meanwhile held back advances in technology. Only the Government-backed attempt to win the Schneider Trophy for Britain in perpetuity had ensured a lead in aerodynamic and propulsion design.

Not until 1932, when Adolf Hitler's National Socialist party gained power in Germany, did a real threat begin to emerge. With this, the RAF initiated a programme of expansion, not only for the regular service, but also for the 'week-end fliers' of the Auxiliary Air Force, and by the formation of the Volunteer Reserve. In the event of war, these could be rapidly mobilised and absorbed into the main force. To meet the demand for aircrew, the flying training organisation was also considerably expanded.

RAF doctrine in those peacetime years was based on offensive action. Exercises showed that fighter interception of 'enemy' bombing raids was far from effective, due to the difficulty of bringing the fighters into contact with the raiding bombers. It was therefore accepted that the bomber offered the best means of exercising air power, both as a deterrent and as a strategic weapon of war. Consequently, bombers far outnumbered fighters in the pre-war RAF.

With Germany now clearly established as the potential threat, the next task was to predict the form which an aerial assault on the British Isles would take, together with the best means of countering it. Raids on Britain from across the Channel could hardly be expected if the raiding force had first to run the gauntlet of the numerically formidable French air defences. This appeared to leave only one offensive option open to Germany: massed bomber attacks across the North Sea.

The *Luftwaffe* raids would have to be unescorted, simply because no fighter of the period had the range to accompany them; nor at that time was there any realistic possibility of such a fighter being developed. The possibility of the military collapse of France, giving the *Luftwaffe* access to bases just across the Channel, was not seriously considered. It was, however, expected that Germany might violate the neutrality of the Low Countries, but that reinforcements from Britain and France would limit their gains.

The perceived threat was therefore large bomber formations, defended by cross-fire from their gunners, approaching across the North Sea. As it was not a practical proposition to entirely prevent large bomber formations from reaching their targets, the aim was to inflict unacceptable levels of attrition on them. If this could be done, raids would soon cease. With the benefit of hindsight, we now know that this theory was flawed, and for many reasons. But at the time, it seemed to make sense.

Tactically, pre-war RAF doctrine, based as it was on the offensive, was unsound. One of the cardinal rules of warfare is security of one's base, and unless this is obtained the possibility of offensive action cannot be assured. Yet interception, given the difficulty of bringing fighters into contact with a raiding force, looked a dubious proposition. From a purely tactical viewpoint, standing patrols provided the best solution, but these were prodigal of resources, and required a huge number of fighters to be even moderately effective. What was needed was a system which could give at least 20 minutes' warning of the approach of the bombers, giving time to get the fighters off the ground, up to altitude, and into position. Observation positions on the coast were inadequate, and, in any case, dependent on good visibility. Sound locators were far too short-ranged and inaccurate. Something better was needed.

The answer lay in what was initially called radiolocation, or later radar, in which electronic wizardry produced a series of contacts, which in turn provided the range, direction, course, and to a lesser degree altitude and numbers, of a raiding force. This information was passed to a control centre which in turn steered intercepting fighters directly towards the inbound raid. This system was gradually developed, and constant practice had already brought it to a high state of efficiency before the war.

Fighting Area Attacks

With a fair degree of confidence that raids could now be intercepted, RAF Fighter Command concentrated on developing set-piece attacks against massed bomber formations. These duly emerged as Fighting Area Attacks 1 to 3, plus Attacks A and B for the ill-conceived Defiant turret

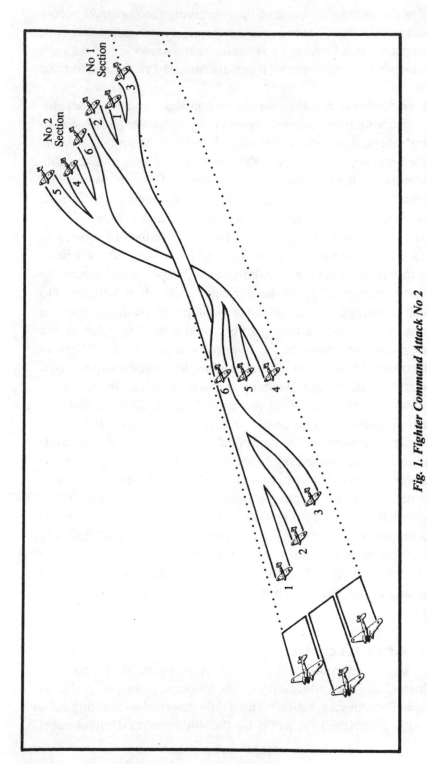

Fig. 1. Fighter Command Attack No 2

The No 2 Attack was designed to allow six fighters to attack three bombers, whilst the others covered different combinations of fighters and bombers. They were far too inflexible, and totally impractical in the presence of enemy fighters.

fighter. A further three FA attacks were later developed to meet other possible scenarios, with variations on a theme, such as if the bombers were above or below cloud. In all, they ranged from a section of three fighters versus a lone bomber, to a complete squadron of 12 fighters against a large bomber formation.

The FA Attacks generally involved a considerable amount of initial jockeying for position, including changing from squadron formation to sections line astern, sometimes even aircraft line astern, and back again, then possibly deploying into echelon for the final attack. Care was taken to avoid mid-air collisions between friendly fighters, generally at the expense of bringing massed fire-power to bear. They were slow to execute, unwieldy, and inflexible.

It had been calculated that in combat, the average fighter pilot would not be able to hold his sights on target for more than two seconds. Consequently the maximum number of hits had to be scored during this time. The new breed of fast monoplane fighters entering service in the late 1930s, the Hurricane and Spitfire, both carried eight rifle calibre (.303in/7.7mm) machine-guns with a cyclic rate of fire of 1,150 rounds per minute. Given that the average fighter pilot was not much of a marksman, the eight guns were harmonised to produce a broad pattern at a range of 1,350ft (411m), which theoretically ensured that a fair proportion of the 300 bullets fired in a two-second burst would hit a bomber-sized target. Against the unarmoured, fabric-covered bombers of the period when the calculation was made, this should have been sufficient to hit some vital point.

FA attacks stipulated that fire should be opened at the range for which the guns were harmonised, and as too much respect was paid to the cross-fire of the defending gunners, the attack was to be broken off once the range closed to 900ft (274m), which was the distance at which the average fighter pilot might have been able to hit something.

Manoeuvre Combat

While manoeuvre combat between fighters was not entirely neglected at the time, neither was its practice encouraged. The 1938 Training Manual, Chapter VIII, *Air Fighting Tactics*, stated:

> Manoeuvre at high speeds in air fighting is not now practicable, because the effect of gravity on the human body during rapid changes of direction at high speeds causes a temporary loss of consciousness... Single-seater fighter attacks at high speeds must be confined to a variety of attacks from astern.

21

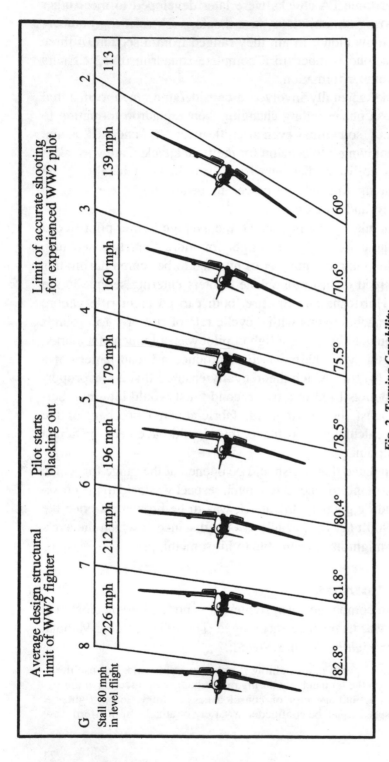

Fig. 2. Turning Capability

Turn capability is usually measured in multiples of the force of gravity, or 'g', and is directly related to the angle of bank. As can be seen here, this operates on a law of diminishing returns, with 60° needed for 2g and 82.8° needed for 8g. It is limited by two factors:: speed and structural strength, with 8g as a practical maximum, although at this level it was purely defensive. Few pilots could shoot accurately at more than 4g, while greyout started at about 6g. Stalling speed increased with g as shown here, doubling at 4g and nearly tripling at 8g.

The fact was that no-one knew whether grey-out or black-out caused by high-g manoeuvring would have any long-term effect, so it was treated with caution. In any case, it was considered that a pilot suffering in this way was vulnerable to attack. Fighter versus fighter combat training largely consisted of the high speed bounce from above and astern. Occasionally this was followed by a short period of manoeuvring for position, but as it generally consisted of one-versus-one encounters between members of the same squadron, flying the same type of aircraft, this reduced it to a contest of flying skill and experience.

Fleet Air Arm

Until 1938, the Fleet Air Arm was manned almost entirely by RAF personnel. At that time, flying from aircraft carriers was widely deemed to be an unnatural activity, to be engaged in only by consenting adults. Consequently, naval aircraft were procured mainly on the basis of how suitable (safe) they were for flying from a heaving deck in mid-ocean, rather than how effective they were as engines of war.

There was, of course, another viewpoint. At first the aircraft carrier was regarded purely as an accessory of the battle fleet. Taking this to its not very logical extreme, it was therefore assumed that carrier aircraft would only be called upon to oppose other carrier aircraft. Therefore, providing that British carrier fighters were rather better than enemy carrier aircraft, they would be good enough. This theory was based on the unwise premise that fleet actions would always be fought well away from land, and that the carriers would never be called upon to support amphibious operations, nor operate within the range of hostile land-based air power. The Royal Navy, with its long tradition of going wherever it was needed, should really have known better. The result was that Fleet Air Arm fighters were inevitably of far lower performance than their land-based counterparts. When war came, not only were they often hard-pressed to intercept enemy bombers, but they were completely outclassed by most enemy fighters.

From 1938 on, the Royal Navy became responsible for its own air power, but it was to be many years before the aircraft on strength were good enough to tackle their land-based equivalents on equal terms, and when they were, most were of American origin.

United States Army Air Corps

The USAAC, which, when elevated to the status of a force in mid-1941, became the USAAF, was far more interested in long-range bombers than fighters during the 1930s. Given the strategic location of the country, this was understandable. Neither Canada to the north nor Mexico to the south could, by any stretch of the imagination, be regarded as posing an air threat to the continental USA. To east and west, the country was bounded by the vast Atlantic and Pacific oceans. Only from these directions could a threat emerge, in the shape of a hostile fleet, and according to the thinking of the time, this was best countered by the long-range bomber. The rapid reinforcement of the Alaskan and Hawaiian defences from the continental USA was another important consideration.

Inasmuch as bombers—particularly the huge four-engined heavies ordered in the mid-1930s—cost considerably more than fighters, not only to acquire, but to operate, limited defence budgets kept numerical air strengths low. Given the doctrinaire ascendancy of bombardment over pursuit in the minds of the high command, fighters were acquired primarily for coastal defence and close air support of land forces. Fortunately the USA had defence commitments overseas—in Panama, to guard the canal, the vital link between the US Atlantic and Pacific Fleets; and in Hawaii and the Philippines, to protect local US naval bases. Had it not been for these, the USAAC fighter situation at the outbreak of the Second World War might have been far worse than it was. In 1939 the main USAAC fighters in service were considerably inferior to those of the main combatants, the British Spitfire and the German Bf 109E. It was perhaps fortunate that the USA was not to enter the war for another two years.

United States Navy and Marine Corps

To many theorists, battleships were still the supreme arbiter of naval power. That they could be sunk by air attack was unarguable, following the well-publicised experiments of USAAC General Billy Mitchell in 1921, but it was equally evident that had his targets been manoeuvring on the open sea, protected by a screen of destroyers, and able to shoot back with their own high-angle guns, the task would have been far more difficult.

The USN soon realised that an aircraft carrier's lack of defensive armour made it vulnerable in a fleet surface action, while its relatively high speed was wasted by having to keep station with the slower battleships. The correct usage was therefore to deploy separate carrier battle groups with fast cruiser and destroyer escorts, using its superior speed to keep out of gun-range of enemy surface units.

The USN also realised that carrier fighters had to have the best possible performance. Power for power, carrier fighters were never quite as good as their land-based counterparts. The reasons were not hard to find. Operating in mid-ocean, from an airfield that might easily have moved 50 miles (80km) since they left it, with bad weather to be taken into account and no possibility of a diversion to an alternate landing place, they needed much greater fuel capacity, with tanks, piping etc. They also needed a stronger structure to withstand the shock of repeated arrested deck-landings. The landing-gear had to be stronger and heavier, an arrestor hook carried, and in many cases provision had to be made for wing-folding, to enable the aircraft to be struck below on the lift. Compared to its land-based counterparts, the carrier fighter was inherently heavier and aerodynamic drag was higher, factors which conspired to reduce performance. Be that as it may, by December 1941, when the Japanese air attack on Pearl Harbor pitchforked the USA into the war, the Navy had a carrier fighter in widespread service that was at least 'good enough', and much better than that to many of those who flew it.

One area in which the US Navy differed from most other air arms of the period was in the widespread use of high angle-off deflection shooting. Whereas everyone else sought the easy no-deflection shot from astern or, at a pinch, head-on, US Naval and Marine aviators were taught attacks from the quarter and beam as standard, and spent considerable time and effort practising them. When the time came for theory to be put into practice, this was to stand them in good stead.

I. FRANCE, SEPTEMBER 1939–JUNE 1940

The Second World War began on 1 September 1939, when Germany invaded Poland. Britain and France had signed a treaty of alliance pledging themselves to come to Poland's aid if Germany attacked, but, like so many political resolutions, this guarantee was useless. Apart from a declaration of war against Germany, there was virtually nothing that either country could do to bring pressure to bear against the aggressor. In a few short weeks, Poland was overrun from the west by Germany, aided by the Soviet Union invading from the east, and was partitioned between the victors. This left the strange situation of two European countries at war with a third, none of which was initially able to take any decisive offensive action. This resulted in the period variously called the Phoney War or *Sitzkrieg* by the British, and the *Drôle de Guerre* by the French.

The French had built the supposedly impregnable Maginot Line, a heavily fortified system which ran the entire length of the German border, which was in turn paralleled by the German Siegfried Line. There was little chance of offensive ground action being successful in this area, but the Maginot Line could easily be turned if it was politically or militarily acceptable for Germany to violate the neutral states of Luxembourg, Belgium or Holland.

Before the war, Adolf Hitler had declared on more than one occasion that Germany would respect the neutrality of the Low Countries. He was not believed. When, shortly after the outbreak of war the British Expeditionary Force (BEF) was despatched to France, it was deployed, together with considerable French forces, along the Belgian border. If the Germans took this invasion route, the plan was to cross the border and advance, to assist the Belgian army to repel them.

Sitzkrieg

When the British Expeditionary Force was despatched to France in September 1939, it was accompanied by two RAF groups. The first was

26

the Air Component, Nos 85 and 87 Squadrons, tasked with providing air cover and support for the BEF. The second was the Advanced Air Striking Force, composed of Battle and Blenheim light bombers, with Nos 1 and 73 Squadrons to supply fighter escort. All four fighter squadrons were equipped with Hurricanes. In November, they were reinforced by two Gladiator squadrons, Nos 607 and 615, of the Royal Auxiliary Air Force. Though these last were scheduled to exchange their antiquated biplanes for Hurricanes, this had not been completed by May 1940.

At first there was little action in the West, as the expected German onslaught failed to materialise. The truth was that none of the combatants were in a position to launch really effective attacks at this stage, so did not wish to escalate the air war before they were able to properly retaliate in kind. For this reason, provocation in the form of collateral damage and civilian casualties had to be avoided. It has since been suggested that international opprobrium was also a factor, but in the German case the bombing of Warsaw in September 1939 makes this a ludicrous proposition.

This left naval units at sea as the only legitimate targets, and both the RAF and the *Luftwaffe* were quick to exploit this. On 16 October 1939, nine Junkers Ju 88A dive-bombers attacked elements of the British fleet near the Firth of Forth. They were intercepted by Spitfires of No 603 Squadron, which shot down two of them and badly damaged a third. The first British fighter victory of the war, this was the precursor of many such minor actions that took place around the coast of Britain over the next few months.

In France, frequent reconnaisance missions were flown by all three nations, including many over Belgium. Weeks and months passed in relative inactivity. Only on the frontier was there any real action, when French and German fighter patrols clashed, giving rise to some bitter skirmishes.

Interception of German reconnaissance aircraft over France was difficult. The French had *Detection Electromagnetique* (DEM), a bistatic radar system with widely separated transmitter and receiver stations, but this was short-ranged, reliant on a ramshackle communications system, and generally useless. Longer-ranged British radars were shipped out to help, but a combination of poor siting, technical faults, and inadequate communications conspired to make them ineffective. Consequently the few British interceptions of German reconnaissance aircraft made during this early period were largely fortuitous.

Chafing at the lack of action, the RAF fighter pilots irreverently translated *Blitzkrieg* as 'lightning that never strikes the same place once'. They had to wait until the final day of October 1939 to open their account, when 'Boy' Mould of No 1 Squadron shot down a reconnaissance Dornier Do 17P near Toul, the first of his eventual eight confirmed victories.

Against the *Luftwaffe*

The RAF was independent of the army and navy, and Fighter Command had, as we have seen, developed tactics for the defence of Great Britain. There is an old saying: One never fights the war for which one is equipped and for which one has trained. One fights the war which one has, with what one has. This was very true of the British fighter squadrons deployed to France in 1939–40. They now faced the vaunted *Luftwaffe*, arguably the strongest air force in the world, in a tactical rather than a strategic defence scenario. What were the Germans worth?

The *Luftwaffe* had been conceived primarily as an offensive force to support the *Wehrmacht*. Its first task was to gain air superiority over the battlefield. Once this was done, bombers and strike aircraft could attack unmolested to soften up enemy strongpoints, clearing the way for the advancing army.

The fighter arm of the *Luftwaffe*, the *Jagdwaffe*, had a tremendous tactical advantage over Fighter Command in the early stages of the war. Many of its personnel had fought with the entirely German *Legion Kondor* in the Spanish Civil War during the late 1930s. This conflict had allowed them to do two things: gain combat experience, and refine their tactics. Of the two, the latter was the more important. Like every other air arm of the time, the *Legion Kondor* started out using the basic three-aircraft section, or *Kette*, which normally flew in a tight Vic formation. This was actually a left-over from pre-radio days, when pilots needed to be able to see the leader's hand signals.

When the Messerschmitt Bf 109 arrived in Spain, a shortage of aircraft initially forced them to be flown in pairs (*Rotte*) rather than threes. An American saying has it that 'when you've got a lemon, the best thing to do is to make lemonade', and this is precisely what the German fighter commanders did. Forced by circumstances to use pairs, they quickly discovered that it was a far more flexible formation than the three-plane *Kette*, while the advent of air-to-air radio made it unnecessary to fly in very close formation. They now exploited this to the limit.

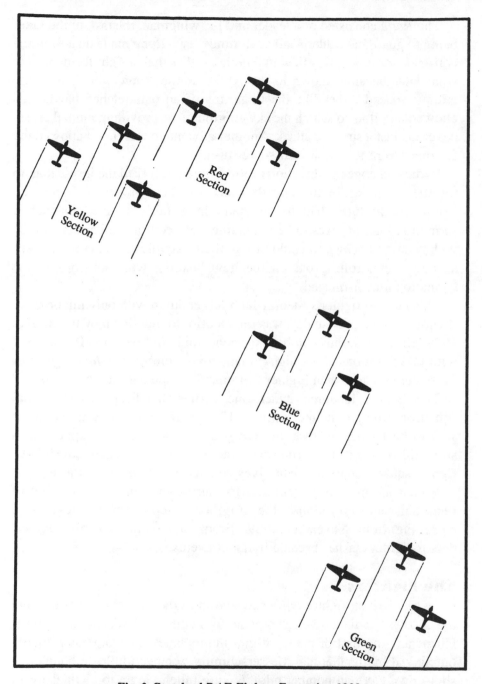

Fig. 3. Standard RAF Fighter Formation 1939
The tight Vic was good for allowing formations to penetrate cloud but was less useful when combat was joined. Normally one or two weavers, or even a whole section, would be detached as tail guards.

The *Rotte* consisted of a leader and his wingman, the task of the latter being to guard his leader's tail at all times. Two *Rotte* made up a four-aircraft *Schwarm*, and this flew in an open rather than a tight formation, in what later became known to the Allies as the 'finger four', with the aircraft spaced rather like the fingertips of an outstretched hand. This allowed all pilots to search the sky continuously, providing mutual cross-cover against a surprise attack. Another advantage was that it allowed the Germans to re-invent the cross-over turn.

Radical changes of direction in Vic formation forced the inside man to throttle back, while the outside man was hard-pressed to keep up. Consequently turns had to be made in a fairly relaxed manner if formation integrity was to be maintained. By contrast, all aircraft in the widely spaced *Schwarm* could turn at their maximum rate, crossing over as they went, rolling out on the new heading with positions in the formation mirror-imaged.

This tactical fighter system, which has endured with only minor modifications to the present day, was far superior to that flown by the RAF in 1939. Given this, plus combat experience in both Spain and Poland, and with no inhibitions about high-g manoeuvre combat, the *Jagdwaffe* was far better prepared than Fighter Command for the conflict that followed.

The British laboured under one further handicap. Their normal squadron strength in the air was 12 aircraft. By contrast, the basic *Jagdwaffe* flying unit was the *Gruppe*, which frequently appeared in strengths of 30 or more. Time and time again in the years to come, RAF fighter squadrons found themselves heavily outnumbered in the air.

Whilst the most important activity during the *Sitzkrieg* consisted of reconnaissance missions, the *Jagdwaffe* commenced aggressive patrolling from November 1939. From this point onwards, fighter-versus-fighter clashes became frequent events.

The Fighters

Only two British fighter types saw action in the first phase. These were the Gloster Gladiator, the last biplane fighter in the RAF, and the Hawker Hurricane, the first of the eight-gun monoplanes. The Gladiator, totally outclassed by the German Messerschmitts, achieved little, although one shot-down German bomber pilot, having fallen victim to a Gladiator of the Auxiliary Air Force (the 'week-end flyers'), expressed himself forcibly in fluent English when apprised of the circumstances: 'I don't believe it. Shot down by a bloody biplane flown by a bloody barrister!'

This notwithstanding, the main burden of the air fighting over France fell upon the squadrons equipped with Hurricanes.

In terms of sheer performance, the Hurricane was slightly better than the Messerschmitt Bf 109D, of which a small number were in service, but it was outclassed by the Bf 109E, although the difference was less marked at lower altitudes. Speed for speed, it could generally out-turn the German single-seater at normal combat altitudes. In most areas it was superior to the twin-engined Messerschmitt Bf 110 *Zerstörer* (Destroyer) heavy fighter, although problems were posed by the powerful forward armament of the latter, which made head-on attacks rather less than advisable; and by the rear gunner, who not only defended against attacks from astern, but made the Bf 110 much more difficult to take by surprise.

Whatever the Hurricane lacked in performance, it made up for by virtues of its own. Although a bit 'lazy' on the ailerons, which made it slow in the rolling plane, it could comfortably out-turn both German fighters. It could absorb a considerable amount of battle damage— indeed, Ginger Lacey of No 501 Squadron once described it as 'a collection of non-essential parts'; it was easy to fly, and forgiving of a ham-fisted pilot; very much so compared with its Bf 109 opponent; and its wide-track main gear was well-suited to rough temporary airfields. Finally, it was an exceptionally stable gun platform, which made for accurate shooting, while the nose sloped down from the windshield, allowing a reasonable degree of deflection to be taken when aiming at manoeuvring targets.

By orthodox single-seater standards, the Hurricane was large, it was heavy, and drag was high, with the result that the Rolls-Royce Merlin engine gave it a lower performance than the similarly-powered Spitfire. This notwithstanding, the Hurricane was at that time an entirely suitable vehicle with which to pursue the King's enemies.

Cockpit check—thumbs up—switches on—press the starter button. A few turns of the two-bladed airscrew, blue-grey smoke puffs from the exhausts and the Merlin roars into life ... At take-off power the Hurricane needs a fair bit of right rudder, then, almost unexpectedly, she leaps eagerly off the grass and flies. Unconsciously moving the stick when reaching for the undercarriage lever, I immediately have to pick up the nose and port wing—God! but these controls are sensitive. But what a beautiful aeroplane—instant obedience to the controls, superb view, and what power. So much in fact that one's leg aches holding her in a prolonged climb.

Graham Leggett, No 46 Squadron, 1940

31

Table 1. Fighter Data, France September 1939–June 1940

	Hawker Hurricane I	Messerschmitt Bf 109E-3	Messerschmitt Bf 110C-4
Wingspan	40ft 0in	32ft 4in	53ft 5in
Length	31ft 5in	28ft 4in	39ft 9in
Height	13ft 2in	11ft 2in	11ft 6in
Wing area	258 sq ft	174 sq ft	413 sq ft
Engine	Rolls-Royce Merlin II carburetted inline rated at 1,030hp	Daimler-Benz fuel-injected BD 601A inline rated at 1,100hp	2 x Daimler-Benz fuel-injected inlines rates at 1,100hp
Loaded weight	6,600lb	5,523lb	14,884lb
Wing loading	26lb/sq ft	32lb/sq ft	36lb/sq ft
Power loading	0.156hp/lb	0.199hp/lb	0.148hp/lb
Maximum speed	316mph	354mph	349mph
Service ceiling	33,200ft	36,091ft	32,800ft
Rate of climb	2,300ft/min	3,281ft/min	2,165ft/min
Range	425 miles	412 miles	481 miles

Note: Range is a purely theoretical figure, given for comparison. What really matters is combat radius, which necessarily includes combat time at full throttle, and a margin for delay in landing. Effective combat radius is generally rather less than one-third of the stated range.

In comparing the above figures, rate of climb is generally in direct proportion to acceleration, while maximum speed divided by power loading gives a vague indication of aerodynamic drag. Wing loading gives an indication of comparative turning ability once the fighter is established in the turn, although acceleration into the roll, allowing the turn to be established quickly, is rather more important.

The Opposition

The *Luftwaffe* single-seater fighter, the Messerschmitt Bf 109E, was smaller than the Hurricane, making it more difficult to see at a distance and providing a smaller target. It was faster, with a higher ceiling, a higher rate of climb, and better acceleration than the Hurricane. Its armament included two 20mm Oerlikon cannon, which gave it greater hitting power than the British fighter. Its other great advantage was a fuel-injected engine, which at times of need enabled it to stuff its nose straight down without the engine cutting under the influence of negative-g. By contrast, the conventionally-aspirated British fighters of the period were forced to roll inverted before pulling through into a vertical dive, losing valuable seconds before they could follow a Messerschmitt down.

However, the advantages were not all on the German side. The heavy framing of the side-opening cockpit canopy gave a poor view 'out of the window', and did not permit of being opened in flight to improve the view, such as was often done in the Hurricane. The Bf 109 was tricky to handle, and unforgiving of pilot error; take-off and landing on the flimsy narrow-track main gear posed particular problems, and resulted in many accidents. Wing loading was on the high side, making for an inferior turn radius and rate *vis-à-vis* its RAF opponent; while leading edge slots, which deployed automatically as the aircraft neared the stall, had a habit of opening asymmetrically during high-g manoeuvring, ruining the pilot's aim.

The Messerschmitt Bf 110 was indubitably the best of the generation of heavy fighters that had arisen in the 1930s. As in other fields, fashion had held sway, and fashion had dictated the need for a long-range fighter. The degree to which this fad had taken hold is illustrated by the fact that *Zerstörer* units were regarded as an elite by the *Luftwaffe*. The Bf 110C was a large and heavy twin-engined two-seater. Its performance was decidedly inferior to that of the Bf 109; its dogfighting capability was poor, yet it was expected to be the spearhead of the *Jagdwaffe*. Although far more docile than its single-seater stable-mate, and described by one British pilot who flew a captured example as a 'twin-engined Tiger Moth', it proved to be extremely vulnerable when pitted against the Hurricane, even though it was rather faster and more heavily armed.

In terms of armament, the German fighters held an advantage. The Bf 109E had two 20mm Oerlikon MGFF cannon mounted in the wings, and two 7.9mm machine-guns above the engine. One hit from a cannon shell was, of course, far more destructive than several hits from rifle calibre machine-guns. On the other hand, the rate of fire of the MGFF was a mere 350 rounds per minute, making it less likely to score hits on an evading target, while muzzle velocity was low, reducing effective range. The engine-mounted machine-guns were of comparable performance to the Colt-Brownings of the Hurricane, with greater accuracy conferred by their solid location, although the need for interrupter gear reduced the rate of fire somewhat. The accuracy of wing-mounted guns was degraded a little under combat conditions by wing flexing during hard manoeuvring. This was more evident in the thin-winged Spitfire than the sturdy Hurricane, although as most shooting was carried out while flying more or less in a straight line, this was no great problem.

The main armament of the Bf 110C was all nose-mounted: two 20mm cannon and four MG 17s, giving a weight of fire more than half as great again as that of the Hurricane. This made it unwise to stand toe-to-toe with it in a head-on pass, although this could not always be avoided. Rear defence was provided by a single swivel-mounted MG17.

Gunsights for both British and German fighters were remarkably similar; the British Barr & Stroud GM2 and the German Revi were both reflector sights, comprising a small glass screen on which was reflected a circle, adjustable ranging bars, and an aiming dot, all focused at infinity. Much has been made of the secrets of the GM2 being revealed to visiting German Generals Milch and Udet at Hornchurch before the war, by a high-ranking RAF officer. He probably knew something the troops didn't. With British companies unable to cope with the flood of orders, a production contract for the GM2 had been placed with C.P. Goerz of Vienna. In a notable contribution to British rearmament, the Austrian company delivered 700 excellent reflector sights to the RAF prior to the outbreak of war.

Into Action

As we saw earlier, the training and tactics of RAF Fighter Command were unimaginative and inflexible in the extreme. But while many squadron commanders played it 'by the book', others refused to be hide-bound by rules and regulations. One such, who used his initiative to out-standing effect, was 'Bull' Halahan, commanding No 1 Squadron. He started by scrapping the standard harmonisation bullet pattern, which was calculated to give a few hits at long range, and ordered all his squadron's Hurricanes to have their guns point-harmonised at 750ft (229m). In theory, this meant that all bullets from all eight guns would go through the same hole which, if the initial aim was true, and the much closer range demanded would assist this, would concentrate the damage caused enormously. Even before the squadron left England, the effec-tiveness of point harmonisation had been demonstrated against towed drogue targets.

Other innovations were wider spacing in the Vic formation, which allowed all pilots to search the sky rather than having to concentrate on holding station, and the introduction of back armour. When the latter was first requested, Hawker Aircraft refused to comply, on the grounds that the extra weight would alter the centre of gravity and lead to handling problems. Taking an empirical approach, Halahan scrounged the pilot's back armour from a written-off Battle bomber, and had it fitted to a Hurricane which was then flight-tested. No problems were found; the machine was then checked out at the Royal Aircraft Establishment, Farnborough, with the same result. Consequently all Hurricanes there-after were provided with back-armour, which saved many lives.

Nor was Halahan averse to learning from other nations. *L'Armée de l'Air* fighter units used 'weavers' to guard their tails: the main body of the formation flew a straight course, with two aircraft above and astern weaving continually, looking over their shoulders to cover the blind spot behind them. Shortly after its move to Eastern France, Halahan's squadron adopted the same system, vulgarly known as 'Arse-End Charlies'. Sources state that No 1 Squadron generally flew with two Charlies, and was never taken by surprise during the French campaign. Later, of course, the system was proved fallible and fell into abeyance, as we shall see in the next chapter, but in France it certainly seems to have contributed to the unit's success.

The other remarkable thing about No 1 Squadron was the results achieved by its personnel. Not only did it wrack up the highest score of any RAF squadron in France for relatively few casualties; it had an exceptionally high proportion of aces. The normal ratio of fighter aces to ordinary pilots was rather less than 20:1. Of the 14 pilots who flew to France under Halahan's leadership, no less than nine qualified as aces, with a combined score of 83 confirmed individual victories, not counting shared scores. Five of them reached double figures, although not all with this squadron, and certainly not all in France. In effect, the usual proportion of aces, which was slightly less than five percent, exceeded 60 percent in this one squadron.

As we shall see in the following chapter, Battle of Britain squadron scores varied according to opportunity, but typically just two pilots accounted for nearly half the totals; a far cry from No 1 Squadron in France, in which about 40 percent of the pilots were high scorers.

While many RAF fighter pilots opened their accounts during the *Sitzkrieg*, only two achieved the 'magic five' victories before the air war started in earnest. New Zealander 'Cobber' Kain, identified by the press in spite of the service's desire for anonymity, was the first RAF fighter ace of the war, followed shortly after by 'Fanny' Orton. Both flew with No 73 Squadron. Their exploits were not without their tribulations; it

Table 2. Aces who flew with No 1 Squadron in France (Confirmed)

Name	Total	Score with No 1 Sqn in France	Score other units/theatres
Billy Drake	18	3	15, mainly N. Africa/Malta
Leslie Clisby	16	16	nil
Hilly Brown	15	14	1 (BoB 1 Squadron)
Prosser Hanks	13	7	6 (BoB/Malta)
F.W. Soper	10	8	2 (257 Squadron)
Paul Richey	10	8	2 (609 Squadron)
Taffy Clowes	9	6	3 (BoB)
Boy Mould	8	7	1 (Malta)

appears that both fell victim to *Luftwaffe Experte* Werner Mölders at different times.

Blitzkrieg

With hindsight, the *Sitzkrieg* was a blessing for the RAF fighters in France. It provided a gradual introduction to combat, and when, on 10 May 1940, the long-awaited German assault began, most of them had gained some experience. They had encountered the enemy, fired their guns, and been fired at in their turn. They had learned to keep a sharp look-out, and also that manoeuvre combat was perfectly feasible. Above all, they had learned to have confidence in themselves and their machines.

As the *Luftwaffe* had demonstrated in Poland, air superiority is most easily gained by destroying enemy aircraft on the ground. The first day of the *Blitzkrieg* in the West saw attacks made on no less than 72 airfields, mainly French, but Dutch and Belgian also. Caught unprepared, the Belgian air force was quickly reduced to near-impotence. Heavily outnumbered, the Dutch fared little better, but further south, only 31 of 47 French airfields attacked held first-line units. This can only have been due to faulty intelligence—the constant harassing of *Luftwaffe* reconnaissance machines during the *Sitzkrieg* had paid off.

From this moment on the sky was never still. Large German bomber formations crossed the frontier constantly, their escorting Messerschmitts never far away. There was no lack of opportunity for the Hurricane pilots, many of whom took full advantage, even though heavily outnumbered. Four more Hurricane squadrons were rushed to France: 501 (which was in action within an hour of arrival) and 504 on 10 May; 3 and 79 a day later.

The new arrivals were subjected to a very rapid learning process. On 13 May, Ginger Lacey, a young sergeant pilot with No 501 Squadron, had difficulty in starting his Hurricane, took off late, and failed to find his section. Stooging around near Sedan, he sighted his first German aircraft, a Heinkel He 111 bomber, several thousand feet below. With no combat experience, and no leader to tell him what to do, he hesitated. As he did so, he spotted a Bf 109E which was apparently escorting the bomber. Finally deciding that he must attack, he opened his throttle and went down on the fighter. The combination of full throttle and a steep dive accelerated the Hurricane rapidly, but the closing speed of around 500ft/sec was too great. Lacey was unable to line up his sights and fire in the brief interval between maximum range and overshooting. Fortunately the German pilot failed to spot him as he flashed past.

Lacey carefully clambered back into position, and, still unseen, closed steadily from astern. From 750ft the 109 looked far too small to hit. He crept closer. At 150ft it at last filled his sight in a satisfactory manner, and he thumbed the firing button. Noise, flames, and smoke, and bullets from the eight Colt-Brownings tore into the German fighter, leaving only drifting smoke and fluttering metal parts.

Having disposed of the fighter, Lacey turned his attention to the Heinkel, which by now was feeling rather unhappy. Evasive action availed it little, and a long burst from 600ft closing to 60ft chewed off a wing. Lacey returned to base to be greeted by disbelief, which was only dispelled that afternoon when a French gun battery confirmed his successes.

Ginger Lacey was not an average squadron pilot. A pre-war flying instructor with over 600 hours in his logbook, he was an outstanding aircraft handler who needed combat experience to give him the necessary confidence to succeed and become the fourth-ranking British ace. We shall meet him again in later chapters.

In the confused melees that took place during the next few weeks, the shortcomings of RAF fighter tactics were ruthlessly exposed. Many leaders persisted in trying to use the standard attacks, even against fighters, for which they were not designed. Ian 'Widge' Gleed (final score 13) was posted to No 87 Squadron as a Flight Commander shortly after the start of the German offensive. His first sortie was on 18 May:

> I waggle my wings, 'Line astern, line astern. Go.' Messerschmitt 110s; nine of us against five of them. This looks easy... The enemy are flying in rather a wide Vic formation. I decide on the right-hand 'plane. 'Echelon port, echelon port. Go...' They still haven't seen us. We are diving steeply now, doing about 300 on the clock.
>
> Throttle back a bit; otherwise you'll overshoot them. Hell! they've broken. What the Hell! they've turned to meet us. Steady, now; get your sights on before you fire. Rat tat tat, rat tat tat. Hell! you can hear their cannons firing. Blast it! I am going too fast; they are past me, on either side—so close that I thought we would hit.

Inexperienced in combat as Widge Gleed was at this time, it was a trifle optimistic to expect that the rearward-facing gunners of the 110s had not seen his formation, especially after the time consumed in manoeuvring from Vic to line astern, then into echelon prior to the attack, which

37

was launched from sufficiently far away to give the German fighters time to reverse into it, making it a head-on pass. The fight ended, as they usually did, in a free-for-all, and Gleed opened his score with two 110s.

On one of Gleed's early sorties, three Hurricane squadrons were combined into a wing of 36 fighters, probably in an attempt to offset the numerical advantage of the *Luftwaffe Gruppen*, which far outnumbered a single RAF squadron:

> On we droned. Out of the corner of my eye I saw nine dots high above us. 'Hell, Jerries!' All of a sudden about five people were speaking at the same time on the RT; the weaving at the back became fiercer than ever. 'Hell! what the devil does that section think it's doing?' Right at the back of the formation one section of three was flying in close Vic formation, as though they were doing a show for the Hendon air pageant. Even as I craned round I saw three of the black dots swinging behind us come diving down. 'Hell, blast! What the Hell can we do?' Another babble of voices on the RT. Too late—the sky was suddenly lit up by two burning Hurricanes. Down, down; a trail of smoke on the ground; no-one had baled out.

The large British formation, with squadrons in line astern and sections of three aircraft in Vics, had tried to wheel to meet the attack, but was too cumbersome to respond effectively to the much smaller threat from above and astern. Not one British fighter was so much as able to bring its guns to bear as the Germans disengaged at high speed.

There was a lesson to be learned from this minor skirmish, which was that without operational flexibility, and mutual cross-cover, superior numbers counted for little against the enemy's positional advantage and superior tactics.

Well though the RAF pilots fought during this phase, events on land rendered their efforts vain. On 13 May, German armoured forces broke through at Sedan and began what virtually amounted to a race for the sea. Outflanked, the Allied armies fell back on all sides, and the RAF squadrons were forced to retreat to avoid being over-run on the ground. Communications were poor, and without ground control interception became a haphazard business. The squadrons were moved hither and thither at short notice; damaged aircraft were abandoned, causing losses to reach record levels, and logistics became a nightmare. Under the circumstances, it was hardly surprising that operational effectiveness was reduced.

Worse still was to come. By 23 May, the *Wehrmacht* had reached the sea near Abbeville, cutting off the BEF and French forces to the north. Evacuation from Dunkirk became inevitable.

Dunkirk

The rescue of over 300,000 troops from Dunkirk was an epic feat of arms. It was carried out under the noses of the *Luftwaffe* and was marked by the most intense air fighting to date. For the first time in the French campaign, the air war moved within range of British-based single-seater fighters..

Initially, sixteen squadrons operated as continuously as possible during daylight hours, patrolling the area inland from the port. There was, of course, little point in flying above the beaches: they had to intercept the *Luftwaffe* before they arrived over the target. Often they saw nothing; sometimes they encountered German bomber formations; at other times they were overwhelmed by hordes of Messerschmitts coming out of the sun. After a few days, it was decided to double the strength of patrols to offset this, even though it meant that no air cover could be provided for lengthy periods. For the British-based fighters, as with the Hurricane squadrons in France, it was a learning time, and many were the future aces who scored their first victories over Dunkirk, among them Bob Stanford Tuck, 'Sailor' Malan, Douglas Bader, and Al Deere.

For the first time, Spitfires encountered German fighters. However, the statistics from the Dunkirk fighting are inconclusive; only in the coming months, as the Spitfire pilots gained experience, would comparative worth become evident.

Aces of the French Campaign

Only rarely can all the victory claims of the aces of any nation, and in any theatre, be verified from surviving records of both sides. The debacle in France resulted in the loss of many squadron records and diaries, and in some cases the pilot's logbooks. Consequently actual·

Table 3. Sorties/Losses, Dunkirk 27 May–2 June 1940

	Sorties	Losses
Royal Air Force		
Hurricane	906	49
Spitfire	746	48
Defiant/Blenheim	112	9
Totals	1,764	106
Luftwaffe		
Bf 109E	1,595	29
Bf 110C & D	405	8
Bombers (Do 17, He 111, Ju 88)	1,010	45
Dive Bombers (Ju 87)	805	10
Totals	3,815	92

scores are in some cases debatable. This notwithstanding, all figures listed have been accepted in good faith by the author.

EDGAR JAMES 'COBBER' KAIN   A New Zealander, Cobber Kain was the first RAF fighter ace of the war. Posted to the Gladiator-equipped No 73 Squadron, he was selected to give an aerobatic exhibition at the Empire Air Day at Hendon in 1938. Having converted to Hurricanes, No 73 Squadron arrived in France in September 1939.

At first there was little doing, but on 8 November, Kain stalked a high-flying reconnaissance Dornier Do 17P of 1(F)/123. Hit, the German aircraft fell into a near-vertical dive, with Cobber in hot pursuit. He only just pulled out in time as the Dornier went straight into the ground near Metz, for his—and the squadron's—first victory. Just over a fortnight later, he shot down another Dornier.

Over the next three months there was little air activity, and Cobber had to wait until 2 March 1940 for his next success. Patrolling at 20,000ft with one other Hurricane, he spotted seven Heinkel He 111s high over Thionville and climbed to engage. While hotly pursuing the bombers, he was bounced from above and astern by Bf 109s of *III/JG53*. Hit by cannon fire, he broke hard to the right, and then, as his assailant overshot, he turned back and opened fire. Almost immediately he was hit by a second 109, which also overshot him. Pulling in behind it, he fired three bursts, and was rewarded by seeing it go down pouring black smoke. But again he had neglected his rear, and he was hit for the third time; his cockpit filled with smoke, and his engine cut out. His assailant was probably *Luftwaffe Experte* Werner Mölders, one of the most successful of the German fighter pilots. Engine-less, he was left over Germany with a burning aircraft. Somehow he coaxed his stricken bird back across the frontier, and fortunately the flames subsided, allowing him to make a good landing on a French airfield.

Cobber had an even narrower escape on 26 March, when, leading a section of three Hurricanes, he once more encountered *III/JG53*. Undeterred by superior numbers, he immediately attacked and claimed two 109s in quick succession, which made him the first RAF ace of the war. *Paddy* (all his aircraft were called *Paddy*) was then hit on the cockpit canopy, the engine caught fire, and he was wounded in one leg. This time there was no alternative to baling out, which he just managed before losing consciousness. He came down in no man's land, and managed to limp painfully to the French lines.

40

The 17 days following the opening of the *Blitzkrieg* on 10 May saw Kain claim 11 more victories. He has been described as a type-hunter who spent hours searching for a Henschel Hs 126 observation aircraft to add to his collection, but this seems highly unlikely. Like all other pilots of the period, he engaged whatever turned up, in his case mainly Dorniers and 109s. His final total included two Hs 126s, but not one Ju 87 or He 111; types that were hardly in short supply at the time.

Impetuous by nature, Cobber Kain showed little finesse in his fighting. Whatever he saw he attacked, regardless of position or odds. Operationally very tired, he was ordered back to England on 6 June. Taking off from his base at Echemines, he attempted a final low-level beat-up. For once his judgement failed him; his aircraft hit the ground and he was killed, his final score standing at 16.

FRANK CAREY The press acclaimed Carey as 'the Cockney Ace', but as it is highly unlikely that the sound of Bow Bells ever carried the five miles to Brixton, this is a misnomer. A sergeant pilot with No 43 Squadron from September 1936, in the pre-war period he was, with Peter Townsend (9 victories), and Caesar Hull (4 victories), part of a strictly unofficial aerobatic team, in which Townsend generously admitted that Carey flew the most difficult position.

In the first three months of 1940 he shared in three interceptions of Heinkel He 111s off the north-east coast of Britain. On the third occasion, Carey was one of four pilots of No 43 Squadron which attacked a Heinkel and set it on fire. When it turned back and tried to make the Scottish coast, they escorted it. Carey later commented that he was extremely anxious that the helpless German crew should survive.

In April 1940, Carey was commissioned and posted to No 3 Squadron, also with Hurricanes, which was sent to France at the onset of the *Blitzkrieg*. Once there, he rapidly became a bomber specialist, destroying 12 bombers and a solitary fighter, with another four bombers unconfirmed, in the space of five days. It was not planned; it was just that he encountered far more bombers than fighters during this period. It is now one of the enduring myths of the early war years that bombers were easy to shoot down. This was not the case. As slow and unmanoeuvring targets they were relatively easy to hit, providing that one managed to run the gauntlet of return fire from their gunners. Doing sufficient damage with .303 calibre machine-guns was a different matter, which makes Carey's feat the more remarkable. But sometimes, unusual aid was forthcoming:

> I got behind this Ju 88 and pressed the button, and to my utter amazement bits
> flew off and the damage was astonishing! Our .303 guns weren't heavy
> enough to do so much damage. Then I saw fire over my head. There was a
> 109 trying to hit me but shooting high, and we were both knocking the hell
> out of this poor old Ju 88! It went down.

There was a price to be paid. On 14 May, Carey attacked a Dornier Do 17, which did a snap half-roll and dived vertically. Not realising that it was finished and worried that it might escape, he followed close behind, only to be hit and wounded in the leg by its rear gunner. Force-landing in Belgium, he was evacuated to England, only to find that he had been posted missing.

Frank Carey returned to No 43 Squadron in time for the Battle of Britain. Several more victories followed, but on 18 August, shortly after shooting down a Ju 87 in a confused melee off the South Coast, he was hit in the knee by a spent bullet, and force-landed once more. This was his last victory in Europe.

Posted to Mingaladon in Burma in 1942, still flying Hurricanes, he accounted for seven Japanese aircraft during February 1942, five of them supremely agile but under-gunned Nakajima Ki 27 fighters. Most activity from this point on was air-to-ground. Carey's final air combat took place at Chittagong on 25 October, when he was attacked during take-off by a number of Ki 43 Oscar fighters. A desperate battle ensued at zero feet, ending when one of the Oscars appeared to fly into a hill. It was claimed only as a 'possible'. Frank Carey scored hits on a total of 44 German and Japanese aircraft, of which 18 German and seven Japanese were confirmed destroyed.

BOB STANFORD TUCK   A short-service officer, Bob Tuck joined No 65 Squadron in 1936 to fly Gladiators. Having converted to Spitfires before the war, he was posted to No 92 Squadron on 1 May 1940 as a Flight Commander, just in time to take part in operations over Dunkirk. The first patrol over the French port on 23 May nearly ended in disaster as No 92 Squadron droned up and down in the regulation tight Vic formations. With too much attention paid to holding position, it was sheer luck that the 109s were spotted as they came snarling in behind the port beam. A Spitfire burst into flame, then the sky was full of turning, twisting fighters all jockeying for position.

Bob Tuck latched onto the German leader, who zoom-climbed through cloud, then levelled off and set course for home. Using emergency power, the Spitfire gradually closed the distance, keeping slightly low, shielded from view by the tailplane of the Messerschmitt. Seconds passed; the range shortened. The red aiming dot of the reflector sight was centred on the canopy; 1,500ft range—fire! Tuck's guns were loaded with a high proportion of De Wilde ammunition, which flashed as it hit. The wings and canopy of the 109 sparkled under the hits; its nose rose gently, and an aileron came fluttering back. Then the entire starboard wing broke away, and the doomed German fighter spiralled down. But with no witnesses, this first victory was not confirmed.

That afternoon, No 92 Squadron returned to Dunkirk. This time they encountered a *Gruppe* of Bf 110s. The *Zerstörer* pilots had not yet learned that they were no match for British single-seaters, and dived to the attack. Once again, the neat formations dissolved into a whirling confused mass. At first Bob Tuck could not settle on a target, but then a 110 rose from the depths just ahead. Bullets from its rear gunner hit the engine cowling and windshield of the Spitfire, but then the fire of its eight Brownings tore into the German fighter. Flames burst from its port engine and it yawed, rolled over and went down vertically.

There was no time to think—already the Spitfire was taking more hits; another 110 was charging at it head-on. Tuck held on, firing back, then just as it seemed that the two aircraft must collide, he ducked. He never knew whether it passed above or below him, but screwing round, he saw it heading inland, and set off in hot pursuit. A minute or two later, he was within range, about 1,500ft (457m), and once more opened fire. The rear-gunner replied, while the German pilot took his aircraft down to just above the ground, jinking violently to throw off his attacker's aim. It was too late; the damage had been done and the 110 belly-landed in a field for Tuck's third victory of the day. But his own aircraft had been badly shot up, and he barely managed to stagger back to base.

The squadron commander had been shot down during this action, and for the next few days Tuck was given command. On May 24 he was back over Dunkirk at the head of eight Spitfires, all that could be made serviceable. Now he made his first tactical experiment, ordering his pilots to open the formation wide for greater flexibility. They encountered a formation of Do 17s, and attacked from astern. Tuck again did the unorthodox; to obtain a longer firing pass, he throttled back and lowered his flaps to match his speed to that of the bombers, then opened fire at 1,200ft range, hitting the port engine of his chosen target. The Dornier slowed, the range closed to 300ft (90m); then two more bursts set it alight. Bob Tuck then shot down a second Dornier, for his fifth victory in two days after three sorties.

By now he had realised that the three-ship section contained one too many aircraft. From this moment on, No 92 Squadron flew in loose pairs. Tuck's usual wingman was Bob Holland (5 victories), with whom he developed a close understanding.

Bob Stanford Tuck scored seven confirmed victories over Dunkirk, plus a one-third share in a Dornier and the unconfirmed 109. He was unusual in that he was a long-range marksman, often scoring from distances which other pilots could not match. He fought in the Battle of Britain, and over France in 1941, flying a Hurricane. In an epic solo engagement with three 109s near the Dutch coast on 21 June 1941, he accounted for two and damaged the third before baling out over the sea. He was finally shot down by ground fire over the Pas-de-Calais in January 1942 and became a prisoner of war. His final confirmed score was 27, but may well have been higher.

2. THE BATTLE OF BRITAIN, JULY–NOVEMBER 1940

With the capitulation of France, Fighter Command braced itself to meet the coming storm. Replacement pilots and aircraft reinforced battered squadrons, newly formed units intensified their training, and many veterans of the French campaign were posted to training units where they could pass on their hard-won experience to newly fledged fighter pilots. Meanwhile the vital detection, reporting, and fighter control system was honed to a fine edge of proficiency.

The mood was one of cautious optimism. Regardless of events in France, Fighter Command was far from defeated. And now it was playing at home, in the defensive role for which it had been created. Although the numerically stronger *Luftwaffe* would retain the initiative, in that it could still choose the time, place, and strength of its attacks, many of the factors which contributed to its earlier successes no longer applied. The British early warning system would to a large degree negate the advantages of surprise and confusion which had been so brilliantly exploited by the *Luftwaffe* in the French campaign. With no ground threat to British airfields, security of base, one of the cardinal axioms of warfare, was relatively assured. And whereas in all previous campaigns the *Luftwaffe* had operated in its primary role—as aerial artillery acting in support of ground forces—it was now asked to carry out a strategic task; one for which it was neither prepared nor equipped.

Detection and Control

The first line of defence was the 18 Chain Home (CH) radar stations, which covered most of the south and east coasts of Great Britain. CH could detect incoming raids at medium and high altitudes at distances of up to 120 miles, and give a rough indication of both numbers and height. However, against low-flying aircraft it was ineffective, and to fill the gap a shorter-wave radar, Chain Home Low (CHL) was used. This gave coverage down to about 600ft at 40 miles, but with no height indications. For emergencies, mobile sets with a range of 90 miles were available.

Radar gave coverage out to sea. Inland, tracking was the responsibility of the Observer Corps, from a network of posts at five mile intervals. Together, radar stations and observer posts provided a mass of information. This was centralised and filtered, and errors and 'double-bookings' removed. The cleaned up information was then passed to Group Headquarters, and simultaneously to the sector stations from which the squadrons were controlled. The time lapse between the first sighting and the plot reaching the sector operations room was just four minutes—roughly 12 miles as the bomber flies. Providing the latter made no radical changes of course, this was not too difficult to predict.

Group HQ, with the full picture before them, exercised central command, instructing sector stations which squadrons to scramble and which raids to intercept, although this was not absolute. Sector stations were allowed a degree of discretion.

Organisation

Fighter Command was organised into four geographical areas or Groups. No 11 Group covered London and south-eastern England; No 12 Group defended East Anglia and the Midlands; and No 13 Group extended across northern England and Scotland. No 10 Group, which came into being during July 1940, was responsible for south-western England and Wales. While the primary task of each Group was to defend its own area, but it could also send squadrons to assist a neighbour.

Each Group was subdivided into sectors, each containing a sector station with an Operations Room similar to that at Group HQ. Each sector station had one or more satellite airfields. Although on a map sectors appeared to be geographical areas, this was not the case. Squadrons based in any sector could operate anywhere within the Group area, or even outside it.

In order to keep track of the defending squadrons, a radio device code-named 'Pip-Squeak' was used. Activated in one fighter per squadron, it transmitted for 14 seconds in every minute, during which ground stations took bearings and provided an exact position. Using 'Pip-Squeak', the maximum number of squadrons that a sector could handle efficiently was four, and was frequently less.

Aims and Attitudes

The Battle of Britain was an emotive phrase coined by Prime Minister Winston Churchill shortly after Dunkirk, to rally the nation. It has been given start and finish dates, but like much else, these are arbitrary. The air fighting that took place in the summer and autumn of 1940 was a campaign rather than a battle, with major engagements on some days and minor skirmishes on others. With few exceptions, the action was confined to south-east and southern England, rather than the whole of the British Isles. But the 'Battle of Kent', or even the 'Battle of South-Eastern England', did not have the same emotive ring.

In the summer of 1940, the aim of the *Luftwaffe* was to create conditions suitable for a successful invasion of England. As the *Kriegsmarine* lacked the strength to fend off the Royal Navy, the only alternative was for the latter to be neutralised by air power. The essential precondition for this was to gain air superiority by defeating Fighter Command. The task of Fighter Command was therefore to remain in being as a viable fighting force, while denying air superiority to the *Luftwaffe*. The latter task, however, must never take precedence over the former; at least, not until the invasion was actually under way.

The attitudes of the opposing fighter pilots were very different. The Germans, buoyed up by their successes so far, confidently expected a swift victory. High-scoring German ace Helmut Wick is on record as saying: 'I want to fight, and die fighting, taking with me as many of the enemy as possible!' Had any RAF pilot uttered similar sentiments, he would have been ordered to take a cold shower and lie down for a while. The typical RAF attitude was that somehow they would beat Jerry and survive until ultimate victory. Dying, no matter how gloriously, would be most unfortunate. A Punch cartoon summed up the spirit of the era perfectly. 'Laburnum Cottage Sir? Down the road, past the two Heinkels, turn left at the Dornier, and it's just past the Messerschmitt 109 on the right!'

Aircraft of the Battle

Comparison of the basic performance figures shows that the German Bf 109E was superior to even the Spitfire in many areas, while the Hurricane appears to be completely outclassed. But once the fighting started, the differences were nowhere near so apparent. In all, 28 Hurricane and 18 Spitfire squadrons took a substantial part—i.e. eight days or more in combat—in the battle, a ratio of 60:40. Recent research shows that of the German losses due to fighter action, 638 can be allocated to Hurricane squadrons and 511 to Spitfire units, a ratio of 55:45. This difference can be accounted for by the fact that the Spitfire squadrons stayed in combat for longer periods before they were replaced, mainly due to a rather lower attrition rate. The conclusions to be drawn from this were that Spitfires and Hurricanes were equally good at shooting down German aircraft, but that the latter, mainly due to its lower performance, was more vulnerable to enemy action.

Later in the battle, Spitfires were tasked with holding off the

Table 4. Fighter Data, Battle of Britain

	Supermarine Spitfire I	Hawker Hurricane I	Messerschmitt Bf 109E-3	Messerschmitt Bf 110C-4
Wingspan	36ft 10in	40ft 0in	32ft 4in	53ft 5in
Length	29ft 11in	31ft 5in	28ft 4in	39ft 9in
Height	11ft 5in	13ft 2in	11ft 2in	11ft 6in
Wing area	242 sq ft	258 sq ft	174 sq ft	413 sq ft
Engine	Rolls-Royce Merlin II rated at 1,030hp	Rolls-Royce Merlin II rated at 1,030hp	Daimler-Benz DB 601A rated at 1,100hp	2 x Daimler-Benz DB 601A rated at 1,100hp
Loaded weight	5,784lb	6,600lb	5,523lb	14,884lb
Wing loading	24lb/sq ft	26lb/sq ft	32lb/sq ft	36lb/sq ft
Maximum speed	355mph	316mph	354mph	349mph
Service ceiling	34,000ft	33,200ft	36,091ft	32,800ft
Rate of climb	2,530ft/min	2,300ft/min	3,281ft/min	2,165ft/min
Range	575 miles	425 miles	412 miles	481 miles

Note: Range is a theoretical 'still air' figure. Combat radius, with a full throttle combat allowance and a safety margin, is typically less than one-third of the range stated.

48

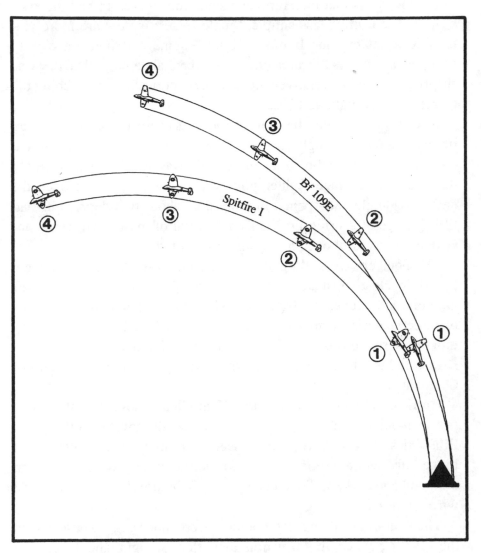

Fig. 4. Comparative Turning Ability, Spitfire I vs Bf 109E
*While it was widely known that speed for speed the Spitfire could out-turn
the German fighter, the margin was smaller than was often realised. Here
it is shown to scale.*

German escort fighters while Hurricanes tackled the bombers. This has added to the Spitfire legend. There is a popular belief that fighters were difficult to shoot down, whereas bombers were easy targets. The inference is that the Hurricane squadrons therefore had the easier task. The truth is less simple. Single-seater fighters are more vulnerable to attack than bombers. Pilot, engine and fuel are closely grouped, and hits in this area often caused lethal damage. The key was surprise, to obtain a relatively easy no-deflection shot by catching the target flying straight and level.

Once manoeuvre combat started, the odds against scoring increased immeasurably. Although the low wing-loaded British fighters could out-turn the 109 at all heights, the margin was smaller than is widely realised. The average fighter pilot was a poor shot, and once the deflection angle had opened to more than about five degrees he had little chance of scoring hits. Only a handful of marksmen were consistently successful once a turning fight started.

The bombers were altogether a different case. Mostly they were found in close formation, protected by the massed fire of their gunners, and with escort fighters lurking close at hand. With upwards of three dozen crewmen in each bomber *Staffel* all keeping a sharp lookout, surprise was not a factor. In the traditional attack from astern British fighters had to brave a storm of crossfire, and the standard of German air gunnery was high.

Hurricane squadron commander Tom Gleave described the tracer fire as looking like 'a cage of gilt wire', while novice Spitfire pilot Ellis Aries of No 602 Squadron, seeing, in his first encounter, what looked like white glinting metal rods accelerating towards him from the bombers, broke radio silence to ask 'Why are they dangling little wires at me?'

The twin-engined German bombers were much bigger targets than the Bf 109; when in formation they flew straight and level, and consequently were easier to hit. On the other hand, they could absorb a lot of battle damage. Many bombers limped back to base after sustaining upwards of 200 hits. Others only succumbed after multiple

> *We were taught a sharp lesson by the enemy rear gunner's excellent shooting.*
> Innes Westmacott (3 victories at least), No 56 Squadron

> *Caught up with five Ju 87s in line astern, opened fire. Two people baled out of No 5 aircraft and a further two from No 4.*
>
> Jim Hallowes (eventual score 17 confirmed), Hurricane pilot, No 43 Squadron, 18 August 1940

attacks by several fighters in succession. The fact is, they were extremely difficult to shoot down with the rifle calibre guns carried by British fighters.

The one exception was the Junkers Ju 87 dive-bomber. Single-engined, rather slower than the level bombers, and with a single gunner for rear protection, the Ju 87 was extremely vulnerable. This was particularly the case just after they had attacked, when their formation had broken up and they were legging it for home with no attempt at mutual support.

To summarise, although six Spitfire squadrons featured in the 'top ten', the records of the aces paints a different picture. Of the 19 pilots who became double aces during the battle, nine flew Spitfires, nine Hurricanes, and one both. While there can be no doubt that the Spitfire was the better fighter, on an individual level the dominant factor was the man rather than the machine.

Table 5. Battle of Britain Top Scorers, 1 July–31 October 1940

Name	Sqn	Aircraft	Score	Bf 109s	War Total
Eric Lock	41	Spitfire	21	13	26
Jim Lacey	501	Hurricane	18	13	28
Archie McKellar	605	Hurricane	17	11	17
Josef Frantisek	303	Hurricane	17	9	17
Brian Carbury	603	Spitfire	15	15	15
Colin Gray	54	Spitfire	15	11	27
Witold Urbanowicz	145/303	Hurricane	15	6	18
Pat Hughes	234	Spitfire	14	12	14
Bob Doe	234/238	Spitfire/Hurricane	14	9	14
Mike Crossley	32	Hurricane	13	6	20
Jim Hallowes	43	Hurricane	11[1]	2[1]	17
Douglas Bader	242	Hurricane	11	1	20
Reg Llewellyn	213	Hurricane	11	1	13
Desmond McMullen	54	Spitfire	10	9	17
John Ellis	610	Spitfire	10	8	13
George Unwin	19	Spitfire	10	7	13
Pancho Villa	72/92	Spitfire	10	4	13
John Dundas	609	Spitfire	10	1	12[2]
Hamilton Upton	43	Hurricane	10	–	10

1 Julius Neumann, a Bf 109E pilot with *JG 27*, believes that he was shot down by Jim Hallowes on 18 August 1940. If so, these figures should be increased by one.

2 Dundas' final victim, on 28 November 1940, was ranking German ace Helmut Wick. Dundas was immediately shot down and killed by Wick's wingman, Rudi Pflanz.

The Hurricane was the better bomber destroyer. It was a more stable gun platform, and it could absorb more battle damage than the Supermarine thoroughbred. This was an important consideration when braving crossfire from the bombers. At the same time, there can be no doubt that the fast and agile Spitfire was better able to deal with the 109s.

'What-ifs'

The conduct of the battle has often been criticised from the safety and comfort of post-war armchairs. It is therefore necessary to dispose of a few old chestnuts.

On 10 July 1940, the official start of the battle, a total of 19 Spitfire squadrons was operational. Yet only five of these were based in the most threatened 11 Group area. It has therefore been suggested that for maximum effectiveness, every available Spitfire should have been deployed to the south-east. There were good reasons why this was not done. September 1940 saw less than 50 replacement Spitfires ready for immediate issue throughout, with a low of 38 in the third week. Flinging all Spitfire squadrons into action at the outset would inevitably have resulted in higher casualties. It is doubtful whether enough replacement aircraft or pilots could have been supplied to keep all 19 squadrons operational. Qualitative expansion of Fighter Command would have been significantly delayed, with a prejudicial effect lasting well into 1941.

The relatively small number of fighter squadrons actively opposing the *Luftwaffe* in the south has also been criticised. Could not more units have been deployed to the threatened areas? After all, there were plenty of other airfields used by other commands available, which could at a pinch have accommodated fighters. Sir Keith Park, commanding 11 Group during the summer of 1940, gave the answer to this question long after the war. It was, he said, due to inadequate communications being available on the airfields in question. Without good communications, extra squadrons could not have been used efficiently, putting them at greater risk. A further factor was that had 12 and 13 Groups been denuded of fighter protection, unescorted bombers could have ranged the length and breadth of the industrial midlands and north with impunity, opposed only by anti-aircraft guns. Retention of squadrons in these areas was amply repaid later.

The next carp was that, as aircraft are far more vulnerable on the ground, why did Fighter Command not send out large fighter sweeps to shoot up known German airfields? After all, *Luftwaffe* fighters strafed airfields in England often enough. The answer here was that the risks far outweighed the rewards. The *Luftwaffe* had brought airfield camouflage to a fine art, making results uncertain, while German light flak guns were both numerous and deadly. By comparison, British airfields were permanent establishments, impossible to hide, and lightly defended. Even then, it should be remembered that the strafing Messerschmitts usually failed to do significant damage. Had Fighter Command adopted this course, it could easily have lost 50 or more pilots in a single afternoon, in return for the destruction of a handful of easily replaced German fighters. In the long term, these losses might have been critical. The next five years were to show that air forces ran out of experienced pilots far more quickly than they ran out of aircraft.

The Hour Approaches

As 1 July 1940 dawned, Fighter Command knew that the expected *Luftwaffe* onslaught could not be long delayed. The exact form it would take could only be guessed at; all the defenders could do was respond once it started. Everything was in place. The radars and the reporting and control system could, if they were allowed to function properly, give the fighters a tremendous advantage. But would it be allowed? All Fighter Command could do was watch, wait, and hope.

Phases of the Battle

The waiting ended during the first week of July, when the *Luftwaffe* opened the ball with a series of reconnaissances and probing attacks around the British coast. At first Fighter Command was unable to discern a pattern against which to plan their defence. This was hardly surprising; at that time there wasn't one. The main body of the German air fleets was still moving into position, while the High Command planned a full-scale assault which would pave the way to ultimate victory.

Table 6. Fighter Command Order of Battle, 10 July 1940

Sector	Base	Sqn	Type	Commander
11 Group (HQ Uxbridge)				
Biggin Hill	Biggin Hill	32	Hurricane	John Worrall
		141	Defiant	William Richardson
	Gravesend	610	Spitfire	A.T. Smith
	Manston	600	Blenheim	David Clark
Debden[1]	Debden	17	Hurricane	R. MacDougall
Hornchurch	Hornchurch	65	Spitfire	Henry Sawyer
		74	Spitfire	Droguer White[2]
	Rochford	54	Spitfire	Prof Leathart[3] (2)
Kenley	Kenley	64	Spitfire	N. Odbert
		615	Hurricane	Joe Kayll (3)
	Croydon	111	Hurricane	John Thompson (6)
		501	Hurricane	Harry Hogan (6½)
Northolt	Northolt	1	Hurricane	David Pemberton (2)
		604	Blenheim	Michael Anderson
	Hendon	257	Hurricane	D. Bayne
North Weald	North Weald	56	Hurricane	Minnie Manton (1)
		151	Hurricane	Teddy Donaldson (1)
	Martlesham	85	Hurricane	Peter Townsend (6)
		25	Blenheim	K. McEwan
Tangmere	Tangmere	43	Hurricane	Tubby Badger (8½)
		145	Hurricane	John Peel (3)
		601	Hurricane	Max Aitken (1)
	Shoreham	FIU3	Blenheim	George Chamberlain
10 Group from 21 July 1940 (HQ Box, previously 11 Group)				
Filton	Pembrey	92	Spitfire	Philip Sanders (4)
	Exeter	87	Hurricane	John Dewar (3½)
		213	Hurricane	H. McGregor (2)
	St Eval	234	Spitfire	R. Barnett
Middle Wallop	Middle Wallop	609	Spitfire	George Darley (3)
		238	Hurricane	Harold Fenton (1)
12 Group (HQ Watnall)				
Church Fenton	Church Fenton	73	Hurricane	Hank More
		616	Spitfire	Marcus Robinson
		249	Hurricane	John Grandy
Digby	Digby	46	Hurricane	A.D. Murray
		611	Spitfire	Big Jim McComb (2)
		29	Blenheim	J.S. Adams
Duxford	Duxford	264	Defiant	Philip Hunter
	Fowlmere	19	Spitfire	Philip Pinkham
	Coltishall	66	Spitfire	Rupert Leigh (1½)
		242	Hurricane	Douglas Bader (11)
Kirton-in-Lindsey	Kirton	222	Spitfire	Tubby Mermagen
Wittering	Wittering	229	Hurricane	H. McGuire
		266	Spitfire	Rodney Wilkinson (2)
	Collyweston	23	Blenheim	L. Bicknell

continued...

Table 6 continued

13 Group (HQ Ponteland)

Catterick	Catterick	41	Spitfire	H. West
		219	Blenheim	J. Little
Dyce	Grangemouth	263	Hurricane	H. Eeles
Turnhouse	Turnhouse	79	Hurricane	Hervey Heyworth
		253	Hurricane	Tom Gleave
		245	Hurricane	E. Whitley
		603	Spitfire	George Denholm (3)
	Drem	602	Spitfire	Sandy Johnstone (8)
		605*	Hurricane	Walter Churchill
Usworth	Usworth	607	Hurricane	James Vick
	Acklington	72	Spitfire	Ronald Lees
		152	Spitfire	Peter Devitt
Wick	Wick	3	Hurricane	S. Godden
	Castletown	504	Hurricane	John Sample (1)

* denotes non-operational at the time. Figures in parentheses after commanders' names are confirmed BoB victories where known.

1 Debden transferred from 12 to 11 Group on 8 August.

2 Droguer (sometimes rendered Drogo) White got his sobriquet from a pre-war incident in which he was towing a target drogue for the Navy. When shells burst ahead of him, he is reported to have radioed 'I am pulling this *#*?*! thing, not pushing it!'

3 Prof Leathart was so named for his mathematical bent.

Gradually the German strategy hardened. Attacks were made on British convoys in the Channel and Thames Estuary, and naval bases on the South Coast were raided. This was ominous. Not only was Britain's mastery of the sea being challenged, but it appeared that the *Luftwaffe* bomber force was honing its anti-shipping skills against the day when it would have to defend the invasion fleet from the might of the Royal Navy. At the same time, large-scale fighter sweeps began over south-east England. These were obviously a prelude to gaining air superiority.

Even with radar, advance warning of attacks on convoys and coastal targets was minimal. To counter this, some squadrons were moved to forward airfields, while patrols were mounted over the convoys. Such patrols normally consisted of a section of three fighters. If the *Luftwaffe* appeared in force, they were often overwhelmed, fighting desperately to survive until reinforcements arrived. The same applied against the German fighter sweeps, or *Freijagd*, which were usually made in *Gruppe* strength. If these were identified in time, they were ignored, and left to suffer the attrition normal with operations over the sea from temporary landing fields. But it wasn't always possible to do so.

Defiants of No 141 Squadron took a heavy beating when they were intercepted by Bf 109s off Folkestone on 19 July. The element of surprise had been with the Defiant during the Dunkirk operations, but now the *Jagdflieger* knew it for what it was: a slow, unmanoeuvrable, under-armed non-starter. A head-on pass, followed by individual attacks from astern and below, downed six out of nine. Only the belated arrival of the Hurricanes of No 111 Squadron prevented the massacre from becoming absolute. At the time, the RAF had no air-sea rescue service. With the majority of actions taking place over the sea, pilot losses were high and replacements were in short supply. Royal Navy pilots were already serving with Fighter Command; now light bomber and army co-operation pilots with single-engine experience were also transferred to fighters.

The nature of the battle changed on 12 August. Heavy attacks were launched against radar stations on the South Coast. Ventnor was badly damaged, and Dover, Pevensey and Rye were hit. While the last three were all repairable within hours, it seemed that follow-up attacks would soon render them unusable. Fighter Command's vital all-seeing radar eyes were in jeopardy. On the same day came the first attacks on fighter airfields, indicating that the entire defensive system was now at risk, not just its eyes.

The Good Fairy who protects the British now worked overtime. Dummy signals were emitted from Ventnor, to give the impression of a fully operational station, while the gap was partially plugged by a mobile set. From this, and the fact that the other stations were soon back on the air, the *Luftwaffe* concluded that radar stations were almost impossible to knock out. It was also seduced by the Richthofen legend, many *Jagdflieger* arguing that anything which brought up the British fighters to be shot down was to the advantage of the Third Reich. For whatever reason, the Germans failed to follow up their advantage. The Good Fairy was also active on behalf of the sector

> *I must admit I had qualms about leading my little band into the midst of a vast horde of the enemy.*
>
> Peter Townsend, No 85 Squadron

> *Advancing towards us was a massive column about a mile and a half high, stepped up wave upon wave.*
>
> Peter Townsend, No 85 Squadron

stations. German intelligence never for a moment suspected that the sources of the interception instructions that they monitored were not deep underground and well away from the airfields. Nor, it became apparent, did they know which airfields housed fighters and which did not. Consequently a great deal of the German bombing effort was dissipated against secondary targets.

The air fighting of August was very heavy. The advantages of single squadrons were speed of reaction and flexibility, but this meant that units of 12 aircraft or less routinely intercepted huge raids of 100 plus. To the pilots it looked and felt frightening, but it worked. Fortunately they were rarely alone, as other squadrons converged on the German *Balbos* from all sides.

Three notable British victories were scored during the month. On 18 August, the Ju 87 Stuka units took a terrible beating, losing 17 aircraft with another seven damaged. After this they were withdrawn from the battle. Spitfires and Hurricanes also carved a deadly swathe through the twin-engined Bf 110 heavy fighters, to the point where they were also deemed to need fighter escort. Finally, rising bomber losses caused the Bf 109s to be ordered to provide close escort. As there were not enough fighters to go round, this resulted in a diminution of the bomber effort. But these factors were not readily apparent to Fighter Command.

By the beginning of September, the outlook for Fighter Command was grim. Manston, the most forward airfield, had been abandoned, while cumulative damage to other airfields had started to reduce efficiency. Many squadrons had been pulled out of the most threatened areas to rest and regroup, and had been replaced by

> *On 6 September victory was within the* Luftwaffe's *grasp. The previous two weeks' offensive on airfields had cost Fighter Command 295 fighters (daily average 21) and 103 pilots killed (over seven daily), with 170 fighters badly damaged.*
>
> Peter Townsend, No 85 Squadron

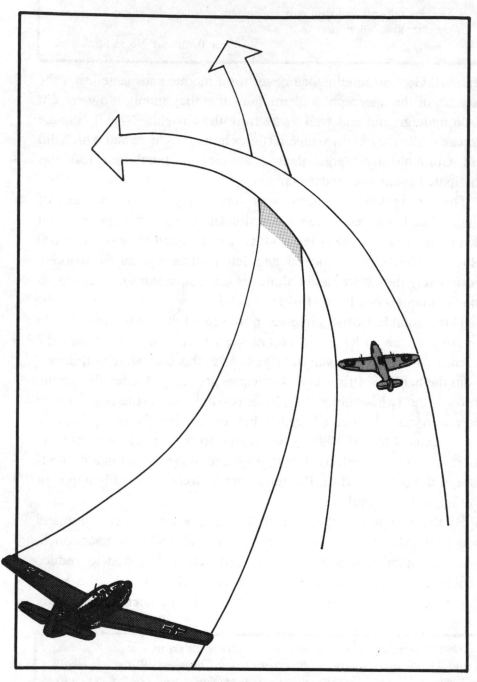

Fig. 5. The Break
The standard evasion against attack from astern was to turn as hard as possible in the direction of the attacker, to increase deflection quickly and make oneself a harder target.

inexperienced units from the north, some of which sustained horrendous casualties before they learned the rules by which the game was being played.

That month, the Air Officer Commanding Fighter Command, Sir Hugh Dowding, categorised his squadrons as A, B and C. 'A' Squadrons remained in 11 Group and on its flanks; 'B' Squadrons, of which there were few, formed a small operational reserve, while 'C' Squadrons, usually those which had sustained severe casualties, were posted to the north, to provide a pool of replacement pilots for those units in the south. Among the old hands, exhaustion was setting in. The strain of waiting for the scramble order, knowing that when it came they would be launched against vastly greater numbers, always with the 109s lurking above, took its toll. No 501 (Hurricane) Squadron was a rarity. It was based in 11 Group from beginning to end, and often flew as many as five missions a day. In all, it engaged the enemy on 35 days; more than any other unit, and sustained the heaviest losses of all—nearly 2.4 times established strength.

> Towards the end of the Battle I had taken about as much as I could bear. My nerves were in ribbons and I was scared stiff that one day I would pull out and avoid combat. That frightened me more than the Germans and I pleaded with my CO (Harry Hogan) for a rest. He was sympathetic but quite adamant that until he got replacements I would have to carry on. I am glad now that he was unable to let me go. If I had been allowed to leave the squadron feeling as I did, I am sure that I would never have flown again.
>
> *Jim Lacey (28 victories), No 501 Squadron*

Nor was it any easier for the novices. Paddy Barthropp of No 602 (Spitfire) Squadron first went into action on 15 September. He flew four sorties, saw lots of German aircraft, and exhausted his ammunition on each occasion, but was unable to see if he hit anything. He was 'milling around, absolutely terrified, looking behind him and firing at something painted with swastikas', a graphic description of a state of total confusion.

The *Luftwaffe* had no means of knowing how hard-pressed Fighter Command was at this time. The siren song of the Richthofen syndrome—enhanced, as always, by overclaiming—lured them into a false move. Seeking to bring on a decisive fighter battle which would ensure the final destruction of Fighter Command, they switched targets from fighter airfields to London. On 7 September, a huge *Luftwaffe* raid, estimated at 348 bombers escorted by 617 fighters, started across the Channel. Twenty-one British squadrons were scrambled to meet it, but their controllers, not having realised that the Germans had changed targets, were deployed to defend the vital fighter airfields. In cloudy conditions most failed to make contact, and the destruction consequently wrought in London's dockland area was horrendous. Over the next few days more heavy raids were launched against the metropolis. For various reasons, the defence against these was ineffective, leading *Luftwaffe* intelligence to conclude that Fighter Command was down to its last 50 fighters.

Then came 15 September 1940, when two large raids were launched against the capital. At noon, a mere 25 Dornier bombers attacked, preceded and escorted by about 150 109s, and supported by an additional small force of 109 fighter-bombers. It is hard not to view the Dorniers as bait. On this occasion the British defences worked at their best. Almost every fighter squadron that was scrambled made contact, harassing the raiders and peeling away their escorts. Then as the bombers arrived over South London, they were confronted with a huge fighter formation: Douglas Bader's five-squadron Big Wing from 12 Group. The fierce opposition while inbound, plus the Big Wing over the target area, clearly demonstrated that Fighter Command was far from being a beaten force. The myth of the 'last 50 fighters' was shattered.

Bader's Big Wing, which will be examined in detail in the next chapter, was always contentious. His idea was to meet force with force, and while it is true that his loss ratio per 100 sorties was relatively low, the results hardly justified the expenditure of effort. But on 15 September, the appearance of the Big Wing—55 fighters in all, but reported by the *Luftwaffe* as 80 plus—resulted in a huge drop in morale in the German air arm. For this reason, if for no other, its existence was justified. The day was an undeniable victory for Fighter Command, even though overclaiming made a nonsense of the actual German losses. Shortly thereafter Hitler's invasion was postponed indefinitely, and after a few more heavy raids on London, the main daylight blitz quietly fizzled out.

Some idea of the intensity of the fighting at the height of the battle can be gained by comparing the Orders of Battle for 10 July and 15 September. After their disastrous debut in 11 Group, the two Defiant squadrons had been transferred to night fighting. Of the 17 Hurricane and Spitfire squadrons in 11 Group on 10 July, only one remained throughout. Of the others, 12 had been withdrawn to the north; two had transferred to 10 Group; and two were temporarily withdrawn to other groups before returning to the fray. The battle was costly in squadron commanders, 14 being killed in all, 10 badly wounded, and many others posted away. Most unfortunate was No 43 Squadron which, by the end of the battle, was on its fourth commander.

Table 7. Fighter Command Day Fighter Order of Battle, 15 September 1940

Sector	Base	Sqn/Score	Type	Commander/Score
11 Group (HQ Uxbridge)				
Biggin Hill	Biggin Hill	72/23^1/$_2$	Spitfire	A.R. Collins
		92/40^1/$_4$	Spitfire	P.J. Sanders (4)
	Gravesend	66/25	Spitfire	Rupert Leigh (1^1/$_2$)
Debden	Debden	17/23^1/$_2$	Hurricane	A.G. Miller
		73/8	Hurricane	Mike Beytagh (1)
	Martlesham	257/16^1/$_4$	Hurricane	Bob Tuck (13^1/$_4$)
Hornchurch	Hornchurch	603/57^3/$_4$	Spitfire	George Denholm (3^1/$_2$)
		41/45^1/$_4$	Spitfire	R.C. Lister
		222/19	Spitfire	John Hill (1)
Kenley	Kenley	253/24	Hurricane	E.R. Bitmead
		501/43^1/$_2$	Hurricane	Harry Hogan (6^1/$_2$)
	Croydon	605/23^3/$_4$	Hurricane	Walter Churchill
Northolt	Northolt	1(Can)/11	Hurricane	Ernest McNab (4^1/$_2$)
		229/11^1/$_2$	Hurricane	H.J. McGuire
		303/44	Hurricane	Ronald Kellett (5)
		504/13	Hurricane	John Sample (1^1/$_2$)
North Weald	North Weald	249/27	Hurricane	John Grandy
	Stapleford	46/12	Hurricane	J.R. McLachlan
Tangmere	Tangmere	213/19	Hurricane	D. Wilson-McDonald
		607/4	Hurricane	James Vick
	Westhampnett	602/37	Spitfire	Sandy Johnstone (8)
10 Group (HQ Box)				
Exeter	Exeter/Bibury	87/17^1/$_4$	Hurricane	R.S. Mills
	Filton	601/37	Hurricane	Archibald Hope (1^1/$_2$)
Filton	Pembrey	79/14^1/$_2$	Hurricane	Hervey Heyworth
Middle Wallop	Middle Wallop	238/32^1/$_2$	Hurricane	Harold Fenton (1^1/$_2$)
	Warmwell	609/48	Spitfire	Horace Darley (3)
		152/27	Spitfire	Peter Devitt
Boscombe Down		56/26^1/$_2$	Hurricane	H.M. Pinfold
St Eval	St Eval	234/32	Spitfire	Minden Blake (6)
	Roborough	247/0	Gladiator	H.A. Chater

continued...

Table 7 continued

12 Group (HQ Watnall)

Church Fenton	Church Fenton	85/29	Hurricane	Peter Townsend (6)
	Leconfield/			
	Ringway	64/11	Spitfire	Don MacDonell (9¹/₂)
Coltishall	Wittering	74/23³/₄	Spitfire	Sailor Malan (12)
Digby	Digby	151/15	Hurricane	*not filled*
		611/10¹/₄	Spitfire	Jim McComb (2¹/₂)
Duxford	Duxford	242/22¹/₂	Hurricane	Douglas Bader (11)
		302/5	Hurricane	Jack Satchell (3)/M.Mümler (1)
		310/14	Hurricane	Doug Blackwood (1)/
				Sasha Hess (2)
	Fowlmere	19/26	Spitfire	Brian Lane (4¹/₂)
Kirton-in-	Kirton	616/12³/₄	Spitfire	Billy Burton
Lindsey				
Wittering	Wittering	1/16¹/₂	Hurricane	David Pemberton (2)
		266/8	Spitfire	*not filled*

13 Group (HQ Ponteland)

Catterick	Catterick	54/34	Spitfire	F.P. Dunworth
Dyce	Dyce/Montrose	145/32¹/₂	Hurricane	John Peel (3)
Turnhouse	Turnhouse	3/1	Hurricane	S.F. Godden
		65/10¹/₂	Spitfire	A.L. Holland
	Prestwick	615/19	Hurricane	Joe Kayll (3)
	Drem	111/32¹/₂	Hurricane	John Thompson (5)
Usworth	Usworth	43/37³/₄	Hurricane	*not filled*
	Acklington	32/23¹/₂	Hurricane	Mike Crossley (14)
		610/30¹/₂	Spitfire	John Ellis (11)
Wick	Sumburgh	232/1	Hurricane	M. Stephens (¹/₂)
Aldergrove	Aldergrove	245/0	Hurricane	E.W. Whitley

Note: All scores are confirmed victories before 31 December 1940. They do not include those gained over France or Dunkirk, or in the defence of Great Britain prior to July 1940.

October saw the widespread use of bomb-carrying Bf 109Es. High and fast, these were difficult to intercept, but the damage they caused was minimal. With the onset of winter adverse weather restricted flying operations. Fighter Command, happy at having withstood the *Luftwaffe*, settled down to a period of training and expansion. Round Two was expected in the early summer of 1941. When it came, Fighter Command would be ready.

RAF Tactics

The frequent German ploy of putting a major force over the Pas-de-Calais, then holding back the start of the raid, was a major problem for British fighters, with their limited endurance. Rather than order the squadrons off too early, it was preferable to delay until no

> *German fighters could do no harm to Britain. German bombers with their deadly loads were the menace. Our orders were to seek them out and to destroy them. Only when their Bf 109 escort interfered did it become a fleeting battle between fighter and fighter. But we tried to avoid them, not to challenge them.*
>
> Peter Townsend, No 85 Squadron

possible doubt remained that the raid was inbound. Delay was the lesser of two evils. Scrambled late, the defenders were often frantically grabbing for height even after the German vanguard crossed the south coast. To have an altitude advantage was rare; to have time to jockey for position when 109s were around was even rarer. There was no time to be fancy.

Against the Bombers

There was no doubt about priorities. Bombers were the primary cause of destruction, and all efforts were directed against them. Late in the battle, Spitfires were directed to tackle the 109s while Hurricanes took on the bombers.

On intercepting, the usual procedure was to charge straight in. Most often this resulted in a head-on attack, pulling into line abreast or flat echelon with all aircraft opening fire at once. While not in the handbook, this proved very effective. The extensively glazed noses of the German bombers offered no frontal protection, and the sight of 12 Hurricanes coming from head-on at a combined closing speed of about 450 mph, with 96 machine-guns spewing out almost 2,000 rounds per second, was terrifying. Added to this was the ever-present risk of collision. As Dornier pilot Wilhelm Raab commented to the author: 'We tried to shrink ourselves small. There was not even a molehill to hide behind!'

> *We levelled out about two miles ahead on a collision course. Ease the throttle to reduce closing speed—which anyway only allowed a few seconds fire. Get a bead on them right away, hold it, and never mind the streams of tracer darting overhead. Just keep on pressing on the button until you think you are going to collide—then stick hard forward. Under the shock of negative-g your stomach jumps into your mouth, dust and muck fly up from the cockpit floor into your eyes and your head cracks on the roof as you break away below.*
>
> Peter Townsend, No 85 Squadron

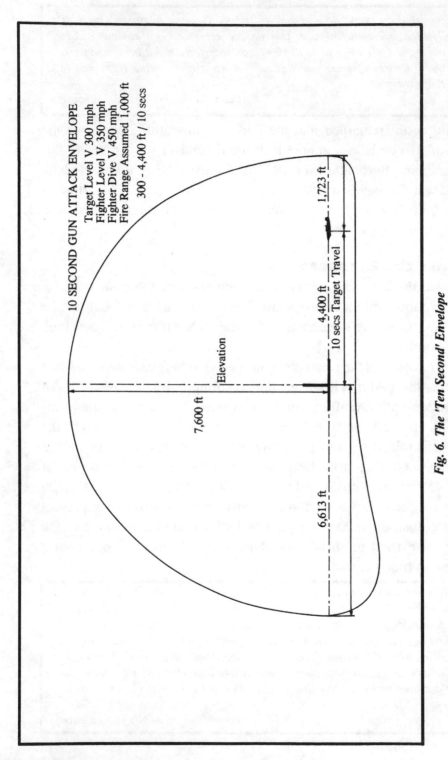

10 SECOND GUN ATTACK ENVELOPE

Target Level V 300 mph
Fighter Level V 350 mph
Fighter Dive V 450 mph
Fire Range Assumed 1,000 ft

300 - 4,400 ft / 10 secs

Elevation

7,600 ft

6,613 ft

4,400 ft

1,723 ft

10 secs Target Travel

Fig. 6. The 'Ten Second' Envelope

From the target 'start point' to the right, the envelope here shows the area from which an attack can be made within ten seconds of a sighting, by which time the target aircraft has reached the centre point.

At such a high closing speed, firing time was very short, and there was little scope for adjusting one's aim. The best that could reasonably be hoped for was that enough damage could be inflicted to break up the formation. Once separated, the bombers could be attacked individually, with a much greater probability of inflicting lethal damage. Nor was the psychological impact of the head-on attack to be scorned. It became ingrained in the minds of German flyers that the mere appearance of British fighters was the immediate prelude to a sudden and vicious assault. This belief quite naturally induced a defensive mind-set.

Against the Fighters

The usual impression of the Battle of Britain is of a fighter selecting an opponent, then whirling and darting around in circles until it succeeded in gaining a position from which it could put in a killing burst of fire. By virtue of their lower wing loading, British fighters could out-turn the Bf 109E, and this should theoretically have given them the advantage in a dogfight. But how true was this? Not very, for various reasons, the first of which was to do with aerodynamics. A small radius of turn is undoubtedly an advantage, but before this can be achieved, the turn has to be established by banking. This involves rate of roll. At moderate speeds, below about 240 mph, rate of roll of the Spitfire was better than 90°/sec, allowing full advantage to be taken of its excellent manoeuvrability. As speed increased the ailerons stiffened, progressively reducing roll rate, until at 400 mph the ailerons became almost immovable. The Messerschmitt fighter was even worse. Aileron response was good below 195 mph but reduced rapidly above this, so that at 300 mph, its roll rate was reduced to a pathetic 11°/sec.

To summarise, both the Spitfire and the Hurricane were superior to the Bf 109E in turn radius (by virtue of their lower wing loading) and in roll rate, the Hurricane less so, throughout the speed range. This is not to say that at very high speeds hard turning was impossible. It was simply much slower to establish. Once in the turn drag built up, slowing the fighter. As speed bled off, rate of roll and rate of turn increased.

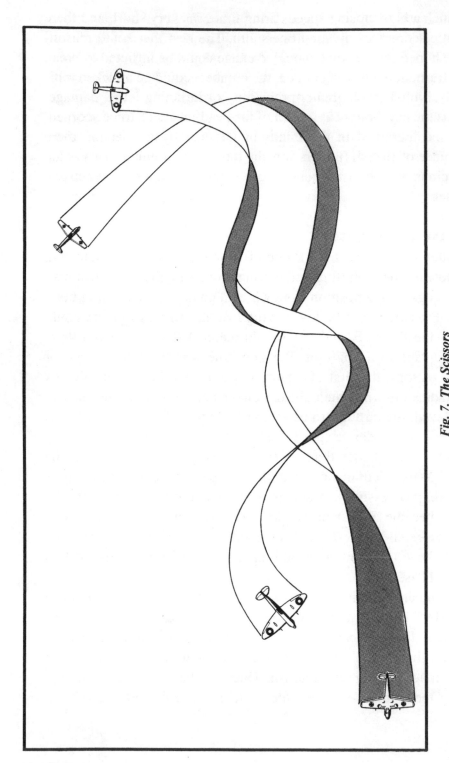

Fig. 7. The Scissors

While there were few references to the scissors in the literature of the period, several photographs of contrails show that it was known. The idea is to force the attacker out in front with a series of turn reversals.

Turning was of more value as a defensive manoeuvre. Few pilots mastered the art of deflection shooting, and once the angle-off increased to more than about 15°, the defender was reasonably safe. An attacker in position astern needed to turn less tightly to maintain a firing position, but assuming that he was 'in the saddle', i.e. flying in the same plane as his target, this often meant that his opponent disappeared beneath his nose. Turning ability is, of course, based on wing lift, which is roughly proportional to wing loading. This was an advantage in the vertical plane, because when pulling out from a high-speed dive, roll rate was not involved. In the companion volume to this book, *Luftwaffe Fighter Aces*, it was made clear that the *Jagdwaffe*, with its normal altitude advantage, preferred to fight in the vertical, using dive and zoom tactics. If it was not hit on the first pass, even the relatively slow Hurricane could take advantage of this:

> I went after a 109 that made a bolt for home. He dived steeply and I lost him in the haze but continued to dive, [he] saw me and dived again. Again I lost him, and pulled the plug in an effort to catch up. Again the 109 gave himself away by climbing vertically against the sky. I caught him this time and the superiority of manoeuvrability of the Hurricane over the 109 stood me in good stead. Every manoeuvre he did I could do but more tightly. I had a burst vertically up at him and another vertically down and a couple of deflection shots on the beam—and then the roof flew off and the pilot baled out successfully.
>
> *George Barclay (6 confirmed victories), No 249 Squadron,*
> *27 September 1940*

In this combat, the Hurricane was able to catch the much faster Bf 109 by pulling tighter out of the dive to reduce the range and take up a position of advantage astern.

Prolonged turning fights were the exception rather than the rule, and only rarely continued long enough for one fighter to gain a decisive advantage:

> He saw me as I turned after him and, putting on full inside rudder as he turned, skidded underneath me. Pulling round half stalled, I tore after him and got in a short burst as I closed on him before he was out of my sights again. That German pilot certainly knew how to handle a 109—I have never seen one thrown about as that one was, and I felt certain his wings would come off at any moment. However, they stayed on, and he continued to lead me a hell of a dance as I strove to get my sights on him again. Twice I managed to get in a short burst but I don't think I hit him, then he managed to get round towards my tail. Pulling hard round I started to gain on him and began to come round

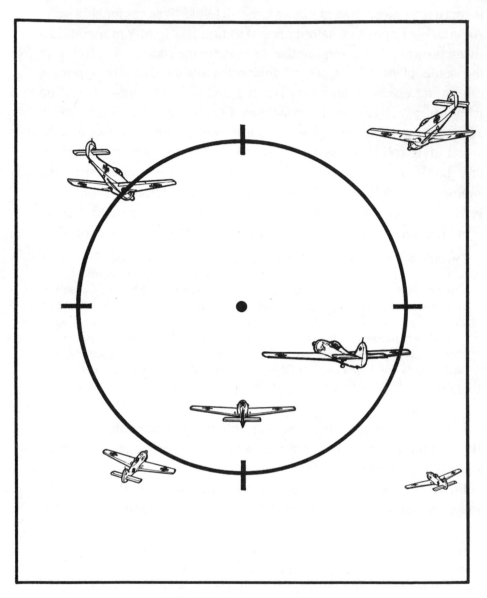

Fig. 8. Deflection Shooting
Range, deflection angle and target speed all had to be estimated in a flash. This is a standard Fighter Command training diagram showing the amount of angle-off needed for targets at varying speeds, angles and ranges.

towards his tail. He was obviously turning as hard as his kite could and I could see that his [leading edge] slots were open, showing that he was nearly stalled. His ailerons were obviously snatching too, as first one wing and then the other would dip violently.

Sandy Lane (6 victories), No 19 Squadron, 15 September 1940

This combat, flown at moderate speeds, clearly demonstrated that a well-handled 109 was no pushover in manoeuvre combat even for the Spitfire. On this occasion the 109 eventually disengaged and vanished into cloud. Lane claimed it as probably destroyed.

This type of thing was fine on the few occasions when two adversaries became separated from the main engagement, but a multi-bogey dogfight involving 30 or so fighters was very different. In this scenario, to engage a single opponent for more than about 20 seconds was to give one of his comrades time to slip in astern. The technique was to select a target, line up quickly, fire a short burst from whatever angle was possible, then break hard. In this sort of fight, sustained manoeuvrability counted for little. Victories were gained only by seizing an opportunity then shooting accurately, preferably at a range short enough to minimise deflection problems. Survival depended largely on being unpredictable.

Fighter Command Tactics

At the start of the battle, fighter tactics were based on the three-aircraft section. Dunkirk saw a move towards using the far more flexible pair, but this remained at the discretion of individual squadron commanders. Often it was a mix of the two. Peter Devitt, commanding No 152 (Spitfire) Squadron, favoured a V-formation using pairs line astern, but frequently put his men into flights of six aircraft abreast, each flight in line astern, before attacking. Equally unhappy with the three-aircraft section was the South African Adolph 'Sailor' Malan, who on taking command of No 74 Squadron, instituted pairs in sections of four in line astern in three files. This was far more flexible than three-aircraft Vics, but, as we shall see, it was far from ideal.

With hindsight, it is possible to wonder why Fighter Command failed to adopt the German *Schwarme* formation. The truth is that they were too busy fighting to worry about clever tactics. In addition,

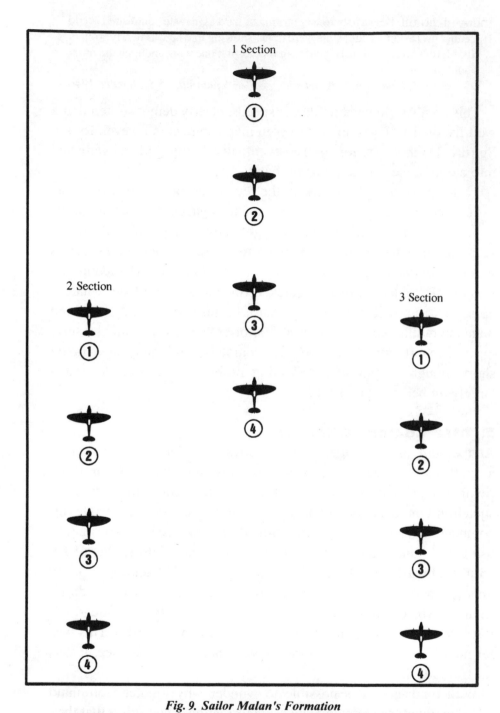

Fig. 9. Sailor Malan's Formation
*This formation was devised by Sailor Malan in the late summer of 1940,
and was based on the pair as the smallest fighting unit. All members
weaved in the combat area. It was not finally superseded until 1943.*

many accounts of the period describe the *Jagdflieger* as flying in three-aircraft Vics. Like the mythical Heinkel He 113 fighter, described as resembling a Spitfire by Hurricane pilots and a Hurricane by Spitfire pilots, this seems to have existed mainly in the mind of the beholder. One consistent observation, however, is that German fighter sections split up rapidly when attacked. This was almost certainly due to the German use of the cross-over turn which, to the uninitiated eye, looked confusing.

The Battle of Britain was unquestionably a British victory. The *Luftwaffe* failed to destroy Fighter Command; it failed to bomb the island race into submission; and most importantly, it failed even to gain air superiority over the invasion area. But, like many past British victories, it was a near-run thing.

The Aces

The Battle of Britain was a battle of attrition, and it was won by those few who gave just a little more than they got. For this reason, the following aces are lesser-known figures.

PETER BROTHERS Peter Malam Brothers joined No 32 (Hurricane) Squadron in October 1936, and was promoted to flight commander in 1938. His first victories came in May 1940; a Bf 109 near Cambrai on the 18th and a Bf 110 over Ieper (Ypres) on the 23rd. In the Battle of Britain he was credited with eight victories, five of which were Bf 109Es.

> One was often aware of being totally outnumbered. We thought 'Oh God! However are we going to cope with this lot?' The enemy bombers often poured a lot of firepower from the rear. But if you could get higher, or at the same level, and attack head-on, you could often split up the formation.
>
> As a Hurricane pilot, I had a certain fear and respect for the 109. For one thing it could dive faster. If a Bf 109 pilot saw you, he could dive down, taking a shot at you, go past, pull the stick back and start climbing very fast. You just couldn't keep up with him. The only way to overcome this was to roll over inverted and dive after him in positive-g. When the 109 pulled up to level out or climb, we'd aileron-turn to right-way-up and see his plan view and get in a perfect shot.

> *I once looked in my mirror and saw the biggest, fattest Bf 109 ever, or so it seemed. All at once his front lit up as he fired at me. The 109 went over the top, to be followed by my No 2, who was firing at me! When we got down I put him on gun practice for two days, and told him 'don't shoot at your friends … and if your shoot at anything, make sure you hit it!'*
>
> Peter Brothers (16 victories)

As the Hurricanes tried to get among the bombers, a surprise bounce by 109s was an ever-present possibility. As a survival tactic against this, Peter Brothers made a practice of trimming his rudder so that his Hurricane crabbed to one side. His reasoning was that this would make it very difficult for an attacker to judge the right amount of deflection, making an apparently easy shot into a far more difficult one. The real answer, of course, was to spot the attacker coming in, but this was not always possible. Brothers observed that 'the Hurricane's visibility was pretty good, except above and below to the rear. The mirror was useful, but not as effective as it might have been. I replaced mine with a curved rear-view mirror, and actually felt it gave me a touch extra speed besides giving me a better view'.

On 9 September he was posted to No 257 Squadron, a Hurricane unit which had taken a fearful beating. With new squadron commander Bob Tuck he pulled the unit round, and led it during the noon action on 15 September, during which he gained two more victories. Against the high-flying 109s of the final stage of the campaign the lower-performing Hurricanes were disadvantaged, and Brothers had no further successes in 1940. He commented on conditions:

> At height cold was a constant problem. The canopy would mist up, and ice used to form inside and out, on the front, bullet-proofed windshield. I often had to scrape ice off the glass in front, but could see out of each side, which was made of perspex. Goggles were a nuisance, uncomfortable. But they were useful if you had to bale out, and helped to prevent burning of the eyes if you were hit.

Rested in January 1941, Brothers commanded No 457 Australian (Spitfire) Squadron from June of that year; then No 602 (Spitfire) Squadron. In October 1942 he became the Wing Leader at Tangmere. After tours at 61 OTU and HQ 10 Group, he led the Exeter Wing in 1944, then the Culmhead Wing at the time of the invasion of

Fig. 10. Peter Brothers' Defensive Measure
*Aware that the greatest danger always came from astern, Hurricane pilot
Peter Brothers trimmed his aircraft so that it was always crabbing to one
side. He reasoned that no attacker would notice this, and that it would
spoil their aim.*

Normandy, with which he scored his 16th and final victory, an FW 190, on 7 August 1944. He survived the war, rose to the rank of Air Commodore, and retired from the RAF in 1973.

BOB DOE   After joining the RAF Volunteer Reserve in March 1938, shortly after his 18th birthday, Bob Doe gained his wings and in November 1939 was posted to No 234 Squadron, which was forming at Leconfield, with a mixture of Blenheims and Battles. In March 1940 these were replaced by Spitfires. For Bob it was love at first sight. He described his first flight in a Spitfire as the greatest joy he had known, rocketing up into the sky, so easy and smooth to fly. In June the squadron moved south to St Eval in Cornwall, where it flew convoy patrols, before moving to Middle Wallop on 15 August.

The standard description of a fighter pilot is a little man with a big wrist-watch and an even bigger ego. This was not the case with Bob. He had only fired his guns once (into the sea on test), and felt that he was the worst pilot in the squadron and was unlikely to survive his first combat. On the same afternoon as it arrived at Middle Wallop the squadron was scrambled to patrol off Swanage. It flew in four Vics of three in sections line astern, which Bob later described as the stupidest formation possible, with one man looking out and all the rest concentrating on staying in close formation. To make matters worse, they patrolled up and down sun, violating the rule of never flying with the sun at one's back. At one point they turned, only to find that the rear section had vanished. Two were missing, and the third had force-landed near Cherbourg. No-one had even noticed their assailants.

Shortly afterwards the rest of the squadron encountered a mixed bag of 109s and 110s. Bob Doe's section leader Pat Hughes (14 victories) fired at a 110, then broke away. Doe found himself on its tail, closed in and kept firing until it went into the sea. As he pulled away, another 110 overshot him; he closed in behind and shot it down also. Realising that he had been very lucky, that night he went early to bed to think. It was apparent that the greatest danger came from astern. The accepted wisdom was always to break into an attack, but Bob could not accept this. He determined that as soon as he saw bullets coming past, he would simply hit the stick and bunt out of the

74

line of fire. He was also shaken by the suddenness with which he had found himself in the midst of the enemy. He had failed to see them in time. In the tight formation flown, this was hardly surprising. He resolved that getting away on his own as much as possible would give him a better chance.

Victories mounted, and Bob's confidence grew. On 18 August, he singled out a Bf 109 which had been shooting down barrage balloons over Portsmouth and chased it out to sea. Down to 100 ft, he hit it, and as it slowed he saw the canopy fly off: 'I flew alongside him, to his right, about 30 or 40 yards away. It was most odd, the first time I had ever seen a German in the air. The impression of him has stuck with me to this day; a big man with fair hair and a round face. As he went down I looked back and saw him splash into the sea.'

Seeing the enemy first gives the initiative, and Bob, blessed with good eyesight, put this to good use. From experience he found that the most effective way to attack was to go straight in and scatter the enemy. Careful jockeying for position simply gave the enemy more time to spot him. Bob also learned the trick of using his peripheral vision; something few ever managed. 'I'd learnt an awful lot about seeing aeroplanes, and was very good at spotting them. You never see an aeroplane if you are looking straight at it. You see it ten degrees off to one side. You might see movement, at one o'clock, two o'clock, then that's it, you've got it'.

As August gave way to September, Bob started flying with Alan 'Budge' Harker (7 victories) for mutual cover, spaced a couple of hundred yards abreast. It worked well; on the first outing, Harker shot a 109 off Bob's tail. But then No 234 Squadron, reduced to just three of its original 21 pilots, went back to St Eval to rest and re-equip.

On 28 September, Bob was posted to fly Hurricanes with No 238 Squadron at Chilbolton. Commenting that the Hurricane was more manoeuvrable and a better gun platform than the Spitfire, he continued to score, but on 10 October he emerged from cloud over Poole only to be hit from behind by a Bf 109. Wounded in an arm and a foot, he baled out. After returning to action, he was badly injured in a night landing in January 1941 following engine failure. When he recovered he joined No 66 Squadron in May 1942, and damaged a Ju 88 during the following month. It was his last air combat victory. Later in the war he flew Mustangs, then Hurricanes in Burma. His final score was 14 confirmed and two shared destroyed, and five damaged. He left the RAF in 1966.

JOSEF FRANTISEK A pre-war pilot in the Czech Air Force, Frantisek escaped to Poland in 1938 when the Germans took over his country. Following the fall of Poland, he escaped to Romania, and thence to France via Syria. Finally he arrived in England in June 1940, joined the RAF, and was posted to the predominantly Polish 303 Squadron. First going into action on 30 August, this was probably the top-scoring Hurricane squadron of the battle, with 44 confirmed victories in exactly six weeks. It was certainly one of the most effective. Frantisek, a single Czech among the Poles, stood out even among this company.

Often described as a 'lone wolf' who would leave the squadron to go hunting on his own account, the truth was more prosaic. If the squadron became scattered after combat, he would, fuel and ammunition permitting, slip off on his own to prowl the German exit routes, looking for stragglers. Often he found one. His first victory came on 2 September, when he attacked two Bf 109s near Dover. A head-on pass damaged one, which he turned and followed, closing right in and shooting it down into the sea. The pilot was rescued.

If success in air fighting can be summed up as opportunity plus marksmanship, then Frantisek's marksmanship must have been of a high order. In the space of exactly four weeks he was credited with 17 confirmed destroyed and one probable. It was not done without risk: on 6 September he tackled two 109s near Sevenoaks, and while he sent one down in flames, the other hit his aircraft with cannon fire. Three days later, in a large multi-bogey fight near Beachy Head, he accounted for a Bf 109 and a He 111, but was then isolated by two 109s and badly shot up. With damage to wings, fuel tank and radiator, and an overheating engine, he was in a desperate situation. Only the arrival of the cavalry in the shape of two Spitfires, enabled him to escape. He eased his stricken Hurricane into a cabbage field near Brighton, then calmly caught a train back to London.

His final victories, on 30 September, were in the true 'lone wolf' tradition. His engine was late in starting, and the rest of the squadron went without him. Finally he got away and chased after them. Heading south, he encountered six 109s, which formed a defensive circle. But the Czech sergeant spotted an opening and pounced. His first burst knocked one of them out of the circle; his second set it ablaze. In the ensuing melee he fired at a second 109, which streamed smoke before vanishing into cloud. Outnumbered four to one, Frantisek also made himself scarce.

It all ended on the morning of 8 October. At the end of an uneventful patrol, his Hurricane crashed on landing at Northolt, turning over and bursting into flames. Josef Frantisek was dead. Some sources state that his total score had reached 28. He has been credited with 11 victories whilst flying with the Polish and French Air Forces, but this is not confirmed by the records, and it seems probable that he has been confused with Frantisek Perina, also a Czech, who while in French service was credited with two whole and nine shared victories.

3. LEANING FORWARD, JANUARY 1941–MAY 1944

As the Battle of Britain drew to a close, its two key commanders, AOC Fighter Command Hugh Dowding and AOC 11 Group Keith Park, were replaced. Dowding was, of course, long overdue for retirement, while Park appeared very tired, but the widespread feeling was that they were shabbily treated. Be that as it may, Fighter Command was taken over by Sholto Douglas, while Trafford Leigh-Mallory moved to 11 Group from 12 Group, where he had been instrumental in forming the Big Wing at Duxford. In the previous conflict Douglas had commanded No 84 Squadron on the Western Front with SE 5a fighters. Leigh-Mallory's background was Army Co-operation rather than fighters.

New brooms sweep clean. Dowding and Park had won the Battle of Britain, which was all that could possibly have been asked, yet had been criticised for their handling of it. Both Sholto Douglas and Trafford Leigh-Mallory were among the leading critics, and were determined to do things differently. That they were able to do so was due to a complete change in circumstances from that of the previous summer. The invasion had been postponed indefinitely, and even if it was possible would now take many months to remount, while *Luftwaffe* activity in daylight was minimal. This allowed the RAF fighter squadrons to rest, re-equip, and train novice pilots. By the end of the year, Fighter Command was stronger than ever before.

As we have already seen, the standard *Luftwaffe* fighter unit was the *Gruppe*, typically 28 aircraft. An RAF sector station and its satellite airfield(s) normally operated three squadrons of day fighters, with an air strength of 36 aircraft. To achieve a numerical advantage, all that was necessary was to combine the three squadrons into a wing.

78

Technical parity was the next priority, which in effect meant that all fighter squadrons should be equipped with the Spitfire. This provided the fighter force with the best weapon available, and simplified tactical control in the air and maintenance on the ground. Of the Hurricane units, some had already been transferred to night fighting; others, notably those with the four-cannon Hurricane IIC, were employed in anti-shipping and intruder roles. The remainder soldiered on, scheduled to be re-equipped with the Supermarine fighter, or with the new Hawker Typhoon when these became available in sufficient quantities.

There were drawbacks as well as advantages to using three-squadron wings. The greater number of aircraft involved meant that taking off and forming up at altitude took longer, although for offensive operations this was not too important. In cloudy conditions involving instrument flying, the wing was more difficult to hold together than a squadron. Finally, the larger the formation, the further away it could be seen and the longer it took to jockey into position. Surprise, the dominant factor in air fighting, was reduced. But the fact that wings brought to the battle far greater firepower and, in a large multi-bogey encounter, far more mutual support, was undeniable.

Sholto Douglas was keenly aware that unless a fighting force is used it loses its edge. Eager to gain the initiative by taking the offensive he initiated probing attacks from the end of 1940. At first these were little more than putting a toe in the water to check the strength of the enemy reaction, but as experience was gained, so the raids became stronger and more formalised. Adverse weather caused the first major operation, planned for Boxing Day 1940, to be post-poned until 10 January 1941. A target a few miles south of Calais was raided by six Blenheim bombers, escorted by three squadrons of Spitfires and three of Hurricanes. The German reaction was feeble, and little opposition was encountered. This was the first 'Circus': a handful of bombers as bait, protected by a mass of fighters, with the aim of bringing on a large-scale fighter-versus-fighter encounter. It was the shape of things to come.

The Circus was not the only type of operation mounted. The 'Rodeo' was a pure fighter sweep by up to six squadrons. If it was

79

identified in time, the *Luftwaffe* left it alone, as the RAF had tried to ignore the *Freijagd* during the previous summer. If the weather was unsuitable for large formations, that was no excuse for letting Jerry have a day off. 'Rhubarbs' and 'Rangers', flown by pairs or fours at low level, sneaked across the Channel, seeking targets of opportunity. But the Circus was the main offensive ploy during 1941.

Wing Leaders

A fighter squadron was a family, with a distinct identity shaped by its commanding officer. On the ground, friendly rivalry between squadrons was normal, and there were few problems. Overall control was the responsibility of the station commander. But in the air, when three squadrons flew together as a wing, misunderstandings occurred, units got in each other's way, and individual commanders often disagreed on tactics. Something better was needed.

The problem was one of co-ordination. Operating together, the squadrons had to think as one and follow the same tactical principles. With one squadron commander leading the wing one day and another the next, this was simply not happening. What was needed was an air leader, someone to provide unified command; to co-ordinate the three squadrons in flight and in battle; and to impose hard and fast tactical principles to which all should adhere. A Wing Leader. Once this was recognised the answer was simple. The three squadrons in each sector were already at least nominally a wing. In March 1941, the first leaders were appointed, with the title Wing Commander Flying, later generally referred to as a Wing Leader. But the selection of a Wing Leader was something else. He had to have a fighting record worthy of respect, he had to be able to lead by example, and he required a dominant personality to impose his own tactical ideas. A man to love and a man to fear, but above all, a man to follow to hell and back.

In the air, a Wing Leader was identified by a blue and red pennant beneath the cockpit canopy, and instead of squadron codes, his initials were painted on the fuselage. He led his wing from one of the squadrons, displacing its commander who either rested, or flew as a section leader. A good wing leader flew with all of his squadrons, frequently favouring the least experienced outfit. This fostered team spirit, and welded them into a martial tribe. The first two Wing Leaders, and in some ways the greatest, were 'Sailor' Malan, formerly of No 74 Squadron, who took command of the Biggin Hill Wing, and Douglas Bader, the only man with experience of handling large formations, who went to Tangmere.

Basic Tactics

During the Battle of Britain, the pilots had been too busy fighting to develop new tactical systems, and the basic section of three aircraft was still in widespread use in 1941. The first task of the new Wing Leaders was to find something better. Malan, whose 74 Squadron had been heavily engaged in the Battle, had made the most progress in 1940. Having established that the three-aircraft section contained one aircraft too many, he built his squadron formation around the pair. Shortly before his appointment to Biggin Hill, he had produced a tactical paper which, while it dealt mainly with defensive considerations, showed the depth of his thinking.

> I am of the opinion that climbing for height underneath enemy fighters over Base, Biggin Hill, is both a dangerous and stupid practice, and believe that the only safe and efficient way of gaining height is to climb in a direction which gives the squadron its height well out of harm's way, bearing in mind the direction of the sun and the existing weather conditions.
>
> Furthermore, it is found that the modern fighter is a difficult machine to climb at its most efficient climbing speed above 15,000ft, and that a spiral climb takes considerably longer than a straight or zigzag course. Experience has proved that to gain height efficiently above 20,000ft in a Spitfire, requires a fair amount of concentration on the instrument panel, particularly when climbing in a turn (which in itself is inefficient) thereby not allowing for an adequate look-out for enemy fighters above, and it is therefore considered inadvisable to have more than one leader concentrating on gaining height for the squadron. From the above it can be seen that it is inadvisable to split the squadron into two flights.

For his squadron, Malan had retained a 12-aircraft formation while abandoning the two flights of six in favour of three fours in line astern, each composed of two pairs. The leader flew the No 1 position in the central four, with the others staggered back to left and right. Not only was this a flexible formation; its relatively narrow frontage made it easy to manoeuvre. Malan spread his tactical gospel far and wide, and by the end of 1940 his line-astern formation was in widespread use. As Wing Commander Flying at Biggin Hill, he imposed it on the squadrons under his command, and it was not finally superseded until well into 1943.

Whilst Malan had done a great deal to improve RAF fighter tactics, it was left to Douglas Bader at Tangmere to take the final steps which led to tactical parity with the *Jagdflieger*. It was he who introduced the 'finger four' to Fighter Command, although it is believed that the original idea was suggested by 'Cocky' Dundas (4 victories). This consisted of two pairs in a fractionally echeloned formation—'sucked abreast', as the Americans would put it—the positions of each fighter corresponding to the fingertips of an outstretched hand. By concentrating their search inwards, they could cover the blind spots behind and below each other. It was, of course, very much a matter of trial and error. When bounced from astern, the two pairs initially broke in opposite directions and lost mutual cover. Later they all broke in the same direction, the outside pair going high while the inside pair stayed low. The 'finger four' stood the test of time and was still in use more than 30 years later.

Policy for 1941

Not until the middle of June 1941 was Circus No 14 flown, but by then Sholto Douglas' ideas had hardened. By now, the top-secret 'Ultra' organisation at Bletchley Park had succeeded in deciphering German signals which indicated that Hitler was about to March on Russia. In effect this meant that there was no danger of invasion in 1941, whilst a fair proportion of the *Luftwaffe* would be transferred to the Eastern Front. It was a green light for offensive action.

Under these circumstances Sholto Douglas was able to issue Tactical Memorandum No 14, outlining a policy of 'leaning forward into France'. His objectives were five-fold. To destroy enemy aircraft; to force the enemy to increase his fighter strength in the West at the expense of other fronts (by this time the *Luftwaffe* was active in Greece, the Mediterranean and North Africa); to dislocate enemy transport and industry (little more than a token objective at this stage); to obtain moral superiority; and to build up and maintain a high

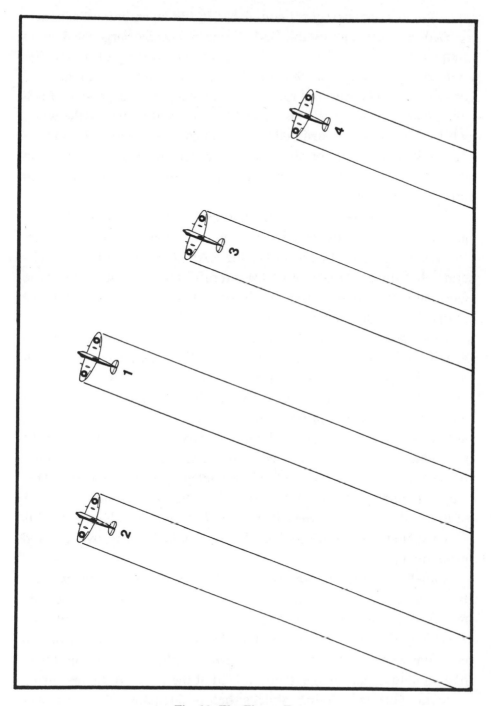

Fig. 11. The Finger Four
Introduced to Fighter Command by Douglas Bader in 1941, the finger four was an extremely flexible formation that stood the test of time.

standard of efficiency in his command. It was an ambitious scheme.

With the principle established, Circuses became larger and more frequent, there often being two a day, each consisting of nearly 300 fighters, which was more than the *Luftwaffe* had in total in France and Belgium. Eight wings of three squadrons was par for the course. Each wing had its own specific task, as had each squadron within the wing, whilst timings were scheduled to keep an area saturated with fighters. To make life even more difficult for the defenders, all units were at different altitudes, with many arriving at different times and from different directions.

The truth, however, was that Circuses were not very effective, although this was obscured by the perennial bogey of overclaiming. In the 20 days from 14 June 1941 the RAF claimed 214 German aircraft shot down for losses of 80 aircraft and 68 pilots, when true German losses were 48 fighters destroyed and 33 damaged, with 32 pilots lost and six wounded.

This was the pattern throughout the year. There were several reasons for this apparent failure. As soon as the pattern became evident, the *Luftwaffe* cobbled together a radar and reporting system. While not as sophisticated nor as effective as that of Fighter Command, it gave plenty of early warning. The approach of a large Circus at high altitude could not be concealed, and the *Jagdflieger* could be brought to readiness, scrambled, and vectored to altitude to intercept in plenty of time. In boxing terms, the RAF was telegraphing its punches. This was not entirely one-sided. British radar reached deep into France at altitude, and the Wings were warned of *Luftwaffe* aerial activity. This was the first campaign in which both sides had radar coverage and ground control.

Sometimes likened to the Battle of Britain in reverse, this was far from the case. The few British bombers were never going to be able to cause damage critical to the conduct of the war, and while the *Jagdflieger* usually tried to get through to them, it was far from an essential objective. More often the German fighters held off until they had an altitude advantage, then nibbled at the flanks of the escorting fighters with fast diving attacks before breaking off. This was extremely difficult to counter.

New Zealand ace Al Deere commented of this period that to get results from the fleeting opportunities offered, marksmanship was essential. An above average pilot but an indifferent shot, he had to get close to score, and against the German slashing attacks this was very difficult. This is borne out by his record: 13 confirmed victories between 23 May and 30 August 1940, but a mere five damaged in the second half of 1941.

The final reason for the adverse success ratio was pilot quality. The two *Luftwaffe Geschwader* left in the West were largely composed of veterans. By contrast, many experienced RAF pilots were rested during this period; others were with training units, passing on their hard-earned skills to newly fledged pilots. Still more had been sent further afield to Malta, the Western Desert and the Far East. This drain on resources, coupled with the expansion of Fighter Command during this period, ensured that a high proportion of RAF fighter pilots on the Western Front between 1941 and 1944 were greenhorns. Some—a few—did well. Others paid a high price for their inexperience.

Changing Times, 1942–May 1944

After No 110 was flown on 8 November 1941, Circuses were discontinued in their original form. Fighter Command had learned (as the *Luftwaffe* had learned in the summer of 1940) that stacking fighters around the bombers to give close protection was ineffective. Nor, for the results obtained, were Circuses productive.

In 1942, a different approach was adopted. RAF expansion saw the light bomber force increased, and the American-built Douglas Boston, which carried a heavier bomb-load faster than the Blenheim, entered service. Then as the year progressed, the USAAF build-up in England began, with both medium and heavy bombers. Slowly but surely, really damaging raids were mounted against targets in the occupied countries.

The method of attack also changed. Increasing use was made of low-level penetration by the bombers, while the supporting fighter wings also took to crossing the Channel at low level, beneath the German radar coverage. Only on approaching the coast of France did they pull into a flat-out climb for altitude. No longer could the

85

Jagdflieger take off at their leisure and climb to an advantageous position. Often, the Spitfires were already high above them.

On 19 August 1942 came the amphibious raid on Dieppe. Mounted to test the feasibility of capturing a working port in the event of a future invasion, air superiority was paramount. To attain this, Leigh-Mallory flung in all his available Spitfires; 48 squadrons of them, three of them USAAF units, denuding other areas to do so. A three-squadron wing of Typhoons, and eight Hurricane squadrons, made up the numbers, the latter allocated to defence suppression and close air support. Opposing this armada were 190 FW 190As and 16 Bf 109Gs of *JG 2* and *JG 26*, and Dornier, Heinkel and Junkers bombers. It resulted in one of the greatest single air battles of the war.

The idea was to put an air umbrella over Dieppe. In practice it was clearly shown that air umbrellas leak. Spitfires flew a total of 2,050 defensive sorties, losing 59 aircraft, with 29 pilots killed and 16 taken prisoner; Typhoons flew 72 sorties, losing two aircraft and no pilots. Total RAF aircraft losses were 106, although only about 70 fell to German fighters. Flak and bomber gunners accounted for at least 34 of the remainder. The *Luftwaffe* flew about 950 sorties, some 800 of these by fighters. Total German losses amounted to 48, of which only 20 were fighters. In spite of the *Luftwaffe*'s numerical inferiority in numbers, Fighter Command was unable to achieve more than tempo-rary local air superiority. When, slightly less than two years later, the invasion of Normandy was mounted, the lessons of Dieppe had been well learned. For this, if nothing else, the operation was worthwhile.

After Dieppe the Circus fell into disuse. B-17 Fortresses of the USAAF started to range into the occupied countries, at first going only so far as the Spitfires could escort them; then with experience, going far deeper. With this, the importance of incursions over France and Belgium diminished. While bitter fighting still took place on occasion, the war moved deep into Germany.

The RAF Wing instituted in 1941 was typically composed of three squadrons. Back in 1940, Douglas Bader had led five, but this was only as a method of bringing large numbers to battle at the same place and the same time. The typical Wing of the 1941–42 period consisted of only three squadrons. While it appears that Bader could handle this effectively, few others had the ability to do so. By 1943 the average Wing consisted of just two squadrons, which was the most that the average Wing Leader could handle in the air.

The Fighters

The 41 months between the beginning of 1941 and the invasion of Normandy in June 1944, saw a race between the adversaries to develop their respective fighters. The spring of 1941 saw the emergence of the Bf 109F, which was subsequently developed into the Bf 109G, which entered service in the summer of 1942. Whereas the 109 was a small aircraft, it did not easily lend itself to development without paying a heavy price. More powerful engines gave it a higher top speed and ceiling, and greater acceleration, but handling became progressively worse. The final variants of this type were difficult to fly, turned like a tram, and had positively dangerous take-off and landing characteristics.

The other *Luftwaffe* fighter that emerged during this period was the Focke-Wulf FW 190A. Whereas the 109 was a thoroughbred racehorse, the 190 was designed to be a cavalry horse; rugged and effective. When it first entered service it gave the Spitfire pilots who came up against it a severe shock: it was faster, climbed and dived better, while its rate of roll was superb. Only in turn radius was it inferior to the British fighter, due to higher wing loading, and its stall characteristics were unforgiving. The stall came without warning, with a tendency to flick and spin. Reefed into a hard turn at low altitude, it was a potential killer, a fact that the Allied pilots were sometimes to use to their advantage.

The increasing use of self-sealing fuel tanks and armour plate quickly made the standard British aircraft gun, the .303 Browning, obsolete. Its high rate of fire and the number of guns carried was insufficient to offset its short effective range and its lack of hitting power. Something better was needed—cannon. As a general rule, early aircraft cannon were all 20mm. The German Oerlikon MG FF, as fitted to the Bf 109E, had both a low rate of fire and a low muzzle velocity. The choice of the RAF settled on the Hispano Suiza which, although it fired a slightly lighter projectile, had double the rate of fire

87

and a muzzle velocity nearly half as great again, giving it double the penetrative power of the German weapon.

First used in the Spitfire I, it caused jamming problems. These were finally cured, and the first model to be generally equipped with cannon was the Spitfire VB, which carried two 20mm cannon and four .303 machine-guns. Fitted with an uprated Merlin engine, and metal rather than fabric-covered ailerons, which improved the rate of roll, the performance of the VB matched that of the Bf 109F fairly closely, while retaining the superior turn performance.

When, late in 1941, the FW 190A entered service, it outclassed the Spitfire VB in almost all respects. Improved Spitfires were under development, but Fighter Command needed something better immediately. The standard method of improving fighter performance was to fit a more powerful engine. The answer was to fit the Series 60 Merlin engine into the airframe of a VC to produce the Spitfire IX, the performance of which was almost identical to that of the FW 190A. External changes were marginal, which meant that German pilots were generally unable to tell which variant they were up against. This carried obvious advantages for the VB. The Spitfire IX was the most numerous variant, and remained in service until the end of the war.

Table 8. Fighter Data, Western Front, 1941–44

	Supermarine Spitfire VB	Supermarine Spitfire IX	Messerschmitt Bf 109F-3	Messerschmitt Bf 109G-6	Focke-Wulf FW 190A-3
Wingspan	36ft 10in	36ft 10in	32ft 6in	32ft 7in	34ft 5¹/₂in
Length	29ft 11in	30ft 6in	29ft 1in	29ft 7in	29ft 0in
Height	12 ft 7in	12ft 7in	11ft 2in	11ft 2in	13ft 0in
Wing area	242 sq ft	242 sq ft	173 sq ft	173 sq ft	197 sq ft
Engine	Rolls-Royce Merlin 1,440hp	Rolls-Royce Merlin 1,710hp	Daimler-Benz DB601E 1,300hp	Daimler-Benz DB605 1,800hp	BMW 801Dg 1,700hp
Loaded weight	6,650lb	7,500lb	6,063lb	6,945lb	7,652lb
Wing loading	28lb/sq ft	31lb/sq ft	35lb/sq ft	40lb/sq ft	39lb/sq ft
Maximum speed	374mph	408mph	391mph	387mph	399mph
Service ceiling	37,000ft	44,000ft	39,370ft	38,550ft	33,800ft
Rate of climb	c.3,650ft/min	c.4,150ft/min	4,291ft/min	4,560ft/min	c.4,100ft/min
Range	470 miles	434 miles	440 miles	450 miles	644 miles

Note: Development of all fighters listed was a continuing process, and there were many sub-types of each, the data for which varies in detail.

The Aces

Whereas in the defensive battles of 1940 there was often little option but to rush headlong into the fray, the offensive actions of the next three and a half years gave scope for more tactical finesse. Memories of the previous summer, with hordes of Messerschmitts spilling out of the sun, were still fresh in the minds of the first RAF Wing Leaders. Now it was their turn, and while the close escort wing had to stay with the bombers, the top cover and target support wings were often able to stalk the prowling *Jagdflieger* and take them by surprise.

The first two years also saw the technological advantage sway first one way and then the other. The Spitfire V, which entered service in February 1941, was superior to the Bf 109E, but lost the performance edge to the Bf 109F, which came out three months later. Occasionally the Messerschmitt pilots turned at bay and a brief dogfight erupted, but as the lightly-loaded Supermarine fighter held the advantage in the turn, this was not a frequent occurrence. Matters changed in September, when the FW 190A entered service. If the 109F was a formidable opponent, the 190A was enough to make the British pilots pass little green apples. Against the Spitfire V, it was faster, better in the climb and dive, and changed direction in the twinkling of an eye.

By spring 1942, the new German fighter was available in large numbers, and the *Jagdflieger* stayed and fought as never before. For the British, this was their hardest period of the campaign, and for the most part they were forced to fight defensively. Survival, in their out-classed aeroplanes, depended on a mixture of caution, teamwork, the ability to turn tightly, and coincidental support.

Even when an FW 190A was captured intact and evaluated, there proved to be no weak points that could be exploited to any degree. Aces who had scored well against the 109F achieved little against the newcomer. Only one pilot, Belgian Yvan Du Monceau, managed to shoot down five FW 190s with the Spitfire V, and that took from mid-March to mid-December. Only with the service entry of the Spitfire IX in July 1942 did parity start to be restored. The performance gap never again became so wide.

ADOLPH GYSBERT 'SAILOR' MALAN   Son of a South African

farmer, young Malan spent his early years in the merchant navy, hence his sobriquet. Dissatisfied with life afloat, he applied for a short-service commission with the RAF, learned to fly, and in November 1936 joined No 74 Squadron at Hornchurch. On the outbreak of war, he was a flight commander, and 74 Squadron was equipped with Spitfires.

Like many others, 'Sailor' made his combat debut over Dunkirk. Also like many others, he fluffed it. To err is human. In training he had been noted for very precise flying, but in his first engagement he closed on a Heinkel bomber much too fast and overshot, fortunately without being hit by the enemy gunners. Hauling off to one side, he lost speed, then came back in astern, opening fire at a range of 150 yards and closing to 50. Like many other aces, shooting from very close range was his trademark. The bomber was hit hard, and its gunners, perhaps wounded, failed to return fire. Black smoke gushed back and the main wheels dropped, a frequent event with damaged Heinkels.

Pulling up, 'Sailor' left it and headed for more action with his two wingmen. In the next few minutes he shot down one Ju 88 and damaged another. After ten patrols over Dunkirk, he had accounted for three confirmed and the Heinkel, which remained unconfirmed; had shared in another two victories; and scored hits on four more. It was a promising start.

The squadron was heavily involved in the Battle of Britain that followed, and in August 1940 'Sailor' was promoted to command it. Now he could give free reign to his tactical ideas—three four-aircraft flights based on the pair; point harmonisation for the guns at 250 yards, etc. By the end of the year his score had risen to 14, with shares in another five, and his reputation for marksmanship against manoeuvring targets at up to 300 deflection angles was established.

His personal combat philosophy was encapsulated in his 'Ten Commandments', drawn up probably late in 1940, to furnish guidelines for the inexperienced. They were:

Ten of my Rules for Air Fighting
1) Wait until you see the whites of his eyes. Fire short bursts of 1 to 2 seconds, and only when your sights are definitely 'ON'.

> *Sailor Malan was the best pilot of the war, a good tactician; above average pilot; and an excellent shot.*
>
> Al Deere (17 victories)

2) Whilst shooting think of nothing else, brace the whole of your body, have both hands on the stick, concentrate on your ring sight.
3) Always keep a sharp lookout. 'Keep your finger out'!
4) Height gives You the initiative.
5) Always turn and face the attack.
6) Make your decisions promptly. It is better to act quickly, even though your tactics are not the best.
7) Never fly straight and level for more than 30 seconds in the combat area.
8) When diving to attack always leave a proportion of your formation above to act as top guard.
9) INITIATIVE, AGGRESSION, AIR DISCIPLINE, and TEAM WORK are words that MEAN something in Air Fighting.
10) Go in quickly—Punch hard—Get out!

So highly regarded were these rules that they were pinned on the notice-board of an American Wing in Korea more than a decade later. With the benefit of hindsight, only one of them seems slightly suspect. At average combat speeds at that time, 30 seconds flying straight and level in the combat area would allow an opponent to cover rather more than two miles. As a purely personal opinion, the author feels that this was far too long.

By the standards of the day, 'Sailor' Malan, who was approaching his 31st birthday in 1941, was an old man. Self-contained and distant, he was a martinet, both in the air and on the ground, and few ever got close to him. Quiet and cool in the air, he rarely got even moderately excited about anything. He was aggressive, of that there can be no doubt, but his aggression was always tempered with caution. As a Wing Leader, he shot down 12 Bf 109s, shared in the destruction of two more, plus two probables and nine damaged. He ended the war with a score of 27 confirmed destroyed with shares in a further seven; two and one shared unconfirmed; three probables; and 16 damaged.

> *What I like about Sailor is his quiet, firm manner and his cold courage. He is gifted with uncanny eyesight and is a natural fighter pilot. When he calls over the R/T 'Let 'em have it! Let 'em have it!' there's no messing. The bastards are for it, particularly the one he has in his own reflector sight.*
>
> Ira Jones, First World War ace

Apart from his cool nature, Malan's greatest asset was his exceptional eyesight. Usually he was the first to sight the enemy, often from great distances.

'Sailor' Malan left the service in 1946 and returned to South Africa. He died of Parkinson's Disease in 1963.

DOUGLAS ROBERT STEWART BADER Arrogant, opinionated, utterly dogmatic, courageous to the point of folly; Douglas Bader was the most inspirational fighter leader of the war. A product of the RAF College at Cranwell, he played cricket and rugger for the RAF. An outstanding pilot, he flew with the RAF aerobatic team at Hendon in 1931. In December of that year he crashed his Bulldog while stunting at low level, was badly injured, and had both legs amputated. Invalided from the service, by sheer force of personality he was once more accepted for flying duties on the outbreak of war. He flew Spitfires with No 19 Squadron, then was posted to No 222 Squadron as a flight commander in time for Dunkirk, where he scored his first victory, a Bf 109.

In July 1940 he was given command of No 242 Squadron, a mainly Canadian outfit which had taken a beating in the French campaign. Morale was low, but under his leadership they became an effective fighting force again. From the outset Bader was convinced that the Fighting Area Attacks were worthless, and that air fighting would follow the pattern laid down in the Great War. To this end he evolved the doggerel: 'He who has the sun creates surprise. He who has the height controls the battle. He who gets in close shoots them down.'

Based in 12 Group, on the fringe of the battle, he became obsessed with the fact that squadrons from 11 Group fought individually, and were often heavily outnumbered by huge German formations. His answer to this was the Big Wing, first of three, then of five squadrons, although in practice this had little success. His personal score during the Battle of Britain was 11 confirmed.

In March 1941 he was appointed Wing Leader at Tangmere, where he quickly made his presence felt. His introduction of the 'finger four' has already been mentioned, and he, more than anyone, was responsible for the improvement in minor tactics. His own favoured attacking position was from below and astern:

> You've got to get behind, for obvious reasons, so he can't see you, and you've got to be slightly underneath because then you have the plan of the aeroplane, not firing at just a silhouette. And it was the same with anything, whether it was a bomber or you were firing at engines or whatever you were doing. The vulnerability was underneath. Of course the 109 was not particularly difficult to shoot down, depending on how you manoeuvred and so on. The pilot was sitting on an L-shaped tank. The petrol tank was the same shape as the seat. Oh, they had armour plating and so on, you know, but I would still keep my cheeks pretty tight if I was sitting on a petrol tank!

It was as a fighter leader that Bader really stood out, on the ground as much as in the air. A few months older than Malan, he was a much more gregarious personality than the South African, and on the ground was generally found in the centre of a group of his pilots. Dogmatic to a degree, he did not take kindly to contradiction, but his circle was not that of a king surrounded by courtiers; more a Viking chief about to lead them on a foray, incongruously wassailing in lemonade while they quaffed their ale. The Tangmere Wing was one happy family.

A major aspect of Bader's leadership was his ability to inspire confidence by trivialising the risks involved with a totally irreverent attitude. The wing was dubbed the Green Line Bus, with the motto 'return tickets only'. His initials, DB, on the side of his Spitfire, were quickly transmuted to 'Dogsbody', and quick to see the underlying morale value in the joke, he adopted this as his callsign in the air.

In the air, inbound high over France, with the prospect of a hard fight ahead, he developed a remarkable habit of making irrelevant comments. Four miles high over Le Touquet, he would remark: 'That eighteenth green could do with mowing, couldn't it?' Eyes crinkled with amusement behind the goggles, and mouths twisted into reluctant grins behind the oxygen masks at the absurdity of it, while the tension drained out of the pilots. Yet another ploy was to smoke his pipe on the return trip. No sane man lit a match in the cockpit of a Spitfire, but it all added to the myth of Bader's indestructibility. For those who have never flown in wartime, the effect is hard to comprehend. Johnnie Johnson of 616 Squadron wrote:

When the leader speaks, his voice is warm and vital, and we know full well that once in the air like this we are bound together by a deeper intimacy than we can ever feel on the ground. Invisible threads of trust and comradeship hold us together and the mantle of Bader's leadership will sustain and protect us throughout the fight ahead.

The end of an era came on 9 August 1941. Leading the Tangmere Wing, Douglas Bader was shot down over France and taken prisoner. His total was 20 confirmed and four shared, with 18 probables and damaged. Of these, eight confirmed, three shared, and 12 probables and damaged—all of them Bf 109s—had been scored as a Wing Leader. He left the RAF in 1946, and died of a heart attack in 1982.

JEAN-FRANCOIS DEMOZAY The era of the lone wolf fighter pilot was widely thought to be over by mid-1917, when team fighting became the order of the day. But there were always exceptions. Frenchman Jean-François Demozay was one. An airline pilot before the war, he joined *L'Armée de l'Air* in 1939, and was seconded as an interpreter to No 1 Squadron RAF. At the end of the French campaign he found a damaged Bombay transport on the airfield at Nantes, carried out makeshift repairs, then flew it to England with 16 British soldiers on board. He then joined the Free French, trained to fly fighters, and was posted to No 1 Squadron at Wittering.

His first encounter came during a training flight on 8 November 1940, when he damaged a Ju 88 over East Anglia. When the squadron moved south, he took part in operations over the Channel, scoring three victories between March and May 1941. A brief spell with No 242 Squadron followed, during which he claimed two 109s. On 28 June he was posted to No 91 Squadron as a flight commander. This unit, originally 421 Flight, was engaged in coastal and other reconnaissance work. These missions were flown at low level, by single aircraft or pairs. *Luftwaffe* fighters often tried to intercept. When they did, bitter small-scale skirmishes took place. This suited the individualistic Frenchman very well.

He took little time to get off the mark. The Spitfire V which he now flew was far superior to the Hurricane which had been his previous mount. By the end of July he had shot down three Bf 109s confirmed and one probable, damaged a fourth, shot up two Hs 126s on the ground, and sunk a minelayer by strafing. His score climbed rapidly, and when in January 1942 he was rested it had reached 15 confirmed, 12 of which were 109s.

He returned to No 91 Squadron to command in June, and in his second tour added three more to his tally, all FW 190s. Little can be said about his methods, except that he was happiest as a lone wolf flyer. He survived the war, only to die in a flying accident in France in December 1945.

4. MALTESE FALCONS, JUNE 1940–NOVEMBER 1942

Some of the most bitter air fighting of the war took place over the tiny island of Malta. Situated athwart the Mediterranean between Sicily and North Africa, it was ideally placed to allow British forces to interdict Italian supply routes to their army in Libya. But as a corollary, its very proximity to enemy air bases made keeping the island supplied a matter of considerable difficulty. For 30 months, Malta was effectively under siege.

Initially the air defence was minuscule: a handful of Sea Gladiators which were barely able to catch the Italian bombers, reinforced by a few Hurricanes pilfered from the trickle of reinforcements bound for Egypt. It was more than seven weeks before a dozen Hurricanes were flown in from the carrier HMS *Argus*, to give Malta its first real fighter defence. More Hurricanes followed later in the year but there were never enough.

The nearest Italian air bases were on Sicily, less than 20 minutes' flying time from Malta. With so little early warning, the British fighters were hard pressed to gain sufficient altitude in time. Fortunately the *Regia Aeronautica*, or Italian air force, was not a particularly aggressive foe, and until the end of 1940 the scanty British fighter force sufficed. While this was the case, Malta remained home to bombers, warships and submarines, all of which cut a deadly swathe through Italian supply convoys to North Africa.

Early in 1941, circumstances changed with the arrival of the *Luftwaffe* in Sicily. Attacks on the island now intensified. The Italian fighters consisted of Fiat CR.42 biplanes and Macchi MC 200 monoplanes, reinforced by a single *Staffel* of Bf 109Es. The latter, led by high-scoring ace Joachim Müncheberg, wrought havoc among the

A tight pre-war formation by Spitfires of No 19 Squadron at Duxford. Far too much time was spent holding position, and not enough in keeping a look-out. *(Bruce Robertson)*

(Above) Fleet Air Arm fighters lacked performance. Despite this, William Lucy managed to share in seven victories and a probable, all bombers, by 14 May 1940, flying the antiquated Skua. *(Bruce Robertson)*

(Below) In the early war years the Fulmar was the best British naval fighter, but this was not saying much. Stan Orr managed to claim six victories with the Fulmar plus five shared. When in 1944 he flew the Hellcat, opportunities were rare. *(Bruce Robertson)*

(Right) Bob Tuck, in the nearest aircraft, leads a formation of Spitfires of No 65 Squadron.

(Above) No 1 Squadron in France 1940. L to R: Billy Drake (18 victories); Leslie Clisby (16); Lorimer; 'Prosser' Hanks (13); 'Boy' Mould (8); 'Bull' Halahan; Johnny Walker (3); Medical Officer; Paul Richey (10); 'Killy' Kilmartin (12 or 13); Stratton (2); 'Pussy' Palmer (2). This picture is of particular interest, as between Halahan and Walker can be seen the *Armée de l'Air* liaison officer, Jean-François Demozay. On the fall of France, Demozay escaped to England, became a fighter pilot with the RAF taking the *nom-de-guerre* of Moses Morlaix, and scored 18 victories.

(Above) This early photograph of No 43 Squadron contains four future aces. From the right: Hamilton Upton (10 victories); John Simpson (9 victories); Peter Townsend (9 victories); and Jim Hallowes (17 victories).

(Left) On the outbreak of war, Frank Carey was, at 27, a fairly elderly sergeant pilot. This notwithstanding, he scored a total of 25 victories during the war plus four unconfirmed, 14 of them in France. He added another seven in Burma in 1942. All were scored with the Hurricane. *(Norman Franks)*

Eric Lock of No 41 Squadron opened his score on August 1940, and over the next three months gained another 22 victories. Wounded, he was off operations until July 1941, when he gained a further three victories. Days later he went missing while strafing.
(Norman Franks)

(Above) When RAF Fighter Command was disbanded in April 1968, a few of the Few gathered for the ceremony. Right to left: Peter Brothers (16 victories), Douglas Bader (20), 'Al' Deere (17), Sir Frederick Rosier, Bob Tuck (27), Peter Townsend (9), and 'Johnnie' Johnson (34).
(Bruce Robertson)

(Right) World War I fighter ace Keith Park commanded 11 Group during the Battle of Britain, then Malta in 1942. His handling of limited resources in both campaigns was exemplary.
(Norman Franks)

(Left) 'Sailor' Malan (27 victories), seen here as Biggin Hill Wing Leader. He is considered by many to be the foremost tactician and outstanding fighter pilot of the war. *(Norman Franks)*

(Below) Big Wing advocate Douglas Bader (fourth from right), seen here surrounded by pilots of No 242 Squadron. L to R: Denis Crowley-Milling (4 victories); Hugh Tamblyn (5); Stan Turner (10); Saville (on wing); Campbell; Willie McKnight (17); Bader; Eric Ball (6); Homer; and Brown.

(Left) Deadly duo from No 54 Squadron, New Zealanders 'Al' Deere (left) and Colin Gray (right). Deere was credited with seven victories over Dunkirk, six more in the Battle of Britain, and four over France. Colin Gray got one over Dunkirk, 15 in the Battle of Britain, one over France in 1941, and 10 more over North Africa and Italy.
(Norman Franks)

(Above) Mass take-off by Spitfire Vs of No 122 Squadron, 1941. *(Bruce Robertson)*

(Right) Desert ace 'Killer' Caldwell, who scored 16 of his 27 victories in the Tomahawk and a further three with the Kittyhawk. Transferred to the Pacific in 1943, he flew Spitfire Vs against the Japanese, claiming a further eight victories. *(Norman Franks)*

(Below) Kittyhawk of No 112 Squadron in the desert. The man on the wing was needed to guide it through the dust clouds raised by other aircraft while taxying. *(Bruce Robertson)*

(Left) George Beurling (31 victories) adds white outlines to the black crosses on his Spitfire in Malta. Undoubtedly one of the greatest individualists of the war, he could not come to terms with authority, and was released by the RCAF in October 1944.
(Bruce Robertson)

(Below) 'How on earth they ever shoe-horned a big fella like Reade Tilley into a Spitfire beats me!' (General Mike Rogers, USAF). They did though, as this photo proves. Tilley (7 victories) was the author of *Hints on Hun Hunting,* one of the best tactical papers of the war.

(Right) Paddy Finucane, centre, here flanked by Bluey Truscott (14), and Flight Lieutenant Smith, both of No 454 Squadron. (*Bruce Robertson*)

(Below) Biggin Hill, L to R: Raoul Duval; 'Sailor' Malan; unknown; Pierre Montet, *nom-de-guerre* Christian Martell (7 victories) and Bill Crawford-Compton (20 or 21). (*Norman Franks*)

(Left) Neville Duke (26 victories), seen here with his 112 Squadron Tomahawk. The back-up ring and bead sight can just be seen ahead of the windshield. Allied top-scorer over Tunisia, he ended the war in Italy, then became chief test pilot for Hawker Aircraft.
(Norman Franks)

(Below) The Blenheim was the first night fighter to be fitted with radar, but its performance was too poor and its armament too light for it to be really effective.
(Bruce Robertson)

(Right) John Cunningham (20 victories) was the top-scoring Allied night fighter pilot of the war on defensive operations, and more than anyone, showed the way to defeat the night bomber. He is seen here post-war with the modified Vampire, with which he had just set a world record for absolute altitude.
(Maurice Allward)

(Below) Bob Braham (29 victories), seen outside Buckingham Palace with his wife. The photographer is 'Jacko' Jacobs, one of his regular radar operators.
(Bruce Robertson)

(Left) The business end of a Beaufighter, showing the arrowhead aerial of the Mk IV radar and the sealed muzzles of the four 20mm Hispano cannon. *(Bruce Robertson)*

(Below) 'Flying Tigers': Top 'Tiger' Tex Hill is third from the right in the front row; he scored six more victories with 23rd Fighter Group in China for a total of 18¼. *(Jeff Ethell)*

(Above) The P-51 Mustang was the greatest long-range fighter of the war. This factory-fresh late model features the bubble canopy which gave first-class all-round vision. *(Rockwell)*

(Above) Thunderbolt ace Bob Johnson also scored 28 victories in Europe flying the Thunderbolt, in just 91 sorties. *(Roger Freeman)*

(Above) Gabby Gabreski was equal USAF top-scorer in Europe with 28 victories, all with the supposedly inferior Thunderbolt. Taken prisoner after being hit by flak in July 1944, he went on to fly F-86 Sabres in Korea, downing $6^{1}/_{2}$ MiG-15s. *(Roger Freeman)*

(Above) The top-scoring Hellcat pilot was David McCampbell (left), seen here with his plane captain. His 34 victories were unmatched in the US Navy.

(Above) Obviously in his best uniform, Mustang ace John C. Meyer (23 victories) poses self-consciously in the cockpit of his fighter, which carries some very fancy artwork. *(Roger Freeman)*

(Below) Dick Bong was the American top-scorer of the war with 40 victories, flying the P-40 and P-38 against the Japanese. *(Jeff Ethell)*

(Above) The Hellcat was the fighter which turned the tide of battle in the Pacific. Robust and hard-hitting, it outclassed the Zero. *(Grumman)*

(Right) Former 'Flying Tiger' and later Corsair pilot, 'Pappy' Boyington (28 victories) was notable for his use of ruses. *(Jeff Ethell)*

(Top) Once its deck-landing faults were cured, the Corsair was arguably the best carrier fighter of the war. It handily outperformed the Hellcat. *(Vought)*

(Above) Spitfire development never ceased. This is the Griffon-engined Mk XIV, the final major variant to see service in the war. *(Bruce Robertson)*

(Left) 'Johnnie' Johnson was the most successful of the RAF Wing Leaders. All of his 34 victories were gained on the Spitfire, 27 of them with the Spitfire IX. He was the master of the careful stalk and the swift bounce.

(Right) Don Blakeslee was the outstanding American fighter leader of the war, despite his relatively modest score of victories. Even today he is spoken of with awe by those who flew with him.
(Roger Freeman)

(Below) The Tempest V was a superb medium and low altitude fighter during the final months of the war. *(Bruce Robertson)*

Hurricanes, which were unable to counter the bombers. Before long Malta had been neutralised as an offensive base. In the late spring, however, the build-up for the invasion of Russia drew off most of the German effectives. This coincided with an accession of air strength on the beleaguered island, and by mid-1941 the unsinkable aircraft carrier was back in business. Axis shipping losses soared, and German and Italian forces in North Africa, starved of supplies, were forced to retreat.

From the Axis viewpoint, this could not be allowed to continue. Once more the *Luftwaffe* returned in force to Sicily, determined to smoke out the British hornets' nest. This time the German fighter was the Bf 109F, while the *Regia Aeronautica* introduced the superb Macchi MC 202. The Hurricanes were totally outclassed, and fought a gallant but losing battle in the sky over the island. The figures tell the story: RAF claims during January and February 1942 totalled 10, against 19 Hurricanes lost.

To redress the balance, 15 Spitfires were flown in on 7 March. They were too few to make much difference, and further small deliveries served only to replace losses. The blitz continued apace, and as in the Battle of Britain, the RAF fighter pilots were ordered to concentrate on the bombers and avoid combat with the 109s.

This was difficult. The total area of the Maltese islands was rather smaller than the Isle of Wight, which allowed the raiders to saturate the area with their fighters. All too often the defenders became embroiled with the patrolling 109s, and failed to reach the bombers. And it was the bombers which reduced the British fighter strength. Serviceability, aggravated by a shortage of spares, kept all too many Spitfires and Hurricanes on the ground, where they were destroyed or

---

Reached Takali and entered the circuit warily. Took a good look around before dropping my wheels and noticed two airtcraft above and behind me. I'd just decided they were Hurricanes when I noticed red tracer flying all around them. I whipped round so fast I almost spun and they passed overhead; heard afterwards they were 109s and had fired a quick, wild burst at me.

Tim Johnston (5 victories)

---

damaged by bombs or strafing. Others came to grief while landing on cratered runways while constantly harassed by relays of 109s patrolling the airfield approaches, looking for easy victims.

Odds of five to one, or even ten to one, were quite normal. The consensus of veterans of the Battle of Britain was that the Malta fighting was far more intense. For most the odds were frightening. For a few, the fact that whenever they flew there was no shortage of targets turned Malta into fighter pilot Valhalla.

However, the Malta experience differed from the Battle of Britain in one major respect. Although fighters were in short supply, there was an abundance of pilots, and the usual rota was one day on and the next off. This was just as well; many were debilitated by 'Malta Dog', a virulent form of the 'trots', not helped by the absence of a balanced diet. American volunteer Reade Tilley praised Lena, the No 126 Squadron Maltese cook, for the number of variations of corned beef that she could devise. And he wasn't joking.

In an attempt to break the vicious circle, the British 'borrowed' the American carrier USS *Wasp*, to fly off 47 Spitfires in one go. Predictably the *Luftwaffe* reacted to the challenge, catching many of them on the ground. Raid followed furious raid, and by the end of the month only a handful of defending fighters remained.

The turning point came in May, when *Wasp*, accompanied by the British carrier HMS *Eagle*, flew off 64 Spitfires. The lessons of the earlier attempt had been learned; no fighter was worth much on the ground. As they arrived over the island low on fuel, every available machine was up to cover them. Then as soon as they touched down, they were refuelled and rearmed in record time, and taken straight back into the air by veteran Malta pilots. The *Luftwaffe*, used to dealing with penny packets of defenders, now found its hands full as a large and confusing multi-bogey fight swirled across Malta. The following day again saw the attackers defeated.

Gradually the pace of operations slackened, while more and more Spitfires flooded in, which over the next few months enabled supply convoys to be fought through. Once again the demands of the Western Desert and the Russian Front caused the withdrawal of many German units from Sicily. They were replaced by units of the *Regia Aeronautica*.

It had always been obvious to the Axis powers that Malta was the key to success in North Africa, but they had signally failed to reduce it by air attack alone. Now, with Rommel's *Deutsche Afrika Korps* halted near an obscure place called El Alamein, and his supply lines at the mercy of Malta's air power, they decided on one last try. A massive *Luftwaffe* influx of six *Gruppen* of bombers and three of fighters reinforced the already sizeable Italian contingent, and in October 1942 they struck. Opposed by five full-strength squadrons of Spitfire Vs, in just seven days they lost at least 42 aircraft, three-quarters of which were bombers. Spitfire losses were also heavy, but the raids were beaten off, and the assault finally faded away.

Within a matter of weeks, Axis forces in the desert were in head-long retreat, and a huge Allied landing had taken place at the far end of North Africa. For the Axis forces in the theatre it was the beginning of the end. Never again was Malta threatened, and the unsinkable aircraft carrier became a platform for offensive action against Sicily during the following year.

The Fighters

The role of the Sea Gladiator over Malta was insignificant, while Hurricane Is and IIs have been described earlier. The most important British fighter type here was the Spitfire V. But whereas in Western Europe the VB was the most widely-used variant, in Malta it was the VC.

Whereas the VB was armed with two 20mm Hispano cannon and four Browning machine-guns, the VC arrived with four 20mm cannon. The extra weight increased wing loading, and, with ammunition often in short supply, the usual practice was to leave two of the

---

Some 109s arrived—four of them I think—and I began to mill around with them. I'd never flown a VC before, and found it a little heavy; tried to out-turn one of them but gave it up because I was afraid if I continued to go round in uniform circles, one of his friends would begin to practice his deflection shooting without my being able to see him; only saw one of them fire.

Tim Johnston (5 victories)

115

> *I had to leave my bomber and pull up into the 109s. All but the last overshot me. I pulled up 30 or 40ft underneath him. It was point-blank range, and every detail of his machine stood out vividly. I could see his markings, his twin radiators, his retracted wheels, even the rivet heads on his fuselage. I gave him a second and a half with all four cannon. The result gave me a terrible fright. His starboard wing snapped off near the fuselage. It folded back, and banged against his fuselage. For a moment I thought it was going to tear away from his machine and come hurtling into my aircraft. I broke down very violently so as to avoid it.*
>
> Paul Brennan (10 victories)

cannon unloaded, but not always. The extra firepower could be devastating.

Other differences were heavier armour protection, a strengthened main gear leg, and often a Vokes filter beneath the nose. Dust in the Mediterranean theatre of operations was a constant problem, causing excessive engine wear. While the Vokes filter countered this problem, its drag reduced performance, but this had to be accepted. The Spitfire VC was inferior to the Messerschmitt Bf 109F and G in rate of climb and maximum speed, but it was always able to out-turn them.

Of the Italian fighter types, the Fiat CR.42 played a minor role over Malta, and in any case will be described in Chapter 5. This leaves the two Macchis—the MC 200 Saetta and the MC 202 Folgore. A close contemporary of the Hurricane and Spitfire, the design of the Saetta was hampered by the lack of a really good Italian engine. The only possible choice was the Fiat A.74 radial, which produced a mere 870hp. Another drawback was an official requirement for the best possible view for the pilot. While this allowed the gun-sight to be kept on target at quite high deflection angles (in both the Spitfire and the 109, at high angles off the target was usually invisible under the nose), the consequence was that the cockpit had to be raised, giving a distinct hump-backed appearance and considerable extra drag.

With these disadvantages, the Saetta could hardly be fast, but it out-climbed and out-turned the Hurricane; handling was excellent, and stability in a high-speed dive was exceptional. As designed it had an enclosed cockpit, but in service the canopy was removed to improve visibility. (Many British pilots liked to fly with the hood open for the same reason.) It was, however, seriously under-gunned, with just two 12.7mm Breda-SAFAT heavy machine-guns mounted in the front fuselage, although the final production model also carried a 7.7mm gun in each wing.

The Folgore was a horse of a different colour. Even as the American Mustang was transformed by the British Merlin engine later in the war, so a developed (and low drag) variant of the Saetta was equally transformed by the German Daimler-Benz DB 601A engine, to become a sleek and racy-looking fighter. Much faster and rather heavier, it retained the excellent all-round handling of its predecessor. Armament consisted of two fuselage and two wing-mounted guns. Allied pilots who flew against the Folgore were impressed with its performance and manoeuvrability.

The Aces

'We were too busy fighting to bother about clever tactics!' This remark, by First World War veteran Harold Balfour, sums up the situation on Malta quite accurately. Heavily outnumbered for most of the time, the defenders could do little other than fly with their heads on swivels and take what shooting chances were offered. This was easier said than done, and the result was almost invariably a large and extremely messy multi-bogey dogfight, in which it was hard to keep track of friend or foe. It was not made any easier by the German

Table 9. Italian Fighters 1940–43, Mediterranean Theatre		
	MC 200 Saetta	**MC 202 Folgore**
Wingspan	34ft 8½in	34ft 8½in
Length	26ft 10½in	29ft 0½in
Height	11ft 5¾in	9ft 11½in
Wing area	181 sq ft	181 sq ft
Engine	Fiat A.74 radial rated at 870hp	Daimler-Benz V-12 rated at 1,175hp
Loaded weight	5,597lb	6,459lb
Wing loading	31lb/sq ft	36lb/sq ft
Maximum speed	312mph	370mph
Service ceiling	29,200ft	37,730ft
Rate of climb	3,125ft/min	c.3,750ft/min
Range	354 miles	475 miles

penchant for head-on or front quartering attacks, which compounded the difficulties of timely recognition. When they opened fire, it was a trifle late.

A standard ploy was for the British fighters to gain height over the sea to the south of the island, then, when vectored in to attack by ground control, make a fast run in to intercept the bombers. A major problem was that this move was rather obvious, and all too often gaggles of 109s would be lurking up-sun in this area, waiting for the Spitfires to come out to play. Avoiding these while waiting to go in against the bombers was not easy, and all too often the defenders became embroiled with the 109s, and were unable to break away to engage the bombers.

By the spring of 1942, the standard British formation had moved from the 'finger four' to fours in line abreast. This was equally good when using the cross-over turn, ensured to a degree that there were no laggards, and when attacking bombers enabled all aircraft to attack simultaneously.

GEORGE F. 'SCREWBALL' BEURLING Montreal-born Beurling was undoubtedly one of the most gifted fighter pilots of the war. He was also an undisciplined individualist; a fact hardly calculated to

Table 10. Leading Allied Fighter Aces over Malta

Name	Country	Malta score	Squadron	War Total	Fate
George Beurling	Canada	26	249	31	KIFA 20.5.48
'Paddy' Schade	Britain	13	126	13	KIFA 31.7.44.
Wally McLeod	Canada	13	603/1435	21	KIA 27.9.44.
Ray Hesselyn	New Zealand	12	249	18	POW Oct 43
'Slim' Yarra	Australia	12	185	12	KIA 10.12.42
Claude Weaver	USA	10	185	12	KIA 28.1.44.
Johnny Plagis	Rhodesia	10	249/185	15	Died post-war
Paul Brennan	Australia	10	249	10	KIFA 13.6.43.
Fred Robertson	Britain	10	261	11	KIFA 31.8.43.
Sandy Rabagliati	Britain	9	46/126	16	KIA 6.7.43.
'Moose' Fumerton	Canada	9	89	14	

NB: Whole victories only. All Spitfires except Rabagliati (Hurricanes), Fumerton (Beaufighters). Interestingly Beurling's score over the island equalled that of top *Luftwaffe Experte* Gerhard Michalski. The confusion of the fighting often made confirmation of claims difficult or impossible.

endear him in RAF squadrons dedicated to team-work. Flying was his only interest from an early age, and the pursuit of perfection in the air became an obsession. After the outbreak of the Second World War, George was forbidden by his family to volunteer for Finland, and rejected by the RCAF on the grounds of inadequate educational standards. Undaunted, he crossed the Atlantic to join the RAF.

In September 1940 he was accepted by the RAF, and quickly found that his precision flying was appreciated. Having survived one or two aerial misdemeanours, he reached the Operational Training Unit at Hawarden in September 1941. There he came under the influence of the great Ginger Lacey, whose score at that time stood at 27. Lacey later recalled that the first time he led Beurling and another pilot on formation training, they completed the exercise with a fast shallow dive over the airfield. He then waved the pupils away to land individually, while he pulled up into a steep climbing slow roll. Only when he was on his back did he realise that Beurling had stayed with him, tucked tightly in on his left. He commented: 'There are no two ways about it, he was a wonderful pilot; and an even better shot'.

These factors, coupled with exceptional eyesight, were the keys to Beurling's later success. But they did not come without effort. At Hawarden he immersed himself in gunnery; estimation of range, deflection, bullet trail, and bullet drop, imprinting them into his subconscious until they were automatic. For him, flying and shooting became one single action.

Brief spells with No 403 Squadron then No 41 Squadron followed, participating in convoy patrols and huge Circus operations over France. George's first victory came on 1 May 1942, a FW 190, which he shot down with only two machine-guns working. Two days later he got another after breaking formation to attack alone, leaving his element leader unguarded. This made him unpopular with the squadron, and when a chance came of an overseas posting, George jumped at it.

On 9 June 1942, he lifted his Spitfire off the deck of the aircraft carrier *Eagle* and set course for Malta. He arrived in a quiet spell, and apart from an inconclusive brush with a 109 did little flying for a month. Then on 6 July he damaged a Cant bomber and shot down two

MC 202s in the same action. Later that day, he demonstrated amazing marksmanship in bringing down a 109:

> Two Me's dropped on me, but I did a quick wing-over and got on one's tail. He saw me coming and tried to climb away. I figured he must be about 800 yards away from me when I got him in the sights and let go at him. It was a full deflection shot, and I had to make plenty of allowance for cannon-drop. I gave him a three-second burst, smack on his starboard flank, and got him in the glycol tank. He started to stream the stuff, leaving a long white trail of smoke.

This was a simply enormous range at which to open fire, even for a no-deflection shot. But Beurling, his marksmanship honed by hours of unremitting practice, was arguably the finest shot of the entire war on both sides. When big dogfights developed, all pilots took snap-shots when opportunities presented themselves. But whereas most missed, or at best caused minor damage, Beurling's snap-shots more often than not connected, and, even more amazingly, on a specific part of the target. The difference was that he always seemed to have that extra split second in which to make sure of his aim.

Beurling was in many ways unusual; a non-smoking teetotaller who didn't gamble and tried not to swear. In his efforts to avoid the latter, he became addicted to the epithet 'screwball', by which he became widely known. Often he flew without eating, as he believed that hunger sharpened his eyesight. As he once said: 'It's a matter of training your eyes to focus swiftly on any small object, so that when you look around the sky once, you pick up anything that's out there'. So good was his vision that on one occasion he claimed a Macchi as a probable with exactly five cannon hits in the cockpit area. The wreck of the Macchi was duly found on the island. In fact almost every one of his victims succumbed to a single burst.

The nature of the fighting over Malta was such that it was not always possible to play safe. On 14 October, Beurling was forced to disregard enemy fighters while going to the assistance of a friend. His Spitfire was shot down, and he was wounded. Shortly afterwards he was shipped back to England. His score on the island was 26 con-firmed—of which 23 were fighters—one shared, and eight damaged, all achieved in just 27 flying days.

He returned to action over Europe, and added two FW 190s to his total. But he could never settle to the team-work style of flying. British fighter ace and wing leader Johnnie Johnson once said of him that he should have been given a long-range Mustang and sent off to fight his own private war.

George Beurling died in 1948 when his overloaded aircraft crashed on take-off at Rome. At the time he was heading for the new state of Israel, and another war.

RAYMOND 'HESS' HESSELYN 'Hess' joined the RNZAF in 1940, arrived in England in September 1941, attended OTU at Hendon, and after a brief spell with No 234 Squadron was sent to Malta. Flying from HMS *Eagle*, he arrived on 9 March 1942, just as things got tough. He gained valuable experience but achieved nothing until 1 April, when his luck changed:

> I chose the one on the extreme right, and as I dived on him, I could see the rest of the boys going in, line abreast. I quickly caught my 109, but I was coming in too fast, and overshot him. However, I got a good bead on the one ahead. It was a lucky break. This 109 was turning at the time, and I had him dead in my sights. Opening fire from about 50 yards, I gave him a four-second burst. He flipped on his back immediately and went straight into the drink. I was excited as hell. I told everybody, including Woody [Group Captain Woodhall, the controller], that I had shot down my first, screaming over the R/T: 'I've got one! I've got one!' My number one, Buck (Buchanan, 6 victories), called up: 'Shut up Hess, We all know you've got one.'
>
> When I landed I found that I had pressed the wrong gun button, and had shot down my first Hun with machine-guns alone.'

This was the first victory of many. A second followed on 20 April, when the inexperienced 'Hess' was almost caught napping. Forced to engage the 109s, he turned behind what he thought was the rear aircraft, only to find that it was the leader:

> I was surprised to find him in my sights, as I had turned very quickly, but had the presence of mind to press my gun button. I caught him with a lucky climbing deflection shot. The Hun disintegrated in the air...
>
> The fact that I had turned into the leader by mistake gave the other Hun his opportunity. He got on my tail, and in my mirror I could see him firing for all he was worth. I broke down promptly, and aileron-turned to about 2,000ft, with the Hun following all the way. Johnny Plagis was on the 109's tail, but we were all so close together that he could not fire for fear of hitting me. At 2,000ft, however, the Hun gave up the chase and climbed away out to sea.

Having destroyed 12 aircraft, including seven 109s, probably destroyed another one, and damaged six, 'Hess' was withdrawn in July. He added a further six to his tally over Western Europe before being shot down and taken prisoner in October 1943. He died in 1963.

READE TILLEY An American from Florida, Reade Tilley joined the RCAF in June 1940, and after training became a member of No 121 Eagle Squadron in May 1941. His sole score with this unit was a FW 190 probably destroyed on 24 March 1942. The following month he flew from the carrier *Wasp*, arriving on Malta on 20 April. Between then and July he accounted for seven Axis aircraft destroyed, six of them fighters, plus two probables and six damaged.

His particular interest is that after transfer to the USAAF later that year, he wrote a tactical paper entitled 'Hints on Hun Hunting', which encapsulated his experiences on the island. Extracts from this follow.

When fighters are scrambled to intercept an approaching enemy, every minute wasted in getting off the ground and forming up means 3,000ft of altitude you won't have when you need it most. Thus an elaborate cockpit check is out. It is sufficient to see that you are in fine pitch [propeller setting] and that the motor is running properly. Don't do a Training School circuit before joining up. As you roll down the runway take a quick look up for the man ahead of you: when you have sufficient airspeed give him about six rings of deflection and you will be alongside in a flash.

Red section leads with the squadron commander at Red One. Red Three, the second in command, flies next to the squadron commander on his left; he will take over the lead in case the squadron commander's radio fails, or he has to leave the squadron because his aircraft is unserviceable.

Always note the bearing of the sun before taking off; then if you get into a scrap miles out to sea and a cannon shell prangs your compass, you may be able to save yourself a lot of unnecessary walking or paddling. Never climb down sun. If it is necessary to fly down sun, do so in a series of 45 degree tacks.

Never fly directly on top of layer cloud, as you stand out like a sore thumb, even to those as far as 10 miles away, if they are slightly above you.

A tactic the 109s are very keen on is 'Boxing'. 109s come over the top and split into two groups, one on either side of you. Suddenly one group will peel down and attack from the beam. You turn to meet the attack, the other group will come and sit on your tail... When you are alone and two box you, it's easy provided you work fast. As the first one starts his dive, chop the throttle, yank

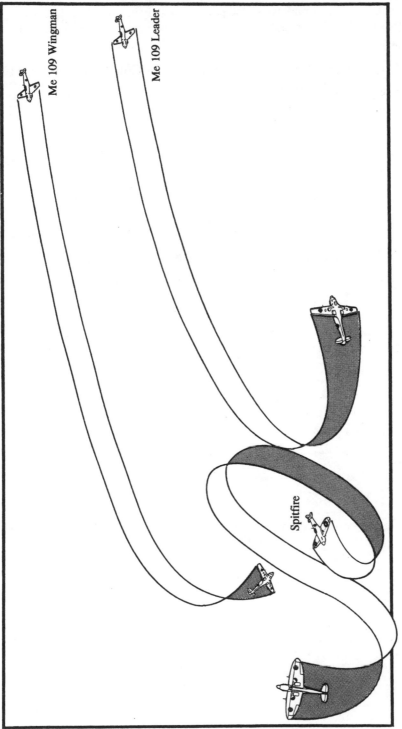

Me 109 Wingman

Me 109 Leader

Spitfire

Fig. 12. Beating the Box

Over Malta the Luftwaffe was fond of the tactic known as boxing, where two 109s took station astern and on either side of a solitary Spitfire. The counter was to throttle back gently, then as the German leader approached, turn violently towards him, fire a quick burst, then turn down and under the wingman.

the nose around, fire a quick squirt in front of him, then skid into a sloppy half-roll, keep the stick well back, and pull out quickly in a skidding turn. The second 109 will have lost sight of you beneath his wing. You should be in a good position to pull up and give him a burst at close range.

Reade Tilley survived the war, and retired as a Colonel in the USAF. He lives at Colorado Springs.

5. NORTH AFRICA, JUNE 1940–AUGUST 1943

When Italy entered the war in June 1940, the British position in the Middle East, centred on Egypt, became extremely precarious. Italian air power on Sardinia and Sicily made passage through the Mediterranean a hazardous undertaking, forcing most reinforcements to go the long way, round the Cape of Good Hope. A large Italian army occupied most of Abyssinia and Somalia, a central position from which it was able to threaten Sudan to the west, British Somaliland to the north, and Kenya to the south. Fortunately this adopted an almost completely defensive stance, and was effectively defeated by March 1941. The main threat was to Egypt from Libya, where a numerically strong Italian force was based. But since much of this was deployed to counter an expected French attack from Tunisia, it was in no position to move against Egypt for some considerable time.

Initial skirmishing was followed by a British thrust in December 1940, which, supported by the RAF, routed the Italian army and took literally tens of thousands of prisoners. By February 1941, the road to Tripoli, and total victory, was clear.

At this point the advance was halted, and forces were detached to assist Greece against an Italian invasion from Albania. This was a disaster on two counts. Although British intervention in Greece halted the Italians, German reinforcements poured in and were quickly decisive. What was left of the British force was evacuated, minus most of its equipment. Leaving Tripoli in Italian hands had also allowed the German *Deutsche Afrika Korps*, under its dynamic commander Erwin Rommel, to land unopposed. Once established, it quickly gathered strength and pushed the depleted British forces back even faster than they had advanced.

This ebb and flow was typical of the Desert War; each army advanced in turn, outran its supplies, and ground to a halt. Its adversary, benefiting from shortened lines of communication, then gathered strength in turn and retook the offensive. So often did this occur that it became known as the Benghazi Handicap. The sequence was not broken until the end of 1942, when the Eighth Army and Desert Air Force combined to win their brilliant victory at El Alamein. At much the same time a combined British and American force landed at the other end of North Africa in Operation Torch. The Axis forces were now caught between a hammer and a hard place, and the end was inevitable.

Air operations in the desert were essentially tactical in nature, in support of the ground forces. Consequently most of the air fighting took place at medium and low altitudes and consisted of encounter battles. This was perhaps as well for the Allies, as it reduced much of the altitude performance advantage of the German Bf 109s.

Conditions were harsh. Blowing sand was a continual enemy, causing excessive wear on all moving parts. Airfields were for the most part ad hoc affairs, with tents set up wherever a level piece of ground presented itself. Take-offs were done by flights of six aircraft in a wide shallow echelon, raising blinding clouds of dust which had to disperse before the next lot could go. At the other extreme, heavy rain turned the makeshift airfields into quagmires, preventing all flying until they dried out.

The ebb and flow of battle over hundreds of miles meant that supplies of fuel, spares, munitions, and even food and water, were often critical. Operationally, fighter control was minimal, and although mobile radar stations were available, for the most part information was gleaned by the RAF's 'Y' service, which monitored enemy radio transmissions. A perennial problem was navigation over the featureless wastes, although near the coast the few roads could be followed. Homing beacons aided a safe return.

The Fighters

In June 1940, the fighter defence of Egypt consisted of just three squadrons of Gladiators: No 33 based forward at Mersah Matruh; No

80 at Amriya near Alexandria; and No 112 at Helwan outside Cairo. As in the early days over Malta, Gladiators were hard-pressed to catch the Italian S.79 bombers, and Hurricanes were urgently sought. But re-equipment was a slow process.

The *Regia Aeronautica* also flew biplane fighters. The 10° *Stormo* fielded three *Squadriglie* of Fiat CR.42s at Castel Benito, while hundreds of miles away at Tripoli, the 2° Stormo was equipped with three *Squadriglie* of CR.32s and three of CR.42s. The elderly CR.32 was clearly inferior to the Gladiator, whereas the CR.42 Falco was slightly better than the British fighter in some respects. It was moderately faster, and its armament of two 12.7mm machine-guns provided a slightly heavier weight of fire than did the four .303 Brownings of the Gladiator.

Some Gladiator pilots nevertheless ran up remarkable scores with their antiquated biplanes, even against monoplane opposition. As always, it was pilot quality that counted most in combat.

The *Regia Aeronautica* operated biplane fighters because, with few exceptions, that was all it had at the time. By contrast, the Desert Air Force flew Gladiators essentially because it was the poor relation; the defence of the mother country naturally took priority. Only slowly did Hurricanes trickle through to Egypt, and not until August 1940 was the first Hurricane squadron formed there. Others followed slowly.

The Desert Air Force remained the poor relation for years to come. The RAF ordered the American-built P-40 Tomahawk in quantity,

Table 11. Gladiator Aces (S/E = single-engined; M/E = multi-engined)

Name	Sqn	Score	S/E	M/E	Total	Notes
Pat Pattle	80	15	13	2	c.50	KIA 20.4.41
Cherry Vale	33/80	10	8	2	30	Died post-war
Joe Fraser	112	9	8	1	9	Died post-war
Don Gregory	80	8	8	0	8	Died post-war
Cas Casbolt	80	7	7	0	13	Retired
Homer Cochrane	112	7	7	0	7	Retired
Alan Boyd	3RAAF	6	6	0	6	Retired
Ape Cullen	80	6	3	3	15	KIA 4.3.41
Paddy Donaldson	112	6	6	0	6	Died post-war
Algy Schwab	112	6	4	2	6	Retired
Heimar Stuckey	80	5	4	1	5	KIA 20.1.41
Tap Jones	80	5	5	0	5	Retired

only to find that its performance was too poor for anything other than low-level tactical reconnaissance operations over Europe. But it was a modern monoplane fighter, faster than the Hurricane, and in the desert, high-altitude performance was of lesser importance than in Europe. Consequently many were sent to Egypt. The first of eight squadrons to re-equip with them was No 112, in June 1941.

The Tomahawk was essentially the Hawk 75, as successfully used by the French in 1940, re-engined with the Allison V-1710-33. The engine was never too reliable, and pilots developed 'oil pressure and temperature eyes'; the slightest movement of the gauges up or down registered immediately. This apart, the pleasant handling of the earlier aircraft had been retained, with low lateral stick forces. The only faults were a vicious wing-drop at the stall, which came entirely without warning, and a tendency to ground-loop if a three-point landing was attempted, as future Hawker Chief Test Pilot Neville Duke discovered the hard way. Landings were generally made with power on and tail up.

The cockpit was spacious by British standards, but two factors were redolent of the biplane era. Two of its six .300 machine-guns were mounted over the engine, and their breeches protruded into the cockpit. When fired, they gave off lots of exciting-smelling cordite smoke. And incredibly, as a back-up to the reflector gun-sight, a fixed ring and bead sight was mounted.

Six months later the Tomahawk was followed into action by its more powerful stable-mate, the Kittyhawk. Rather faster, but essentially similar, the nose guns were deleted and it sported six .50 Brownings in the wings, giving it much greater hitting power. It served with 11 squadrons in all, and was finally phased out in mid-1944 in favour of the Mustang.

The final British fighter used in the desert was the Spitfire, which first became available in mid-1942. In the main these were Spitfire Vs, joined late in the campaign by Mk IXs.

The *Regia Aeronautica* also introduced monoplane fighters as fast as possible, which was not very. The radial-engined Fiat G.50*bis* Freccia, designed to the same format as the Saetta, and of similar hump-backed appearance, made its combat debut at the end of 1940.

The Saetta itself was introduced in July 1941, followed by the superb Folgore in December.

The Italian fighter pilots were of variable quality. Some seemed reluctant to fight, whereas others were more than ready to 'mix it' with Allied fighters. This was in contrast to the more battle-wise Germans, who mostly employed the fast plunge from a high perch, followed by immediate disengagement. In fact it was not unknown for shot-down Italians to complain that the Germans left them to do all the fighting.

However, against better-turning opponents mixing it was tactically quite wrong. Monoplane Freccias made up over a quarter of the single-engined victims of biplane Gladiators of similar power, slower aircraft but with half the wing loading. Then again, many Italian pilots failed to understand that conventional aerobatics have no place in combat; some were even observed to perform slow rolls and loops while under fire. The former did little to make them a difficult target, while the slow pull over the top in the latter made them almost equally vulnerable.

The *Luftwaffe*, which entered the Desert War theatre in 1941, flew the usual Bf 109Es, Fs and Gs; the twin-engined Bf 110; and, from late in 1942, the FW 190A, all of which have been detailed in previous chapters. The Americans, who arrived in Algeria and Tunisia late in 1942, operated P-38 Lightnings, P-40 Warhawks, and P-39 or 400

Table 12. Fighters in North Africa				
	Gloster Gladiator II	Fiat CR 42 Falco	Fiat G 50*bis* Freccia	Curtiss P–40 Kittyhawk
Wingspan	32ft 3in	31ft 10in	36ft 0^1/4 in	37ft 4in
Length	27ft 5in	27ft 1^1/2in	25ft 7in	31ft 2in
Height	10ft 4in	11ft 9^1/2in	9ft 8^1/2in	10ft 7in
Wing area	323 sq ft	241 sq ft	196 sq ft	236 sq ft
Engine	Mercury radial rated at 840hp	Fiat A 74R radial rated at 840hp	Fiat A 74R radial rated at 870hp	Allison V-1710 rated at 1,600hp
Loaded weight	4,790lb	5,033lb	5,963lb	8,500lb
Wing loading	15lb/sq ft	21lb/sq ft	30lb/sq ft	36lb/sq ft
Maximum speed	246mph	267mph	294mph	362mph
Service ceiling	32,900ft	33,465ft	29,000ft	30,000ft
Rate of climb	2,430ft/min	c.2,500ft/min	c.2,600ft/min	c.2,700ft/min
Range	410 miles	482 miles	620 miles	700 miles

129

Airacobras. The Airacobra was not a particularly important combat type in this theatre; the Warhawk differed little from the Kittyhawk; and the Lightning played a more important part over Europe, and is described in a later chapter.

The Aces

On the world stage, the Greek campaign ranked as a side-show, but in the air the intensity of the fighting often exceeded that of the Desert War. Mountainous terrain, often blanketed by cloud, aided the element of surprise which was so hard to come by in the clear skies of North Africa. All RAF fighter sorties were tied to gaining air superiority, while the operational area was relatively small. These factors combined to give the fighter pilots a glut of opportunities to score. And score they did, although the loss of records in the subsequent evacuation makes for an element of uncertainty. 'Pat' Pattle is believed to have notched up about 50 victories before falling in action. Nor was Pattle unique; 'Cherry' Vale scored 19 of his eventual total of 30 victories over Greece.

The Desert War was altogether different. The Hurricanes and P-40s were outclassed by Bf 109s, which could always take position above and strike from the sun. Another factor was that the British fighters were all too frequently used as bomb trucks, attacking ground targets. Heavily laden, they were automatically disadvantaged when intercepted, while many potential aces fell to ground fire. Compared to Greece, opportunities were lacking, and even when they did occur, the *Jagdflieger* held the trump cards of altitude, position and performance. But as always, pilot quality proved decisive, and a few gifted individuals beat the odds to run up scores which would have been

---

Turning round in a stall turn, I observed the leader diving vertically whilst the remaining two had split, No 2 going up, No 3 down. As I had the advantage over the lower aircraft I decided to attack this first. He attempted to come up under me but as I was so near to stalling, I had no difficulty in bringing my sight round to get in a deflection shot and then turn astern on him.

Don Gregory (8 victories), No 80 Squadron, versus three CR.42s, 21 December 1940

130

good under any circumstances. Hamish Dodds of No 274 Squadron was the top Hurricane ace in the desert, with 14 destroyed, six of which were 109s, plus six probables and seven damaged. His particular method was to climb above the main engagement, select a victim, and dive to the attack.

Dodds, a sergeant pilot, was closely followed by Ernest 'Imshi' Mason, also of No 274 Squadron, with 13 (his sobriquet is Arabic for 'kindly remove yourself from my presence', an expression useful with local beggars), and Lance Wade of No 33 Squadron with 12. Posted to command No 94 Squadron with Kittyhawks, Mason fell to the guns of Otto Schulz on 15 February 1942, his total bag being 15 and two shared. 'Wildcat' Wade, a Texan, went on to score 10 more victories flying Spitfires with No 145 Squadron. He died in an accident in January 1944 while flying an Auster. 'Deadstick' Dyson of No 33 Squadron, so called for his frequent engine-out landings, set a record on 11 December 1940 when he was credited with seven victories in a single mission—six CR.42s and a S.79 bomber. Two more CR.42s followed on 19 December. Although Dyson flew extensively in Greece, he was shot down twice without adding to his score.

The outstanding Tomahawk pilot was Australian Clive 'Killer' Caldwell with 16; followed at a respectful distance by Bob Whittle with nine and Neville Bowker with eight. The two leading Kittyhawk pilots were Billy Drake of No 112 Squadron with 13, and Eddie Edwards of Nos 94 and 260 Squadrons with 12. Drake's final score was at least 18, and may have been higher, while Edwards amassed 15. His first victim, on 2 March 1942, was 59-victory *Experte* Otto Schulz. One other P-40 pilot deserves mention: Levi Chase of the 33rd Fighter Group scored 10 victories over Tunisia, the only USAAF pilot to reach double figures in North Africa.

MARMADUKE 'PAT' PATTLE A South African, Pattle joined the RAF in 1936, and in the following year joined No 80 Squadron to fly Gladiators. The squadron was sent to Egypt in April 1938, and by the outbreak of war he was a flight commander. A gifted flyer and natural marksman, he took infinite pains to improve both talents, doing exercises to improve his distance vision and sharpen his reflexes.

His first victories, a Breda Ba 65 and a CR.32, came on 4 August 1940, but after a lengthy fight against heavy odds he was forced to bale out at low level. It was a long walk home through the desert. Four days later he claimed two CR.42s in a set-piece ambush. Then in September he damaged a Savoia Marchetti S.79 trimotor bomber, though the speed of the latter enabled it to escape. Pattle then evolved a tactic for dealing with S.79s. The attack was to be made from above and head-on by a flight of Gladiators in line abreast. The initial aim was to knock out an engine, which would slow the bomber down. With this accomplished, a traditional attack from astern could be made. The next priority was to silence the rear gunner, after which a burst would be aimed at the petrol tank in the starboard wing root; a few seconds to allow the fuel to spray out, then a final burst of incendiary to ignite it. Like many neat ideas it was too complicated in practice, depending on no less than four accurate bursts of fire, and no interruptions from the escorting fighters. Pattle's huge total contained just three S-79s.

Flying Gladiators over Greece, he brought his score to 15 before No 80 Squadron was equipped with Hurricanes on 20 February 1941. Nine more victories followed before he was posted to command No 33 Squadron on 12 March, shortly before the *Luftwaffe* joined the fray. Over the next 39 days, insofar as his score can be reconstructed from surviving records and diaries, Pattle shot down no less than 26 enemy aircraft. Of these, 23 were German, nine of them the formidable Bf 109. The end came on 20 April, when 'Timber' Woods (6 victories) was hard pressed by a Bf 110 over Eleusis Bay. Pattle, flying even though sick and exhausted, went to his aid, but was set upon by other 110s and killed.

Keen vision and marksmanship apart, Pattle's secret was an ability to get just that bit more out of his aircraft. He could handle the controls roughly, but without ever over-stressing the wings or straying into the regions of a high-speed stall. This generally enabled him to get in close before shooting. What he might have done with a Spitfire over Europe we shall never know.

CLIVE 'KILLER' CALDWELL An Australian, Caldwell was

probably the 'fightingest' pilot of the Desert War. Flying Tomahawks with No 250 Squadron he scored 16 victories, eight of them 109s, including *Experte* Wolfgang Lippert. On 5 December he claimed five Ju 87s in one action, then on 24 December he claimed a Bf 109 damaged; this was apparently 67-victory *Experte* Erbo *Graf* von Kageneck, who died of wounds 19 days later. In January 1942 he was given command of No 112 Squadron, flying Kittyhawks, with which he scored another three victories. One of these was 59-victory *Experte* 'Fifi' Stahlschmidt, who force-landed on 24 February 1942.

While Caldwell was basically interested in getting stuck in, his specific method of evading attack from the rear was similar to that of *Luftwaffe Experte* Erich Hartmann. It was to 'shove everything into one corner, even though it hurts'. This involved pushing the stick forward and to one side, while kicking the rudder hard, sending the fighter into a negative-g spiral which induced red-out (the opposite of black-out), with the pilot pressed hard against his straps. An opponent trying to follow him would be unable to continue tracking. After a count of three, centralising the controls followed by a hard pull on the stick produced a climb, from which Caldwell would arrive in a position above his attacker.

In January 1943 Caldwell became Wing Leader at Darwin, Australia, flying Spitfire Vbs. Against the Japanese he scored a further eight victories, to bring his total to 27, with three shared, six probables and 15 damaged.

NEVILLE DUKE Neville Duke joined the RAF in June 1940, after being rejected by the Fleet Air Arm. Posted to No 92 Squadron in April 1941, he learned a great deal from the experienced members of this illustrious unit. At first he flew as wingman to Allan Wright (11 victories) and Don Kingaby (21 victories); then after a while was selected to fly as No 2 to the Biggin Hill Wing Leader 'Sailor' Malan. This was great experience:

> Once I suddenly found myself flying through bits of a 109 before I even realised that [Malan] had fired his guns and once he showered me with spent cartridge cases and links, which was awkward, for they were known to crack hoods, pierce radiators and damage airscrews. Neither Sailor or Don flew straight and level for a second once they became separated from the main

133

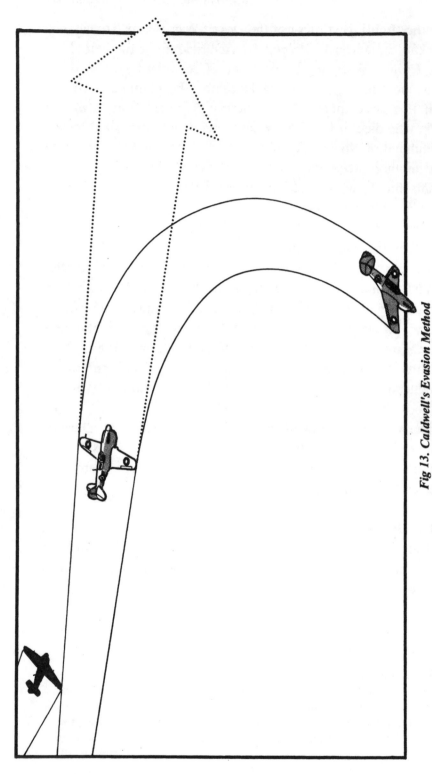

Fig 13. Caldwell's Evasion Method

Killer Caldwell's proven method of shaking an attacker off his tail was to 'stuff everything into the corner, stick, rudder and throttle, even though it hurts!' This sent him into a negative-g uncoordinated bunt which was almost impossible to follow.

body of the squadron. They were masters in the air, and got everything out of their aircraft; with Sailor especially, it was full throttle work most of the time. From such men as these I soon learned to weave and to search the sky continuously, never relaxing until we had landed.

With two confirmed victories, Duke was posted to No 112 Squadron in the desert. His first flight in a Tomahawk was not encouraging; when he landed, he broke off both main gear legs and ended in a heap, fortunately unhurt. However, he soon got to grips with his new mount, shooting down a 109F using the ring and bead when his reflector sight failed.

On 30 November he was downed by Otto Schulz of *II/JG 27*, who hit him with a full 90° deflection shot. Five days later, hampered by a heavily sanded canopy which reduced visibility, he was downed again by a 109. But his own score steadily rose, and at the end of his tour had risen by four, three with the Tomahawk and one with the Kittyhawk. After a 'rest' spell as an instructor, Neville Duke rejoined No 92 Squadron, and was in action over Tunisia in January 1943, flying Spitfire VBs. By the end of the campaign, he had accounted for 14 enemy aircraft, making him the top scorer over Tunisia.

Leading No 145 Squadron over Italy, Duke brought his final score to 26 confirmed and two shared, with one probable and six damaged. After the war he became a test pilot with Hawker, and on 7 September 1953 he set a new World Air Speed record in a modified Hunter.

6. NIGHT FIGHTERS OVER EUROPE

The key to successful night air defence was detection and tracking; not only the raiders, but also the defending fighters. There was little point in knowing exactly where an enemy bomber was, if the intercepting fighter was unsure of its own position. In the late 1930s radar seemed to offer a solution to this problem, but progress was slow. It was nearly 18 months after the outbreak of war before a really effective night fighter force came into being. Until that time, the RAF used what it had, however unsuitable.

At first the threat was not very formidable—a handful of bombers attacking targets in the Midlands and North which were beyond the range at which day bombers could be escorted. But with the failure of the daylight bombing campaign in the summer of 1940, the *Luftwaffe* was increasingly switched to night raiding. The intensity of this grew rapidly, aided by advanced (for the time) target-finding electronic systems. In the final months of 1940, night raids had begun to cause significant damage, while the defences were only able to inflict minimal losses on the German bombers.

'Catseye' Fighters

With airborne interception (AI) radar far from ready, the first line of defence was the 'catseye' fighter, which relied on what the pilot could see 'out of the window'. Unfortunately this was not a lot. Even on the clearest moonlit night, a pilot was hard-pressed to spot an aircraft more than about half a mile distant, while on a moonless night the best that could be hoped for was to discern a vague unidentifiable shape that blotted out a few stars at perhaps 300ft.

Searchlights were expected to provide a partial answer, but in practice these were ineffective above about 12,000ft, and in hazy conditions became very diffuse. In any case, they only lit up the underside of the bomber. From above it remained invisible. While an illuminated bomber could be clearly seen from below, this meant that the fighter was forced to pursue in a time-consuming climb. Neither were the German pilots co-operative. They tried to evade the beam, and all too often succeeded. Even when they failed, the bomber soon passed beyond the range of the light, and was lost in the darkness long before the fighter could get into an attacking position.

Consequently, most 'catseye' interceptions were a matter of luck. Fighters patrolled set lines for set periods, with a ground controller warning them when any 'trade' appeared to be heading their way. The ground control system had been designed to place fighters within visual distance in daylight; a matter of several miles. At night it was simply too inaccurate. At the height of the Blitz, several fighters were stacked over the target area, above the height of the gun barrage, and spaced vertically at 500ft intervals. Usually they saw nothing. The night sky was a big place.

That the 'catseye' fighters had little success was not their fault. They were being asked to achieve the near-impossible. The main British night fighter of the period was the Blenheim, which was barely fast enough to catch a German bomber even if well placed at the time a sighting was made. Hurricanes and even Spitfires were used, with the added handicap that the exhaust flames from their engines were blinding at night. After its brief and disastrous debut in daylight, the Defiant turret fighter joined them. There were a few successes, and one or two pilots regularly beat the odds, but the attrition inflicted was not enough to stem the tide.

Radar Fighters

AI radar was difficult to use. Quite apart from various technical bugs which had to be ironed out of the system, the presentation of the information called for skilled interpretation if it was to be of any practical value. For example, when a day fighter pilot saw his target, he knew at once where it was and what it was doing in relation to his own aircraft. Using AI radar, echoes on a pair of cathode ray tubes showed only where the target was at any given moment. From a succession of

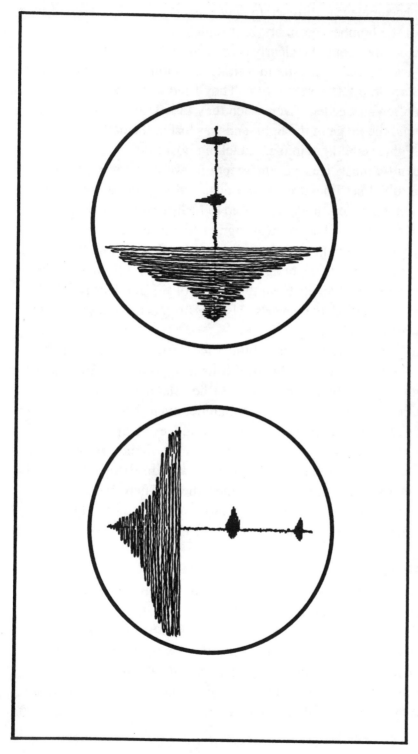

Fig. 14. Early AI Radar Display

From two scopes like these, radar operators had to determine not only where the target was but what it was doing, then guide the pilot into a position from where a sighting could be made. The 'Christmas Tree' at the end of the trace is the ground return.

> *After a while it dawned on me what I had been doing wrong, and I realised that I would have to stop the turn much sooner, and hold a converging course instead of blindly pointing the fighter at the target.*
> Jimmy Rawnsley, No 604 Squadron

these echoes, which changed according to whether the fighter was banking or in level flight, the unfortunate radar operator had to deduce what it was doing, its range, speed and heading, and then steer his pilot in the right direction to intercept. This was far from easy. Successful night fighting was largely a matter of teamwork, with both pilot and operator understanding each other's needs.

The first victory by a fighter equipped with AI came on 22 July 1940. 'Jumbo' Ashfield, flying a Blenheim of the experimental Fighter Interception Unit, was patrolling over Tangmere at 10,000ft when he was informed that a small group of bombers was crossing the coast near Selsey at 6,000ft. Nosing down to pick up speed, he set off in pursuit. His operator, Sergeant Leyland, gained a radar contact at a range of 5,000ft and talked his pilot in behind it. Ashfield finally closed to visual range, identified it as a Dornier Do 17, and opened fire from 400ft. Hit, the Dornier lurched left and vanished into the night, but shortly afterwards was seen burning on the sea. Radar or no, Ashfield had been lucky. He had been well positioned at the outset, with an altitude advantage to convert into speed, without which he might never have caught the lightly laden Dornier. In addition his radar continued to work throughout the interception, something that could not always be guaranteed.

Two more things were needed to make the night defences effective. The first was an aircraft with a turn of speed sufficient to allow it to overhaul enemy bombers with ease, yet large enough to carry a radar set and operator. This eventually materialised in the Beaufighter, a fast twin-engined fighter with a respectable rate of climb and unprecedented hitting power. The second was a ground controlled interception (GCI) system accurate enough to place a night fighter within AI range of its quarry. This finally emerged as a series of overlapping radar stations with steerable antennae giving 360°coverage. By spring 1941, both were in place in growing numbers.

This was just the start. GCI directed the fighter to within about three miles of a target. From here it made AI contact, and used its considerable speed advantage to close the gap swiftly. But with night visual ranges so short, maintaining a high rate of closure for too long was to risk overshooting, or, even worse, a collision. Consequently the rate of closure had to be slowed to little more than walking pace as the distance shortened. The really clever bit was knowing exactly when to slow down. If speed was dumped too far from the bomber, the long pursuit to visual contact became excessive, allowing the bomber time to spot the fighter and escape. Getting it right called for very fine timing on the part of the AI operator.

Even on the darkest night, the sky is slightly lighter than the ground. Once the pursuit was established, the trick was to creep in slightly low, concealing the fighter against the dark ground while outlining the bomber against the lighter sky or the stars. Even then the bomber was difficult to spot—an indistinct patch of darkness, a few stars blotted out. And even with visual contact established, positive identification had to be made. It might be a British bomber returning from a raid, or even a friendly night fighter. Errors inevitably occurred.

Another problem on very dark nights was that AI had a short minimum range of about 400ft. Once the target was within this distance, it vanished from the screens, at a time when visual contact had still not been made. All that the crew knew was that it was somewhere ahead, and very, very close. It was a nerve-racking experience. The level of trust between pilot and radar operator had to be high.

The influx of new equipment combined with experience gained resulted in a startling increase in effectiveness in the first half of 1941. In January RAF night fighters made 78 contacts, claimed just three victories (one claim every 162 sorties), and inflicted a loss rate on the

---

All of which [radar problems] left the unfortunate pilot with several tons of streamlined aeroplane on his hands rushing without any brakes straight at an equally solid and as yet unseen aircraft with an overtaking speed of anything up to 50 mph.

Jimmy Rawnsley, No 604 Squadron

Luftwaffe of 0.02%. In May the same year these figures rose to 371 contacts, 96 victories (one every 21 sorties) and a loss rate inflicted of 3.93%.

This was still not enough to halt the bombing offensive, but it clearly indicated a positive trend. By this time, however, Hitler's thoughts had turned eastward, and much of his bomber force was moved to the Russian Front, considerably depleting the numbers Britain faced. The night threat never again became really serious. German operations flared up from time to time, setting new problems such as low-level penetration, and fast fighter-bombers, but these were all met with a combination of new radars and the superb Mosquito, which by the end of 1943 had virtually supplanted the Beaufighter in the night fighter role. The fast Typhoon single-seater was experimentally equipped with radar, but for various operational reasons this was a failure, leaving the Mossie to reign supreme.

Intruders

One place that German bombers could frequently be found was over their own airfields. Whether taking off heavy-laden, or returning after a sortie, tired and burning their navigation lights in the circuit to avoid colliding, they were vulnerable.

At first Hurricanes, followed later by various twin-engined types— in the early years at least without radar—were tasked with intruding. The secret was not to alert the Germans, who, if they knew intruders were about, turned off the flare-path and warned the bombers to go elsewhere. The trick was to stooge around in the vicinity of two or three airfields waiting for trade. It took a great deal of patience, plus lightning reactions if an opportunity presented itself. Lack of radar was a handicap, but the ban was imposed to prevent it being captured, examined, and compromised.

Bomber Support

The bomber support mission was introduced in May 1943, to counter the activities of the German night fighter force. Prior to this, British intruders patrolled known German fighter bases but, without radar, were unable to obtain decisive results.

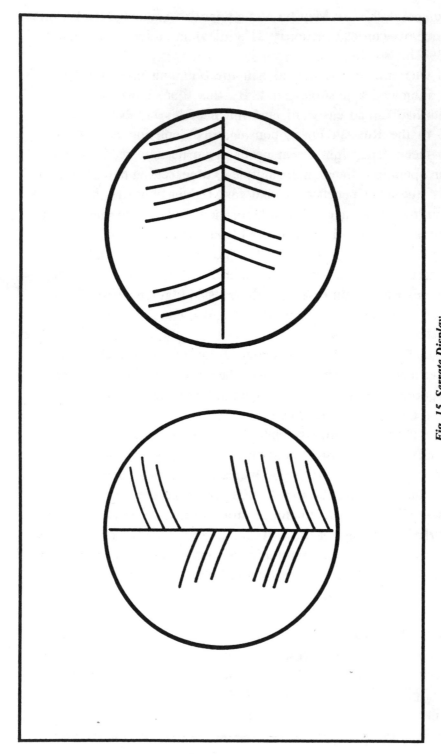

Fig. 15. Serrate Display

Like most AI radars Serrate needed two scopes from which to deduce the direction and relative altitude of a German night fighter. Unfortunately it gave no indication of range.

At this point, the first British radar-equipped fighters were released for service over enemy territory, while intruder patrols were timed to coincide with bomber raids. At much the same time, a gadget called Serrate, which could home on the emissions of German night fighter radars, was introduced. This had the tremendous advantage of positively identifying a radar contact as hostile, obviating the need for visual identification. This and other electronic wizardry put German fighters under threat from the time that their wheels left the ground until they touched down again, inducing a defensive mind-set best reflected in the attrition rates for British bombers at the end of 1944. It fell to 6.6% in October, 1.5% in November, and 0.7% in December. The *Nachtjagdflieger* never recovered from this defeat.

The Fighters

The main German night fighters were the Bf 110G which, laden with a third crew member and external fuel tanks, had a barely adequate performance; the Junkers Ju 88G adapted from the fast day bomber; and the Heinkel He 219, the only purpose-built German night fighter. The latter only served in small numbers, as it not only failed to match its brochure performance, but its extremely high wing loading made it a very hot ship for night operations.

The first really effective RAF night fighter was the Bristol Beaufighter, which began to reach various squadrons in September 1940. Tremendously strong, it was hauled through the air by a pair of Hercules radial engines at over 320mph, and had the unprecedented firepower of four 20mm cannon in the nose and six .303 machine-guns in the wings. If his aim was true, a Beaufighter pilot rarely had to fire twice. The pilot sat in the nose, with a superb view through an optically flat windshield; the radar operator sat amidships.

The best night fighter of the war was without doubt the de Havilland Mosquito, developed from the light bomber variant.

> *The Beaufighter tended to tighten up in turns, and this, accentuating the ever-present difficulty of making accurate turns on instruments, resulted—at least in my experience—in unwitting gains or losses in height in all but gentle turns.*
>
> Rory Chisholm (9 victories)

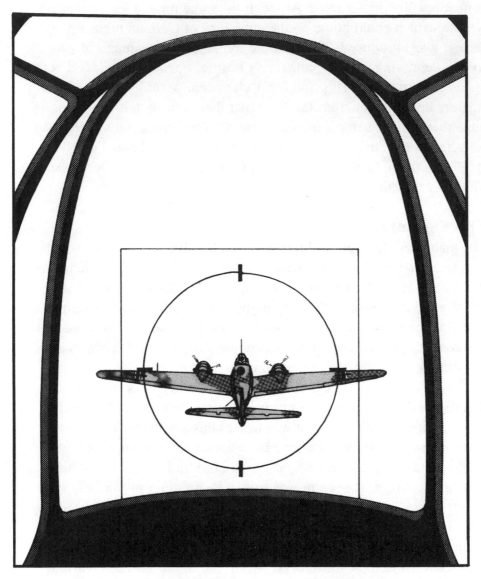

Fig. 16. Shooting Position From The Beaufighter
Because the guns on the Beaufighter were set low, not only was there a
risk that the cannon shells would go beneath the target and miss, but the
recoil tended to tuck the nose down. This was overcome by using an
initial aim high on the target aircraft, as depicted here.

> *It was fast, and had tremendous firepower, but it used to wander laterally at all speeds. The more you tried to correct, the worse it got. In the end, you had to take your feet off the rudder pedals and let it damp out.*
>
> Dickie Haine (3 victories)

Powered by two Rolls-Royce Merlin engines, it was fast, with a good rate of climb, and the range to operate over Germany. Unlike the Beaufighter, it would fly happily on one engine. Initial armament consisted of four 20mm cannon and four .303 machine-guns, but in practice the cannon were found to be sufficient. The crew sat side by side, which made for ease of co-operation. The Mosquito had just one fault as a fighter: aerodynamically clean, it took a long while to slow down, making timing all-important.

The Aces

The circumstances in which the leading night aces gained their victories are so diverse that comparisons are largely meaningless. The early years of the war saw defensive operations predominate; later the offensive took priority. A handful of 'catseye' pilots did well, but for the most part were outshone by the radar-aided crews. Opportunity played a large part; Mosquito pilot John 'Ian' Allan and his operator H. Davidson, of No 256 Squadron, accounted for 13 German and Italian bombers in the space of just 18 nights over Sicily in July 1943, five of them in one night. Allan added one more a month later. But in night ranger operations over Europe in 1944 he failed to score at all.

Table 13. British Night Fighters, 1940–45

	Bristol Beaufighter VIF	DH Mosquito XIX
Wing span	57ft 10in	54ft 2in
Length	41ft 8in	41ft 2in
Height	15ft 10in	15ft 3in
Wing area	503 sq ft	454 sq ft
Engines	2 x Bristol Hercules radials rated at 1,670hp	2 x Rolls-Royce Merlin V-12s rated at 1,620hp
Loaded weight	21,600lb	20,600lb
Wing loading	43lb/sq ft	45lb/sq ft
Maximum speed	333mph	378mph
Service ceiling	26,500ft	29,000ft
Rate of climb	1,850ft/min	2,700ft/min
Range	1,480 miles	1,400 miles

RICHARD STEVENS During most of 1941, the leading night ace was Hurricane pilot Richard Stevens of No 151 Squadron, who between January and October 1941 accounted for 14 German bombers over Britain. A pre-war airline pilot, and at 32 an old man in the fighter world, he had considerable night flying experience before joining the RAF at the outbreak of war.

His background is shrouded in mystery, but what seems certain is that he had a pathological hatred of German bombers. Apparently careless of life, often he closed to such short range that his Hurricane was damaged by debris, while one account has him varnishing over German blood on his wing to preserve it. His decidedly sporty speciality was to fly where the anti-aircraft fire was thickest, there to search visually. Keen vision and accurate shooting did the rest. He was killed over Holland while on an intruder sortie in December 1941.

JOHN CUNNINGHAM Cunningham, who scored the first Beaufighter victory on 19/20 November 1940, went on to become the leading defensive night ace of the war, with a score of 19, plus one in daylight in conditions too bad for the day fighters to operate. This combat was particularly interesting inasmuch as Cunningham did not fire a shot during what was a lengthy engagement, but outflew his opponent, causing him to crash.

His first 16 victories were scored with Beaufighters of No 604 Squadron, after which he and his regular operator, Jimmy Rawnsley, were rested. They returned to operations in mid-1943 to fly Mosquitos with No 85 Squadron. By this time opportunities were scarce, and targets elusive. His last four victories were three FW 190 fighter-bombers and a Me 410. Post-war, he became Chief Test Pilot for de Havilland, and is probably best remembered for testing the Comet jet airliner.

BOB BRAHAM Arguably one of the most aggressive men ever to strap an aeroplane on his back, Bob Braham ended the war with a score of 29 victories, of which 20 were at night. The first of these, made while flying a Blenheim of No 29 Squadron, fell on 24/25

> *Before we had straightened out, Jacko called urgently: 'Hard starboard, there's another only a few hundred yards away!' I hauled the Beau into a tight turn when Jacko called 'Look out, he's only 200 yards ahead and slightly above. You're closing too fast'.*
>
> *'Christ, I've got him,' I yelled. Above me in a tight turn was another Me 110, and at the speed at which we were travelling we looked as though we were going to ram him. I eased back the stick, put the sights on him, and fired at the point-blank range of about 50 yards. There was a blinding flash as the Me exploded in my face.*
>
> Bob Braham, No 141 Squadron

August 1940; the next 12 victories came while flying Beaufighters of the same unit.

Posted to command No 141 Squadron in December 1942, he worked up the squadron with the new and highly secret Serrate during the following year, and became one of its leading exponents, gaining six victories over German night fighters in four months. These included aces Heinz Vinke (54 victories), Georg Kraft (14 victories), and August Geiger (53 victories). Vinke survived, only to fall to the guns of Typhoon pilot Cheval Lallemant a few months later.

Braham's night victories were scored with no less than four different operators, of whom 'Sticks' Gregory and 'Jacko' Jacobs were the most frequent. His nine day victories between 5 March and 12 May 1944 were scored with Mosquitos from four different units. Then on 25 June he was shot down over Denmark by an FW 190 and taken prisoner. After the war he made a career with the Canadian Armed Forces, but died in 1974 aged 53.

BRANSE BURBRIDGE Burbridge joined No 85 Squadron in October 1941, but his first tour, flying Havocs, brought him just one probable. Returning to the squadron in early 1944, which was by now equipped with Mosquitos, he and radar operator Bill Skelton began a 10-month career of mayhem.

Five victories came on home defence. Then, after the invasion of Normandy, No 85 Squadron was assigned to the bomber support role with 100 Group. They flew 30 bomber support sorties in the space of six months, in which time they claimed 16 victories over German night fighters. The first of these was the Ju 188 of *Luftwaffe Experte* Wilhelm Herget (72 victories), which they shot down near Nivelles in southern Belgium.

Their big night came on 4/5 November, when they supported a heavy raid on Bochum in the Rühr. Having accounted for two Ju 88s, they took a turn around a fighter airfield south of Cologne. While still some distance away they saw the landing lights of a fighter touching down. Burbridge's hunting instincts were aroused. He later reported:

> Flt Lt Skelton obtained a contact at 2 miles range, 600 starboard, and at our height which was about 1,000ft above the ground. Following round the south side, we closed in to identify a Me 110. He must have throttled back rather smartly when east of the airfield for we suddenly found ourselves overtaking rapidly, horn [a warning given when the throttles were retarded with the wheels still up] blaring in our ears, and finished up immediately below him about 80ft away. Very gradually we began to drop back and pulling up to dead astern at 400ft range, I fired a very short burst. The whole fuselage was a mass of flame, and the Me 110 went down burning furiously, to crash in a river about five miles north of the airfield...
>
> We flew away to the north for a few minutes, and then turned to approach the airfield again. As we did so, Flt Lt Skelton produced another contact at 2 miles range, 800 to starboard. When we got in behind him he appeared to be doing a close left-hand orbit of the airfield. Again we followed him around the west and south sides, and as he seemed to be preparing to land I selected 10° of flap. I obtained a visual at 1,500ft range: no undercarriage was visible, so I took the flap off again. We identified the target as a Ju 88 and a very short burst from dead astern, 400ft range, caused the fuselage to burst into flames. The cockpit broke away, and we pulled up sharply to avoid debris.

These four victories took only 200 rounds of 20mm ammunition; a tribute to Burbridge's marksmanship. He and Skelton went on to become the leading night fighter crew of the war with 21 night victories, two probables, one damaged, and three V-1s destroyed. Both survived the war to enter the Christian ministry.

7. AGAINST THE RISING SUN, DECEMBER 1941–FEBRUARY 1943

The United States was forced into the war on 7 December 1941, when Japanese naval aircraft from six carriers attacked the American Pacific Fleet at Pearl Harbor. Surprise was complete, and the handful of defending fighters which managed to get off the ground in the teeth of the attack accounted for just five from the shoals of Japanese aircraft. For the Americans it was a rude awakening.

Over the next few months, the Japanese swept across Asia and the Pacific. Through Thailand, Malaya and Burma to the west, and the East Indies to the south, they were supported by the Japanese Army Air Force. Across the Pacific, through the Philippines and other island chains, the Imperial Japanese Navy led the way. While carrier aviation played the leading role at this time, the IJN also deployed strong land-based air units in support of their island-hopping operations. The Allies were everywhere in retreat. How had this happened?

Pre-war, the Allies had consistently made the error of underestimating the Japanese, portraying them as a short-sighted and even shorter-legged nation. Consequently when war came they received some nasty shocks. Instead of encountering second rate pilots in third rate aeroplanes, they found they were up against experienced and battle-hardened veterans, flying aeroplanes that were in many ways superior to their own.

The reasons for this were not hard to find; their opponents had flown against the Chinese since 1937, and for a brief spell in 1938 had also flown against the Russians, emerging victorious from both conflicts. During this time they had refined their tactics, while their operational philosophy had resulted in the development of fighters of adequate performance and astounding manoeuvrability. It was known in the West that Japanese aero engines were nothing special; what they did not allow for was that Japanese airframes were devoid of anything that added unnecessarily to weight. They were stressed for normal fighter manoeuvres, but lacked such refinements as armour, self-sealing tanks, and even radios. The result was what virtually amounted to aerobatic sports planes with relatively high-powered engines and wing loadings far below those of Western fighters. The turning ability of Japanese fighters in the early days of the Pacific War, notably the Mitsubishi Zero, became legendary.

The basic Japanese fighter formation was the three-aircraft *shotai*. This was the standard Vic formation, which, when combat was joined, became an off-set line astern with about 300ft between aircraft. Three *shotai* made up a *chutai*, a loose and flexible formation with all pilots except the leader weaving.

Japanese air discipline was variable; in a more or less controlled situation they stuck together, and an Allied pilot separated from his unit could generally expect to face at least three opponents. While the preferred Japanese tactic was a diving attack followed by a zoom climb, they were aggressive, and not reluctant to 'mix it' in a turning fight. When this happened, however, air discipline broke down completely, with matters not helped by the absence of radio communications. The result was a messy multi-bogey dogfight, with high levels of confusion. This actually gave advantages both ways. For the Japanese, the superior turn capabilities of their fighters gave them an edge both in evading attack and in working their way into an astern shooting position. At the same time it deprived them of anything more than coincidental support. Allied team-work, assisted by radio, to a degree offset the qualitative advantage of their opponents' aircraft. This was particularly true of US Navy fighter squadrons.

Yet another factor played a significant part. While, on a one-versus-one basis, the Japanese fighters could outfly their opponents, their relatively light armament was often unable to inflict decisive damage. By contrast, although the Allied fighters were often hard pressed to obtain a shooting chance, a few hits on the unprotected Zeros and Hayabusas were often enough. The Japanese aircraft were unable to sustain much battle damage.

150

On the mainland of Asia the Japanese were opposed by the RAF with P-36 Mohawks, Hurricanes and Buffaloes, and by the American Volunteer Group (AVG), with P-40 Tomahawks and Warhawks. The AVG, commonly known as the 'Flying Tigers', was an organisation paid for by the Chinese and commanded by American Claire Chennault. It was disbanded on 4 July 1942 and became the 23rd Fighter Group of the USAAF.

In the Pacific, the brunt of the fighting fell on the US Navy. Its primary fighter was the Grumman F4F Wildcat, a sturdy machine which, although it could be outmanoeuvred by the Zero, could hold its own if handled well tactically.

However, for carrier operations there was one tactical consideration which differed widely from land operations. The distances were vast, and the fighter base was mobile and could change position by up to 60 miles during a single sortie. For this reason, aircraft cruised at their most economical speed rather than the faster combat cruise used by their land-based counterparts. This was typically 120–150mph, and made formations more vulnerable to the surprise bounce from above. This extra risk was accepted by both sides, on the basis that while the enemy might rate 50%, the sea always rated 100%. Losses in carrier battles were frequently horrendous; there were no diversionary airfields, no chance of a safe forced landing, and little hope for the crewman forced to bale out, while even if a damaged aircraft or wounded pilot returned to the carrier, the problem remained of a safe deck landing.

Unlike every other Allied air force, the US Navy trained its fighter pilots in deflection shooting. In the Wildcat, the pilot sat up high, with a view of 8° downwards over the nose, which aided him in keeping the target in view at high deflection angles. Four basic textbook attacks were taught: the overhead, side, opposite and astern approaches.

The overhead attack commenced from ahead and at least 2,000ft above the target, on an opposing course. The Wildcat then rolled on its back, before pulling through into a vertical dive. Even the Zero could not turn fast enough to evade this, as a quite small change in direction on the part of the attacking Wildcat was enough to hold it in the gun sight. Optimum range was 600ft or less, after which the

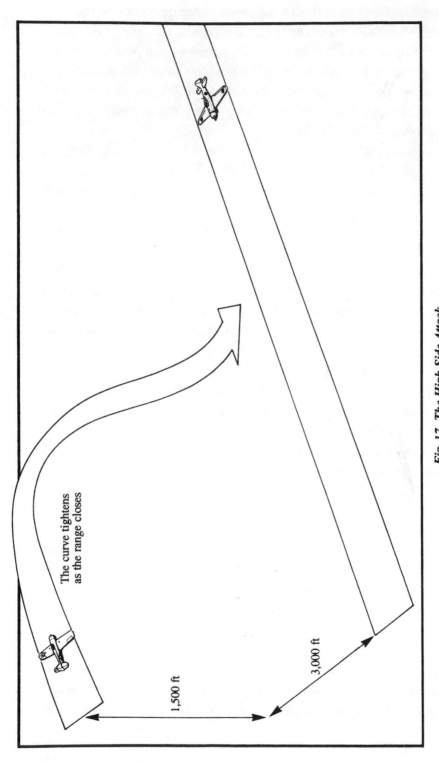

The curve tightens as the range closes

1,500 ft

3,000 ft

Fig. 17. The High Side Attack

The high side attack began from well above and from an offset converging course. As it approached, the USN fighter turned down and made a diving attack from abeam.

breakaway was made astern of the opponent, with a smooth pull-out to convert the excess speed back into altitude.

Side attacks were made from ahead and above, starting with a full-deflection shot, the angle of which rapidly diminished as the range closed. Head-on attacks were also taught, the preferred method being to come in slightly low. This forced the opponent to dip his nose to return fire, thus risking a head-on collision. The basic USN fighter formation was the four-aircraft division, flying in two pairs. This had been widely adopted pre-war as a result of conversations with experienced RAF pilots, sent to the USA for that purpose.

The first great carrier battle of the war took place in the Coral Sea in May 1942, between the Japanese carriers *Zuikaku*, *Shokaku*, and *Shoho*, and the USN carriers *Lexington* and *Yorktown*. This was a hard-fought draw; *Shoho* and *Lexington* were sunk, *Shokaku* badly damaged, and *Yorktown* slightly damaged. This was followed in June by the decisive Battle of Midway, in which the 'Thach Weave' made its combat debut, and in which four Japanese carriers—the *Akagi*, *Kaga*, *Soryu* and *Hiryu*—were sunk, for the sole US carrier loss of the *Yorktown*.

Midway was the turning point of the Pacific War; the first time that the Japanese had been halted. The loss of four aircraft carriers and most of their pilots was equally critical. These were experienced Japanese fighter pilots who could not be easily replaced. From this point on, the IJN was on the defensive; its fighters were outclassed by new American machines entering service, while its pilots were increasingly undertrained and inexperienced. This was underlined by the Battle of Santa Cruz late in 1942, and the protracted struggle for Guadalcanal, which lasted until February 1943.

The Fighters

The primary Japanese Army fighter during this period was the Nakajima Ki 43 Hayabusa, code-named Oscar by the Allies. The main requirements were conflicting: speed and manoeuvrability. To attain this, combat flaps were introduced to improve lift, and thus turning capability. The 14-cylinder Sakae radial engine produced 975hp, and armament was just two 7.7mm machine-guns. The Hayabusa entered

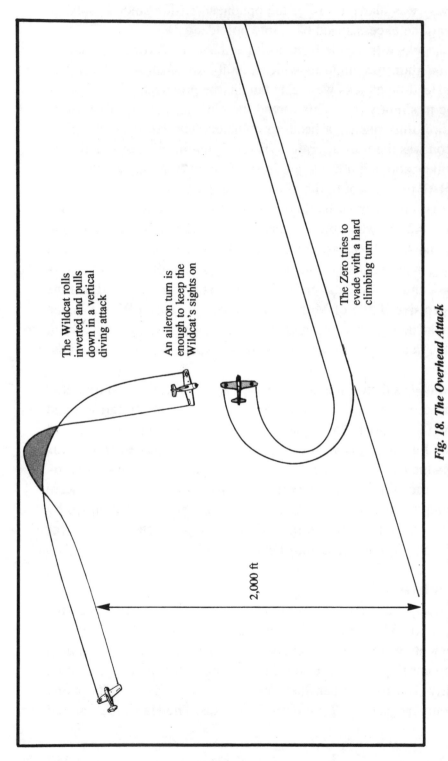

The Wildcat rolls inverted and pulls down in a vertical diving attack

An aileron turn is enough to keep the Wildcat's sights on

The Zero tries to evade with a hard climbing turn

2,000 ft

Fig. 18. The Overhead Attack

Particularly favoured when the approach was from head-on and higher, the overhead attack was made in a near-vertical dive, which needed only small course adjustments to keep the sights on even if the target took evasive action.

service in October 1941. Later production models were armed with two 12.7mm machine-guns, which were still not really adequate. Also at a later date, some armour protection and a more powerful engine were added. No less than 32 *sentais* (roughly 36 aircraft each) flew the type, which, despite increasing obsolescence, remained in service until the end of the war.

Flown by the IJN, the Mitsubishi A6M Type 0, or Zero, was the Japanese equivalent of the Spitfire. Although not as fast as the British fighter, the Zero could out-turn the Spitfire with ease, could sustain a climb at a very steep angle, and could stay in the air for three times as long. Powered by the Sakae radial engine, it was armed with two 20mm cannon and two 7.7mm machine-guns. First flown on 1 April 1939, it entered service in China in mid-1940. Its greatest claim to fame was that it was the first carrier fighter able to out-perform its land-based contemporaries.

The Allied air forces flew the Curtiss P-36 Mohawk, the radial engine of which gave rise to occasional misidentification (the combat report of one RAF Hurricane pilot in Burma stated 'I thought he was a Mohawk; that's why I only gave him a short burst'); the Brewster Buffalo, which could fairly be described as a true air inferiority fighter; the lack-lustre Bell Airacobra; and the P-40 and Hurricane, both of which have been described in previous chapters.

The standard US Navy fighter was the Grumman F4F Wildcat. First flown in September 1937, it was powered by a 1,200hp Pratt & Whitney Twin Wasp radial engine. Basic performance was inferior to that of the Zero, but it had virtues all of its own. The standing joke about Grumman fighters was that they were carved out of a solid, and the rugged Wildcat was certainly no exception. Heavily armed with six .50 machine-guns, and armoured, with self-sealing fuel tanks, it could absorb far more battle damage than the Japanese fighter. This gave it the advantage in a head-on pass. It could also exploit the one serious weakness of the Zero. At speed the ailerons of the latter progressively stiffened, until at about 290mph they became almost immovable. The Wildcat was far more controllable in the rolling plane, and as speed exceeded 250mph, it could easily turn out of the line of fire and escape.

155

Table 14. Fighters of the Early Pacific War

	Nakajima Ki 43 Hayabusa	Mitsubishi A6M Zero	Grumman F4F Wildcat
Wingspan	37ft 6½in	39ft 4½in	38ft 0in
Length	29ft 2½in	29ft 9in	29ft 0in
Height	10ft 1½in	9ft 2in	12ft 1½in
Wing area	237 sq ft	242 sq ft	260 sq ft
Engine	Nakajima Sakae radial rated at 975hp	Nakajima Sakae radial rated at 975hp	Pratt & Whitney Twin Wasp radial rated at 1,200hp
Loaded weight	5,320lb	5,134lb	7,975lb
Wing loading	22lb/sq ft	21lb/sq ft	31lb/sq ft
Maximum speed	320mph	346mph	320mph
Service ceiling	36,800ft	35,100ft	34,000ft
Rate of climb	3,240ft/min	3,140ft/min	2,190ft/min
Range	1,006 miles	1,130 miles	830 miles

The Aces

A feature of the air war against Japan was the number of multiple kills in a single mission, something which was only exceeded by the *Luftwaffe* on the Russian Front. This was aided by two factors: firstly the extreme vulnerability to fire of Japanese aircraft; and secondly the inflexible air discipline of Japanese bomber formations, which they held even as they were chopped from the skies. For example, the first AVG ace was Duke Hedman, who, on his first mission on 23 December 1941, drove his P-40 in close behind a bomber formation. With a total disregard for tactics, he stayed there and shot down five, one after the other. He was badly hit by return fire, and his aircraft was written off on his return. His final score with the AVG was nine.

During the attack on Pearl Harbor, P-40 pilot George 'Wheaties' Welch got off the ground twice in the face of Japanese attacks to claim four. He survived the war with a score of 16, only to die in October 1954 while testing the supersonic F-100 Super Sabre.

The first USAAF ace of the war was 'Buzz' Wagner. A P-40 pilot with the 17th Pursuit Squadron in the Philippines, his flight was bounced by five Zeros on 11 December 1941. Throttling back, he dropped in astern as they overshot, accounting for two of them. His fifth victory came exactly one week later, during a multi-bogey engagement over Vigan, but shortly afterwards eye damage caused by a cannon shell in the cockpit took him out of the battle for several months. He returned to action with the 49th PG, and brought his score to eight.

The first USN ace was Wildcat pilot 'Butch' O'Hare of VF-3, who single-handedly attacked nine Mitsubishi G4M bombers on 20 February 1942. In just three attacking passes he sent three into the sea, set another on fire, and damaged a fifth to the extent that it crashed on its return flight. With his score at 12, he was killed, probably by friendly fire, while flying a Hellcat on a pioneering night interception mission in November 1943.

Another 'ace in a day' was Scott McCuskey, also of VF-3, who at Midway on 4 June 1942 claimed three Aichi D3A dive-bombers and two Zeros in the course of two sorties. He survived the war with a score of 14 victories.

Of course, not all aces against the Japanese were Americans. RAF Hurricane pilot Frank Carey scored eight over Burma, while Sandy Allen, also flying a Hurricane, claimed seven in a month over Singapore, Java and Sumatra. Geoffrey Fisken, an RAF Buffalo pilot from New Zealand, managed six in three weeks over Singapore. After being wounded, he returned to the fray in June 1943 flying Kittyhawks, and increased his score to 11.

DAVID LEE 'TEX' HILL Recruited from the US Navy by the 'Flying Tigers', 'Tex' Hill commanded the 75th Squadron of the AVG, based at Henyang. He recalled of AVG Commander Claire Chennault:

> He trained us. He had these tactical lectures when we first arrived there, and he told us how to use this airplane, and not to engage in a dogfight with them. When they got on your tail, we'd push it over and roll straight down, because there was no [Japanese] airplane in the world that could stay up with a P-40.

His first combat was a genuine learning experience.

> We went over at about 10,000 feet. We hadn't expected to find any people alerted over there, so we were busy lookin' at the airfield. And the first thing I noticed, when we started down to strafe, was that there were more than three of us in the pattern. This guy was on Jim Howard's tail, just really eatin' him up. And so I pulled right in behind him. I didn't even look... We had this ring and bead gunsight on the airplane, but I didn't even look through that. I was just looking through the windscreen there at the tracers and just kinda hosing him down, just kept pullin' the nose right around on him till he just blew up. And in the meantime, this other guy came in. He made an overhead pass—

157

and he came right on down and shot 33 holes in my plane... I got smart after that one and paid a little more attention to what was around me.

Hill's AVG total was 12¼. On the dissolution of the 'Flying Tigers' he joined the 23rd Fighter Group, but as his commission was delayed he scored at least one victory as a civilian. His war total was 18¼.

JOHN S. THACH Jimmy Thach started the war in command of VF-3, 'Butch' O'Hare's squadron. VF-3 flew the F4F-4 Wildcat, which differed from its predecessor in having six .50 Brownings instead of four. Thach was not amused. He said: 'A pilot who cannot hit with four guns will miss with eight!' Against unarmoured Japanese aircraft, this was a valid point. Aware that his mount was outperformed by the Zero, he attempted to redress the balance by tactics. In this he succeeded.

His greatest claim to fame was the introduction of the Beam Defence Manoeuvre. A division of four aircraft flew in two pairs abreast, spaced at about 900–1,200ft. Each pair covered the tails of the other, looking inwards. The first pair to see an attack coming did not wait to transmit a radio call, but broke inwards. On seeing this, the second pair broke towards them, the attacked pair going high, the defending pair beneath them. Zeros that tried to follow one pair round were thus faced with a head-on pass from slightly below by the other pair. And in a head-on pass, the greater armament and survivability of the American fighter gave it the advantage. In the USN, the Beam Defence Manoeuvre became universally known as the 'Thach Weave'.

The 'Thach Weave' was first put to the test during the Battle of Midway in June 1942. Escorting a strike against the Japanese fleet, Thach flew with Brainerd Macomber and two young Ensigns, Bassett and Dibb, all three of whom were newcomers to the squadron; only Dibb had ever heard of the 'Thach Weave'.

Attacked by Zeros, Bassett was shot down and Macomber's radio smashed. Every time Jimmy Thach tried to take up the correct spacing for the Weave, Macomber, unable to communicate, scrambled back into position on his wing. Thach then ordered Dibb out to the flank, and this produced immediate results. In the next 20 minutes, the

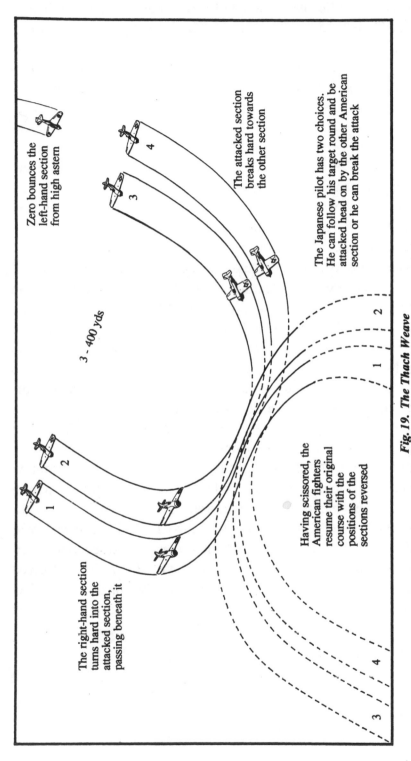

Zero bounces the left-hand section from high astern

The attacked section breaks hard towards the other section

3 - 400 yds

The Japanese pilot has two choices. He can follow his target round and be attacked head on by the other American section or he can break the attack

The right-hand section turns hard into the attacked section, passing beneath it

Having scissored, the American fighters resume their original course with the positions of the sections reversed

Fig. 19. The Thach Weave

To execute the Thach Weave, pairs of Wildcats took station between 900 and 1,200 feet apart. If one pair was bounced from astern, it immediately turned inwards and scissored with the other pair, passing just above them. If the Japanese fighter followed, it became vulnerable to a head-on attack from slightly lower, and could not nose down to meet it without risking a collision.

three remaining Wildcats accounted for four Zeros and tied up a portion of the Japanese defenders, thus keeping them away from the dive-bombers.

The 'Thach Weave' conclusively proved that team-work could off-set the advantages of a superior fighter. Thach became an ace at Midway, and his war total was seven. He retired post-war as an Admiral.

JOSEPH JACOB FOSS The US Marine Corps produced many aces, partly due to their fighting tradition, and partly due to the fact that, as they were mainly land-based, they flew more missions, and had more opportunities, than their ship-based compatriots.

Like many other air aces, Joe Foss grew up with a gun in his hand. This marksmanship cost the Japanese dear. Having joined the US Marine Corps pre-war and learned to fly the Wildcat, he arrived on Guadalcanal on 9 October 1942 with VMF-121. On his first sortie he accounted for a Zero, but was badly damaged by three others and force-landed. From this moment he vowed that he would be known as 'Swivel-Neck Joe'.

Like many other Marines, and in the best tradition of other pilots such as the *Luftwaffe Experte* Walter Krupinski, he became a 'bar-room brawler' type of fighter, often damaged but with at least one victory to show for it. He scored the five victories which made him an ace in just nine days of combat. He later complained that he lost four certain victories because he failed to get close enough before firing. Although hampered by recurrent bouts of malaria, on 15 January 1943 he equalled Eddie Rickenbacker's First World War record of 26 air victories, for which he was awarded America's highest decoration, the Congressional Medal of Honor. Foss survived the war to become a Brigadier in the Air National Guard, and Governor of South Dakota.

8. SEVEN-LEAGUE BOOTS, 1943-45

When in 1942 the USAAF entered the war in Europe, it was committed to a policy of strategic bombing in daylight, even though previous RAF experience had shown that unescorted bomber formations were all too vulnerable to fighter attack. On early raids by the USAAF bomber losses were light, but as the *Jagdflieger* took the measure of their new opponents they rose alarmingly. In a raid on Bremen on 17 April 1943, 16 bombers were lost, 14% of the total force, and a further 48 damaged. This was unsustainable. The only possible answer was escort fighters.

The problem was that those available lacked sufficient range. Spitfires could only reach a portion of Northern France and the Low Countries. In April 1943 longer-legged American P-47 Thunderbolts became operational, but these were still inadequate, even when in the middle of the year a large ventral drop tank allowed them to penetrate (just) the German border. The decision was then taken to escort the bombers as far as possible on the outbound and homeward legs, beyond which they had to fly unprotected. Inevitably the German defenders waited until the escorts were forced to turn back before launching their attacks.

This happened on the notorious Schweinfurt/Regensburg raid of 17 August. Of 377 bombers, 60 were shot down and 55 were stranded in North Africa, too badly damaged to return to England. On 14 October, 294 bombers returned to Schweinfurt, only to lose another 60 of their number, with 138 more moderately or severely damaged. Such loss rates could not be sustained, and unescorted deep penetrations were halted.

Gradually the reach of the P-47 was improved, and the P-38 Lightning became available from October 1943. The Lightning had made its combat debut in North Africa, where it had had mixed fortunes against German fighters. Regardless of its shortcomings, however, it could reach deeper into Germany than the Thunderbolt. But the greatest escort fighter of all was the P-51 Mustang, which became operational from February 1944. A happy marriage of an American airframe and a British engine, the P-51 could not only reach the furthest extremities of the Third Reich, but could meet the Bf 109 and FW 190 on equal terms.

Escort Tactics

For the first year, the USAAF attempted to protect its bombers by packing fighters around them. They soon found, as had others before them, that this restricted their freedom of action, and reduced their effectiveness. In any case, proximity to the bombers was not a good idea when battle was joined, as the aircraft recognition talents of the bomber gunners left something to be desired. The answer was to keep station well out from their charges, and keep their speed relatively high in order to be able to react quickly to a threat.

A large raid typically consisted of several hundred bombers strung out over many miles. There was no way in which even the Mustang could stay with them over the entire trip, and so the escort was carried out in relays. The P-47s could reach central Germany; the P-38s a bit further; and the P-51s handled the rest. This called for fine timing at the changeover points if part of the force was not to be left exposed.

The basic USAAF fighter unit was the Group, composed of three squadrons of 16 aircraft each. Typical escort cover was provided by two flights of eight fighters wide on each side of the bomber formation, and two more about 3,000ft (900m) above. These weaved continually in order to maintain a high cruising speed without outrunning the bombers. In addition there would be an entire squadron lurking up-sun, rather higher, and up to 10 miles (16km) ahead.

Unlike the Battle of Britain, where early warning was short, the *Jagdflieger* were given ample warning by radar. This allowed them time to form up en masse. The initial attack took the form of a head-on charge, which hopefully damaged a few bombers, which would then become detached from their formations. After this they broke up

Table 15. Aircraft of the US 8th Air Force Fighter Groups

	P-38 Lightning	P-47 Thunderbolt	P-51B Mustang	P-51D Mustang
4th FG		Mar 43–Feb 44	Feb 44–Jun 44	Jun 44–May 45
20th FG	Dec 43–Jul 44			Jul 44–May 45
55th FG	Oct 43–Jul 44			Jul 44–May 45
56th FG		Apr 43–May 45		
78th FG		Apr 43–Jan 45		Dec 44–May 45
339th FG			Apr 44–May 45	
352nd FG		Sep 43–Apr 44	Apr 44–May 45	
353rd FG		Aug 43–Nov 44		Oct 44–May 45
355th FG		Sep 43–Mar 44	Mar 44–May 45	
356th FG		Oct 43–Nov 44		Nov 44–May 45
357th FG			Feb 44–May 45	Jul 44–May 45
359th FG		Dec 43–May 44	May 44–May 45	
361st FG		Jan 44–May 44	May 44–May 45	Sep 44–May 45
364th FG	Mar 44–Jul 44			Jul 44–May 45
479th FG	May 44–Sep 44			Sep 44–May 45

into sections which attacked individually, concentrating on the stragglers.

Hopefully the initial attack would be spotted in good time by the leading escort fighter squadron which, from its high perch up-sun, would be well placed to intervene and break them up before they made contact. But often this failed to work as advertised, and the interception turned into a race, with German fighters streaking towards the bombers hotly pursued by the Americans, then both racing past the bombers, whose gunners shot at everything with less than four engines. Once battle was joined, formations were split, with little chance of reforming. While pilots tried to stay in pairs this was not always possible. For a solo pilot, Germany was an unhealthy place to be, and anyone separated from his unit automatically tried to join up with the nearest friendlies.

A feature of the deep escort mission was the protection of stragglers. Only infrequently did a bomber go down as the result of a single attack. Those lost were usually damaged early on; unable to stay in formation for mutual protection, they were easy prey for the scavenging German fighters. Provided that they had sufficient fuel, pairs of American fighters were often detached to provide limited protection to these unfortunates. The more usual alternative was to come home 'on the deck', shooting up targets of opportunity as they did so.

Fig. 20. The Split-S

*A widely used evasion manoeuvre, a roll inverted was followed by a hard
pull into a fast vertical dive, aileron-turning on the way down ready to
pull out into any desired direction.*

Late in the war, German jets posed an almost insoluble problem for the escorts. Too fast to catch, it was almost impossible to head them off. One American leader calculated that it took eight Mustangs to neutralise a single Me 262, by continually cutting across the circle inside it. Against multiple jet attacks effective defence was simply impossible. The best results were obtained by fighters patrolling known Me 262 bases.

The Fighters

The main German fighters were the Bf 109G and the FW 190A, as previously described. While in their standard form they were at least the equal of the American fighters, against heavy bombers their armament was inadequate. Consequently they were upgunned, and in some cases given 21cm rocket-tubes beneath the wings, while a heavily armed and armoured FW 190A was developed to allow the traditional attack from astern to be made. Against unescorted bombers, these measures were adequate. Against agile escort fighters they were disastrous, the extra weight and drag robbing the Germans of much of their performance and manoeuvrability.

The most formidable German fighter of the war was the Me 262 jet. Over 100mph (160km/h) faster than the Mustang, and armed with a formidable battery of four 30mm cannon in the nose, its speed and zoom climb set it in a class apart. It had its weaknesses. It turned poorly, bleeding off speed rapidly as it did so; its endurance was short, forcing it to disengage early; and its engines were unreliable. This apart, it was a worthy opponent, and only the numerical superiority of the USAAF prevented it from cutting a deadly swathe through the bombers.

In the early stages the most widely used American escort fighter was the Republic P-47 Thunderbolt, commonly called the Jug (short for Juggernaut). This was huge, the largest single-engined fighter of the war, the standing joke being that the best way to take evasive action in a Thunderbolt was to undo the straps and run around the cockpit.

Designed around a turbo-supercharged Pratt & Whitney Double Wasp radial engine, rated (in later variants) at 2,300hp at altitude, it was heavily armed with eight .50 Brownings. Rate of climb was poor in early variants, but later improved by using water injection and a paddle-bladed propeller. High wing loading meant that turn capability was poor, but the Jug had three tremendous advantages in combat. Firstly, it was arguably the most survivable fighter of the war; secondly, it could out-dive any German fighter; and thirdly, and rather surprisingly, it had a very fast rate of roll, which could be turned to advantage.

Next into action was the Lockheed P-38 Lightning. A single-seat high-altitude interceptor, it was powered by two Allison turbo-super-charged liquid-cooled engines each capable of delivering 1,425hp. The tail was mounted on twin booms behind the engines, while the cockpit and armament of one 20mm cannon and four .50 Browning machine-guns was located in a central nacelle. Its high wing loading and large span made it no match for German fighters at high altitudes, although at low altitudes and low speeds it could turn with them. Matters were not helped by the fact that it had a yoke control column rather than the more usual stick, and it was rather a 'busy' aircraft to fly, with lots of things to watch and adjust. Its early days were beset with mechanical problems, many brought on by the harsh European climate, and these took some considerable time to sort out. By September 1944, all Lightnings had been withdrawn from the escort groups, but they remained in service with 9th and 15th Air Forces.

The North American P-51 Mustang started life powered by an Allison engine, with which it was deemed unsuitable for high altitude combat. This was rectified by substituting the Rolls-Royce Merlin, which turned it from a 'so-so' fighter into one of the all-time greats. Its aerodynamically clean design, greatly aided by its laminar-flow wing, promised outstanding range performance; this was supplemented by the addition of a large fuel tank in the fuselage. There was, of course, a penalty to be paid, the full tank adversely affecting longitudinal stability: when it was partially emptied the remaining fuel sloshed around, giving rise to a certain amount of twitchiness in handling before it was all finally used.

The P-51B was armed with four wing-mounted .50 Brownings, a bit on the light side for the period. These were prone to stoppages,

Table 16. USAAF Escort Fighters, 1943–45

	Republic P-47D Thunderbolt	Lockheed P-38J Lightning	North American P-51D Mustang
Wingspan	40ft 9in	52ft 0in	37ft 0in
Length	36ft 1in	37ft 10in	32ft 3in
Height	14ft 2in	12ft 10in	13ft 8in
Wing area	300 sq ft	328 sq ft	233 sq ft
Engine(s)	P & W R-2800 Double Wasp radial rated at 2,300hp	2 x Allison V-1710 V-12s rated at 1,425hp	RR/Packard Merlin V-1650 V-12 rated at 1,695hp
Loaded weight	14,600lb	17,500lb	10,100lb
Wing loading	49lb/sq ft	53lb/sq ft	43lb/sq ft
Maximum speed	429mph	420mph	437mph
Service ceiling	40,000ft	40,000ft	40,000ft
Rate of climb	2,780ft/min	2,850ft/min	3,475ft/min
Range	950 miles	1,240 miles	1,650 miles

especially when fired during hard manoeuvres. Many were the times in combat that a pilot would find his guns gradually packing up on him, one by one. This was corrected in the later P-51D, which carried six guns, by redesigning the feed. The P-51D was also fitted with a teardrop canopy, giving a greatly enhanced rearward view from the cockpit.

The Aces

Jug pilots emerged as the top aces of the 8th Air Force, notwithstanding the basic superiority of the Mustang. The fact was that by the time that the Mustang was in widespread service, the German fighter arm was short of experienced pilots and beset by fuel shortages. This meant that Jug pilots generally had more opportunities, while in the later stages of the war some Mustang pilots never even saw an enemy aircraft in the air.

Statistics tell part of the story. In all, some 5,000 fighter pilots flew with 8th Air Force during the war. Of these, nearly 2,900 claimed nothing. Only 261 (5.2%) scored five victories or more, while 57 (2.6%) scored more than ten.

From the middle of the war, American fighter pilots were better trained, and had had more hours on type before entering combat, than those of any other nation. They were tremendously professional. Bud Mahurin of the 56th FG recalled 'sitting in the sack' for hours on end, thinking over what he would do in certain hypothetical situations. His dedication certainly paid off; in 85 sorties he shot down 21 German aircraft before himself being shot down over France by a Dornier gunner. In the Pacific he added one Japanese bomber, and in Korea three and a half MiG-15s. By contrast, the German training programme was bedevilled by fuel shortages, and the newly fledged pilots reaching the *Jagdgeschwader* were of increasingly indifferent quality.

The top-scoring Lightning pilots in the 8th Air Force, with nine apiece, were Robin Olds, who scored a further five while flying Mustangs, and William Morris. Over 20 years later, Olds knocked down four MiGs over Vietnam, where he gained a legendary reputation for his ability to keep track of a fast-moving combat.

The basic USAAF fighter element was the pair, consisting of the leader (shooter) and the wingman (defender). This held good throughout the war, with one notable exception. The 4th FG team of Don Gentile (22 victories) and John Godfrey (18 victories) became legendary for their use of what later became Fluid Two tactics, in which leadership passed from one to the other as required. It should be noted, however, that in multi-bogey fights they stayed with the orthodox welded wing doctrine. Fluid Two could only occur after the squadron formation had broken up, allowing small scale engagements of two-versus-two or two-versus-one to take place. While often compared to teams from legend such as Jonathan and David, or Damon and Pythias, the fact is that Gentile and Godfrey flew together as a pair only about five times.

No fighter pilot is fearless, but few have described the feelings encountered in combat as graphically as Gentile:

> And once the enemy has got you and is clobbering you, that's slow too. It's like lighted matches being slowly dragged across the bunched-up flesh of your brain pan. It feels like your brain is slowly dissolving under the pain on top of it. It's a fight to keep your brain together, and while you're fighting this fight, putting, it seems, your two hands on your mind and holding it with all the strength in your fingers, how long it seems to last and how far away the end you want seems to be.
>
> I've had help in fighting this kind of fight from two Huns with whom I struck up a brief acquaintance on separate occasions. Each fought very well. They were crafty and had courage. One of them I thought was going to be real

serious trouble for me. The other I thought was going to be able to get away to fight another day.

But suddenly, I don't know, something happened in their minds. You could see it plainly. Their brains dissolved under the pressure of fear and had become just dishwater in their heads. They froze to their sticks and straightened out and ran right into their graves like men stricken blind who run, screaming, off a cliff.

It is hard to avoid the conclusion that these two opponents of Gentile actually gave up before they were fatally hit. Their aggression failed; their determination melted away, and even their basic survival instinct deserted them. As Gentile clearly indicates, self-control under pressure is the primary requisite of a fighter pilot.

FRANCIS S. 'GABBY' GABRESKI Of Polish ancestry, 'Gabby' was at Pearl Harbor during the Japanese attack in December 1941, but was unable to take off and intercept in time. Assigned to 56th FG in January 1943, he was detached to No 315 (Polish) Squadron RAF, with whom he flew 13 sorties in Spitfire Vs before returning to 56th FG with P-47 Thunderbolts. On 26 November 1943, after shooting down two Bf 110s, he became separated from his squadron when, short on fuel, he was attacked by a Bf 109G:

As he came down I was going to run him out of ammunition. That was my decision, and I felt that I was good enough to do that. So he came down, and I broke into him. And as he went on by me, firing, I pulled up in a sort of chandelle. As my airspeed was dropping, he came back up again, turned around, and started coming into me. As he was coming up, I gave him a 90° deflection shot. Well, the first deflection shot was great. In other words he fired and I could see the 20mm gun spittin' fire. I broke and he lost his airspeed, and I went down into him and he came down after me and went... I did that twice, and on the third one I had all the confidence now that I was gonna run him out of ammunition.

So the third time I went ahead and did this same thing and he came up with about a 90° deflection shot again, the same shot I'd been giving him. I was very fortunate the first two times, but that last time he rang the bell. I mean, he really hit me! I heard an explosion in the cockpit and I felt my foot grow numb. I lost power in my engine. I says 'Oh Boy!'... So I rolled over in a kinda steep dive, pointed the nose down and I was afraid to look at my foot because with the sight of blood, or something like that, I mighta gone into shock and passed out. So I didn't look.

'Gabby' dived into the undercast, evaded, and managed to creep

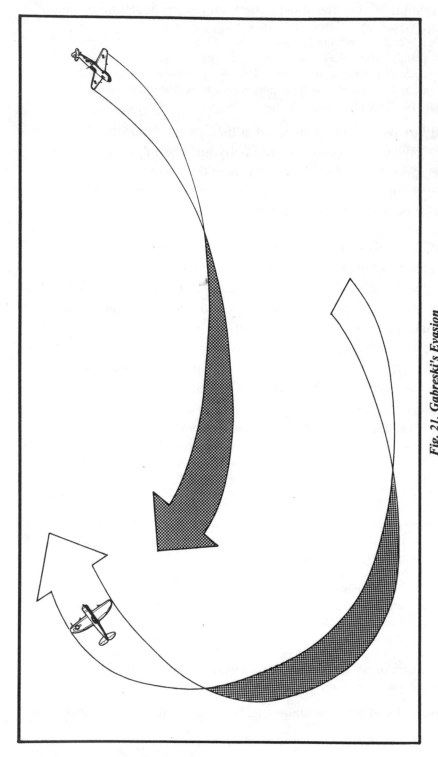

Fig. 21. Gabreski's Evasion

In this particular combat, Thunderbolt ace Francis Gabreski tried to run his opponent out of ammunition. At each attack he pulled into a climbing chandelle towards his opponent, allowing only a fleeting shot at 90° deflection.

home, running out of fuel shortly after landing. He went on to record 28 air victories, 21 of them single-engined fighters, before being downed by flak on 20 July 1944. In Korea he accounted for $6^1/_2$ MiG-15s.

ROBERT S. (BOB) JOHNSON It is not widely realised that a three-dimensional manoeuvre such as the barrel roll could be used to defeat a better-turning aircraft. Thunderbolt ace Bob Johnson (28 victories) used the superb roll capability of his huge mount to advantage on several occasions. The German pilots knew that they could not out-dive the Jug, but thought they could out-turn it. On one occasion Johnson latched onto the tail of a Bf 109 as it disengaged from the bombers in a dive; the German pilot spotted him and prepared to evade by means of a hard turn:

> Almost at once the stream of exhaust smoke stopped: he had cut his throttle and at the same time pulled his fighter into a tight left turn. The same old mistake! The moment the smoke cut out I chopped power, skidded to my right, back on the stick, and rolled inside his turn, firing steadily in short bursts. The Kraut glanced back to see a skyful of Thunderbolt wing spitting fire directly at him. I know he thought I had cut inside of his own turn...

Bob Johnson was an unlikely fighter pilot. He failed the gunnery course during flying training, and was scheduled for bombers. But in the frantic expansion of the USAAF in 1942 he was assigned to the 56th Fighter Group, and arrived in England early in 1943. His first victory came on 13 June, when he broke formation to attack an FW 190A, for which he was sharply criticised for lack of discipline. On 22 June he was attacked and badly shot about by *Luftwaffe Experte* Egon Mayer, barely regaining the airfield at Manston. From October he started to score regularly, his former gunnery failure long forgotten, and by 8 May his total had reached 28 victories, amassed in 91 sorties. When his tour expired he returned to the USA and saw no further action. Post-war he joined Republic Aviation.

JOHN C. MEYER Meyer arrived in England in the summer of 1943 at the head of the 487th Fighter Squadron, part of the 352nd FG. His first three victories came flying P-47Ds, but when, in April 1944, his

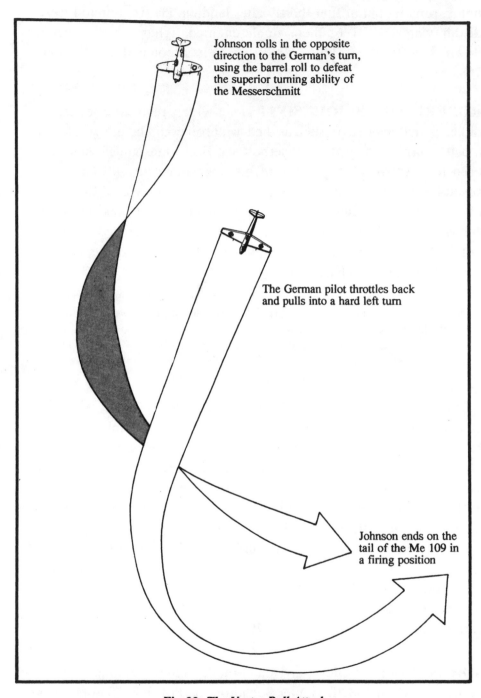

Johnson rolls in the opposite direction to the German's turn, using the barrel roll to defeat the superior turning ability of the Messerschmitt

The German pilot throttles back and pulls into a hard left turn

Johnson ends on the tail of the Me 109 in a firing position

Fig. 22. The Vector Roll Attack
Used to defeat a better-turning adversary, the attacker, in this instance Thunderbolt ace Bob Johnson, barrel-rolled away from his opponent's turn, allowing him to cut inside and achieve a firing position.

unit re-equipped with P-51Bs his score rose rapidly. His outlook was keep it simple:

> I didn't turn with enemy pilots as a rule. I might make one turn—to see what the situation was—but not often. It was too risky... My approach was to attack from above if possible in a fast pass, and to pull back up after firing. I could quickly move out of the other fellow's gun range and wait until he stopped doing whatever he was doing. If he had gone into a turn he would have lost speed and I was in a good position to come back down on him with speed. I should mention that in those days most German pilots I met were not up to stuff. Only seldom at this stage of the war [late 1944] did I meet a really proficient enemy pilot...

Meyer's most memorable encounter took place on 1 January 1945. On that day, the *Luftwaffe* mounted a massive dawn attack on Allied airfields. At Asch in Belgium, surprise was complete. Even as his wheels left the ground, Meyer spotted a FW 190 crossing in front, almost head-on. He pulled his wheels up, aimed and fired almost in the same moment. His bullets struck home, and the German fighter hit the ground. Merlin screaming at full throttle, Meyer desperately sought speed to manoeuvre. At last he latched onto another FW 190, and after a lengthy chase, during which he was hit by 'friendly' ground fire, he brought it down. It was his 23rd victory, plus two shared. A few days later he was injured in a road accident and returned to the USA.

John Meyer remained in the Air Force after the war, flew in Korea, where he destroyed two MiG-15s, and finally rose to the rank of Lieutenant General.

9. VICTORY IN THE PACIFIC, 1943–45

The Japanese defeat at Guadalcanal was the turning point of the Pacific war. Only in Burma did they continue on the offensive for a while longer.

In the spring of 1943, the task faced by the Allies was daunting. The area controlled by the Japanese extended to between 3,000 and 4,000 miles out from the home islands, with interior lines of communication aiding defence in depth. While limited resources did not allow them to be strong everywhere, strongpoints could be swiftly reinforced by air and sea power.

On the mainland of Asia, Allied forces faced the Japanese on the ground, but these offered no viable alternatives. In Burma the British were still on the defensive, and would be for some time to come. To the north of Burma, the Chinese army, although supported by the USAAF 14th Air Force, was ill-equipped and unreliable.

This left the Pacific as the decisive theatre of action. There were two possible courses. The US Army preferred a land campaign, through New Guinea to the Philippines, and then on to Japan. The US Navy wanted an island-hopping campaign through the central Pacific, also heading initially for the Philippines. In the event, both courses were adopted. While the resultant two-pronged attack had the effect of keeping the Japanese in a state of uncertainty and preventing them from concentrating their forces, there was a price to be paid. Greater Allied resources were needed, while preparations took longer. In general the USAAF supported the thrust up past New Guinea to the Philippines, while naval air power, including US Marine aviation, spearheaded island-hopping operations. The two services worked together remarkably well. Inevitably there was some operational overlap, but this caused few problems.

New Guinea is a huge island, over 1,000 miles long and 400 miles across at its widest point, divided by the Owen Stanley mountain range with jungle on both sides. The Japanese held more or less the northern half. A series of amphibious landings up the coastline by the Allies gradually isolated pockets of defenders, which were then cut off from supplies. Thus neutralised, they were simply contained until the end of the war.

Meanwhile the USN was busy taking islands in the Solomons, 400 miles eastwards, in a pincer movement aimed at the Japanese strong-hold of Rabaul. This also was eventually isolated, and in the terminology of the time, left to wither on the vine. The island-hopping thrust then switched 2,000 miles to the north-east. Islands in the Gilberts were the next objective, after which the Marshalls were bypassed with a leap to Eniwetok, to threaten the major Japanese base at Truk. In February 1944 Truk was hit by massive air strikes from nine American carriers. Further devastating raids followed, but Truk was not invaded. Instead it was bypassed while the American fleet went elsewhere.

The spearhead of the US 5th Fleet was Task Force 58. In June 1944 it was tasked with securing bases in the Marianas. For this it could muster seven fleet carriers and eight light carriers, with a total of 894 aircraft of which 473 were fighters. The invasion of the Marianas was a prime strategic move. They lay halfway between Japan and New Guinea; opened the door to the Philippines; and best of all, provided bases from which B-29 heavy bombers could raid the Japanese home-land. An attack here could also be guaranteed to provoke a strong reaction from the Japanese carrier force, which had largely avoided combat for over a year.

It so happened that the Japanese carrier force at this time actively sought a confrontation with TF 58. It mustered its nine remaining car-riers in the area and awaited an opportunity to catch the Task Force within reach of land-based air power. The combination of land and carrier based aircraft would then crush it. The invasion of the Marianas gave them their opportunity. The land-based 1st Air Fleet deployed about 850 aircraft of all types, spread between the Marianas, the Caroline Islands and Truk to the south, and Iwo Jima and Chichi

Jima to the north, while the Japanese carriers deployed a total of 451 aircraft, of which 160 were A6M5 Zero fighters.

The Americans opened the ball on the afternoon of 11 June with large fighter sweeps against airfields on Guam, Saipan and Tinian. The Japanese early warning system was not up to par, and the defending fighters were caught struggling for altitude. American claims were for 81 shot down and 29 destroyed on the ground. It was a promising start.

Little air opposition was encountered over the next few days, and Saipan was invaded on 14 June. The Japanese fleet had sailed the day before, and had been reported. Knowing there was time to spare, two Task Groups dashed far to the north to raid airfields on Iwo Jima and Chichi Jima. Already the Japanese plan was going pear-shaped; most of the land-based air assets were out of the battle even before it began. Reinforcements were rushed to the area, only to meet the same fate.

The Japanese fleet arrived on 19 June, by which time TF 58 had regrouped to the west of the Marianas. The first attack wave was detected by radar at the incredible range of 130 miles, was met by nearly 200 Hellcats, and was cut to pieces. The few attackers that reached the Task Force achieved little. Three more waves met the same fate; in all Admiral Ozawa threw 328 aircraft at TF 58 and lost 220 of them, as well as 23 reconnaissance aircraft. American losses for the day, including operations over Guam and non-combat losses, amounted to just 28 aircraft of all types. This day of what was the fifth and last great carrier action of the war has become known as the Great Marianas Turkey Shoot. Why the enormous discrepancy between the two combatants?

There were four reasons. Firstly, the US Navy had adopted the radar-aided fighter control system perfected in the Battle of Britain, which allowed them to intercept well out from TF 58. Secondly, the land-based threat which would have allowed the Japanese to attack from all points of the compass, had been smashed beforehand. Thirdly, the latest Navy fighter was the F6F Hellcat, which was vastly superior to the most modern Zeros. And finally, Japanese pilot quality had declined. Incredibly, the first attack wave had circled en route while the leader briefed his men.

Leyte in the Philippines was invaded in October 1944, and by mid-November USAAF P-38s were based there. Mindoro and Luzon followed, then Iwo Jima, and finally, in the last great amphibious assault of the war, Okinawa, in April 1945.

Iwo Jima was vital as a base for fighter escorts for B-29 bombers operating from the Marianas. Two Groups of long-range P-51D Mustangs arrived in March 1945, and commenced escort work in April, flying the longest single-seat fighter sorties of all, eight hours or more. Mustangs over Tokyo signalled the beginning of the end for Japan.

The Fighters

The Pacific theatre was unique for the vast distances involved, mainly over water. For this reason the Lockheed P-38 Lightning, with long range and twin-engined safety, largely supplanted the inadequate P-40 Warhawk from 1943. Although found wanting in Europe, it proved very successful against Japan. Until the advent of new and faster Japanese fighters late in the war, its considerable speed advantage allied to dive and zoom tactics and team-work helped keep it out of trouble, while its firepower was more than adequate against the rather fragile 'this side up' Japanese aircraft. The two highest scoring American aces of the war were both Lightning pilots. A few Thunderbolts were used in the Pacific, but the other major USAAF fighter to see service was the very long-ranged North American P-51D Mustang.

The main USN carrier fighter was the Grumman F6F Hellcat, which entered service in the late summer of 1943. Designed around the Pratt & Whitney Double Wasp radial engine, it had a similar configuration to the earlier Wildcat, although it was much larger and heavier. Only moderately wing-loaded, it could still not match the Zero turn for turn, but its better performance and superior roll rate more than compensated for this, while its six .50 Brownings could

> *The P-38 pilots, flying at great heights, chose when and where they wanted to fight ... with disastrous results for our men.*
>
> Saburo Sakai, Zero pilot

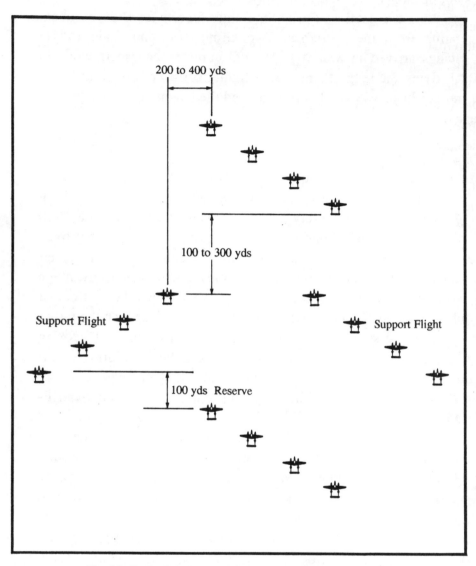

200 to 400 yds

100 to 300 yds

Support Flight

Support Flight

100 yds Reserve

Fig. 23. Typical Lightning Sweep Formation in the Far East
*This varied considerably from formations used over Europe. In the
14th Air Force, the squadron commander led the reserve flight, from
where he could most easily control the opening stages of combat.*

> *These Grummans are beautiful planes. If they could cook, I'd marry one!*
> Gene Valencia (23 victories)

tear up the Japanese fighter in short order. It was credited with the destruction of 5,156 enemy aircraft during the war, with a victory ratio of 19:1. Rugged, viceless, and easy to land on a carrier deck, the Hellcat was popular with its pilots.

The same could not always be said for the Vought F4U Corsair. Designed around the same Double Wasp engine as the Hellcat, its appearance was formidable and its configuration unorthodox. To gain clearance for the massive propeller, yet keep the main gear legs reasonably short, an inverted gull-wing was adopted. Unlike the Hellcat, in which the pilot sat up high, giving him a good view over the nose, the cockpit of the Corsair was set so far back that forward view was minimal. For deck-landing, this was not good. At first it had a deadly reputation. A tendency to bounce made carrier landings hazardous, and its first years were spent ashore with the US Marines. But it was much faster than the Hellcat; it climbed better, and when the bounce was cured and the cockpit view improved, it became arguably the best carrier fighter of the war.

On the Japanese side, both the Zero and Hayabusa were re-engined to improve performance and upgunned to improve hitting power during the conflict, but these improvements did little to offset the basic weaknesses of these types. However, three new fighters entered service in large numbers which in many ways were the equals of Western aircraft.

The Kawasaki Ki.61 Hien was, unusually for a Japanese fighter, powered by a liquid-cooled V-12 engine derived from the Daimler-Benz DB 601A. Similar in appearance to the Macchi C.202, the Allies first encountered it over New Guinea in April 1943. Not only was it fast, but it was armoured, with self-sealing fuel tanks, and carried two 20mm cannon and two 7.7mm machine-guns. In action it could out-dive the Wildcat, which posed problems for that fighter, while high altitude controllability was excellent.

The specification for the Nakajima Ki.84 Hayate stated that it had to be as agile as the Hayabusa, with the speed and climb rate of the

179

> *Unfortunately the Shiden's flight characteristics were treacherous and demanded an experienced pilot.*
>
> Saburo Sakai, Zero pilot

Ki.44 Shoki, a dedicated interceptor. Powered by a Homare 18-cylinder radial engine, it was sturdily built, well protected, and armed with two 20mm cannon and two 12.7mm machine-guns. Its only fault was the unreliable engine, which held back development. It made its operational debut over China in August 1944, followed by the Leyte battles, where, despite less than crisp handling, it proved a formidable opponent. It was certainly able to outclimb and outmanoeuvre the Mustang.

Remarkably, the ancestor of the Kawanishi N1K1 Shiden was a floatplane, the Kyofu. With new Allied types appearing over the Pacific, the Japanese Navy desperately needed a high altitude interceptor. Aircraft were under development, but this was taking too long. The Kyofu, although not 100% suitable for redesign to land-plane configuration, was at least immediately available. An automatic combat flap was fitted, unique for its time, giving it exceptional manoeuvrability, while four 20mm cannon gave it an outstanding punch.

Following service entry in January 1944, experienced Shiden pilots

Table 17. Pacific Theatre Fighters 1943–45

	Grumman F6F-3 Hellcat	Vought F4U-1 Corsair	Kawasaki Ki.61 Hien	Nakajima Ki.84 Hayate	Kawanishi N1K1 Shiden
Wingspan	42ft 10in	41ft 0in	39ft 4in	36ft 10in	39ft 3in
Length	33ft 7in	33ft 4in	29ft 4in	32ft 7in	30ft 8in
Height	11ft 3in	16ft 1in	12ft 2in	11ft 1in	13ft 0in
Wing area	334 sq ft	314 sq ft	215 sq ft	226 sq ft	253 sq ft
Engine	P&W R-2800 Double Wasp radial rated at 2,000hp	P&W R-2800 Double Wasp radial rated at 2,000hp	Ha 40 V-12 rated at 1,160hp	Ha 45 radial rated at 1,900hp	Ha 45 radial rated at 1,990hp
Loaded weight	12,186lb	12,694lb	7,650lb	7,965lb	9,039lb
Wing loading	36lb/sq ft	40lb/sq ft	36lb/sq ft	35lb/sq ft	36lb/sq ft
Maximum speed	376mph	417mph	348mph	388mph	370mph
Service ceiling	37,500ft	37,900ft	32,800ft	34,450ft	39,700ft
Rate of climb	3,240ft/min	2,890ft/min	2,900ft/min	3,400ft/min	3,350ft/min
Range	1,085 miles	1,015 miles	1,118 miles	1,025 miles	1,069 miles

regarded the Hellcat as 'easy meat'. Fortunately for the Allies, they were rare. But the Shiden was difficult to fly, and like so many Japanese fighters it suffered from an unreliable engine.

The Aces

The ascendancy of the Allied fighter pilots gradually increased as the war progressed. Superior numbers, performance and tactics made survival ever more certain, allowing green pilots time to gain experience. The agility of Japanese fighters availed their pilots little when they were forced to fight on the defensive against opponents who could attack and disengage at will. Also, most experienced Japanese pilots were long dead, and their replacements were of poor quality. Of course, the Americans could not take this for granted; an occasional honcho was still encountered. Japanese ace Kinsuke Muto (28 victories), flying a Shiden over Tokyo in 1945, accounted for four Hellcats in a single sortie.

RICHARD BONG Like many high scorers, Dick Bong was a hunter in his youth, and his shooting ability later served him well in a fighter cockpit. He arrived in the Pacific in November 1942 to fly P-40s with 35th FG at Guadalcanal. Victories came quickly, and by 8 January 1943 his score had risen to five. Shortly thereafter he transferred to 49th FG, which was equipped with P-38 Lightnings. Capitalising on the speed and climb rate of his new mount, his score climbed steadily. By the spring of 1944 it stood at 28, but in spite of this he felt that he was not a good shot. A combat report of April 1944 reads:

> Made a 90° deflection shot with no result. Got a tail shot and scored a few hits but he did not go down. Finally got on his tail again and hit him some more and he turned left and down gradually, caught fire behind the engine on the bottom, crashed and exploded on the side of a hill.

It seems probable that Bong felt that had his deflection shooting been better, much of the time and manoeuvring needed to gain an astern position could have been avoided.

He returned to the USA soon afterwards, supposedly to take a course in gunnery. This seems doubtful. With 28 scalps to his credit he would hardly seem to need it.

181

He returned to the Pacific late in 1944, and in just 30 sorties brought his tally to 40. In December he returned to the USA and became a test pilot, only to die in a crash on 6 August 1945, when the engine of his P-80 Shooting Star flamed out shortly after take-off.

DAVID McCAMPBELL With 34 victories, David McCampbell was the top-scoring carrier pilot of the war. He was unusual in other respects: all his victories were scored while flying as a Carrier Air Group Commander; he was an 'old man' of 34 at the time; and he set the Allied record of nine victories in a single sortie.

McCampbell had a big day during the Marianas Turkey Shoot, but even so, things did not go entirely to plan. Leading 10 Hellcats of VF-15, he made a high side attack on a gaggle of Yokosuka D4Y dive-bombers (reporting name Judy):

> My first target was a Judy on the left flank and halfway back in the formation. It was my planned intention after completing the run on this plane to pass under it, retire across the formation and take under fire a plane on the right flank with a low side attack. These plans became upset when the first plane fired at blew up practically in my face and caused a pull-out above the entire formation. I remember being unable to get to the other side fast enough, feeling as though every rear gunner had his fire directed at me.

He recovered his composure sufficiently to down four more Judies, then later in the day he shot down two Zeros over Guam. In combat he was never once shot down. His philosophy was that 'you could never know when you might run into a real top-notch fighter pilot. So I always gave them the benefit of the doubt of being a good pilot, and I engaged him in that fashion... There's no way you can tell whether he's good or bad until you engage him.' On two occasions he disengaged when faced with a top enemy pilot.

On 23 October 1944, McCampbell led seven Hellcats to intercept 20 bombers escorted by 40 fighters over Leyte Gulf. As they met, the bombers passed below cloud, pursued by five of the Hellcats. This left McCampbell and his wingman, Roy Rushing (13 victories), to tackle the fighters.

At his first pass, the Zeros formed a defensive circle. McCampbell found this difficult to crack, so he and Rushing sat above it, waiting for the circle to break up. When it finally did, the Japanese set course

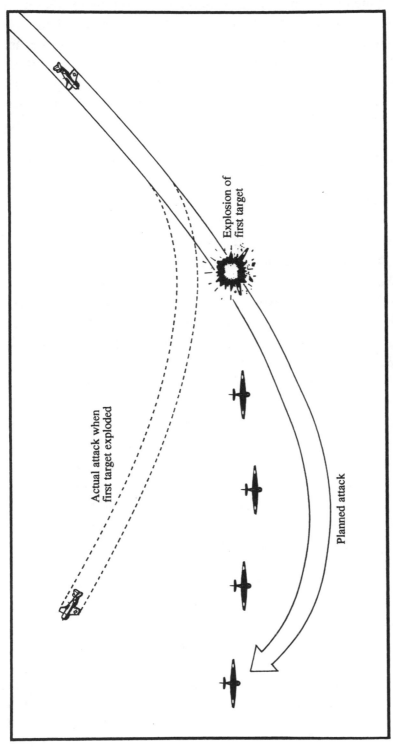

Actual attack when
first target exploded

Explosion of
first target

Planned attack

Fig. 24. The Best Laid Plans

USN ace David McCampbell made a high side run on the nearest bomber in the Japanese formation, intending to pass below it and make a climbing attack on the aircraft of the far side. He was foiled when his first target blew up in his face, forcing him to pull out above the bombers, where he became a target for their gunners. Fortunately for him he was not hit.

for home. One or two tried to climb and engage, but these were easily dealt with, leaving the two Hellcat pilots to make attacking runs on the rest with little opposition. After about five victories between them, McCampbell took out a pencil to record results. It was just as well he did; by the time they broke off, low on ammunition, McCampbell had accounted for nine and Rushing five or six. He retired from the US Navy in 1964.

GREGORY 'PAPPY' BOYINGTON By fighter pilot standards, 'Pappy' Boyington was another 'old man'. Most politely described as a colourful character, he had become a Marine aviator before the war, but by 1941 a tangled personal life had endangered his career. He solved the problem by joining the American Volunteer Group, and between December 1941 and June 1942 shot down six Japanese aircraft over Burma.

Aggressiveness is an essential quality for a fighter pilot, but Boyington was more than this; he was positively belligerent. This did not endear him to Chennault, commander of the 'Flying Tigers', and he returned to the USA to rejoin the Marine Corps. In September 1943 he led VMF-214, the 'Black Sheep', into action over the Solomon Islands.

Boyington was punctilious that the briefed mission came first; only when this had been completed could the squadron go looking for trouble. On the other hand, some of his ideas were totally unorthodox. For example, he advocated removing the camouflage paint from the squadron Corsairs, to allow the enemy to see them easily, and hopefully start a fight. In combat he advised against trying to loop or turn with a Zero, keeping speed high, and disengaging with a fast, shallow climb. But it was in other fields that his unorthodoxy paid off. He excelled in ruses. Once a Japanese came up on the radio, addressed 'Pappy' by name in English, and asked his position. 'Pappy' gave it, but was understandably coy about his altitude. When the Japanese fighters arrived, they were bounced from above.

In October, the Black Sheep flew at high altitude in bomber-style Vics rather than fighter pairs, and discussed fictitious bombing targets over the radio. When the Japanese fighters scrambled to intercept, the

Corsairs reverted to pairs and streaked down on them. The end came on 3 January 1944, when he was shot down trying to protect his stricken wingman. He survived baling out at hair-raisingly low level, but was taken prisoner. His final score was 28, making him the top-scoring USMC pilot of the war.

10. NORMANDY TO BERLIN

Air power cannot take and hold territory. The defeat of Nazi Germany demanded that the Allies invade the continent of Europe. The place selected was Normandy, the date was 6 June 1944, and the operation was called Overlord. Two essential preconditions were that army and navy invasion preparations should be concealed beforehand, and that absolute air superiority be maintained during and after the operation.

Preparations had been in hand since November of the previous year, with the formation of the 2nd Tactical Air Force RAF. This was later joined by the American 9th Air Force. As troops massed in southern England, and the invasion fleet gathered in the Channel ports, an air umbrella was thrown over the area. The Germans knew that an invasion was coming, they could guess at its timing, but with air reconnaissance made impossible, they completely failed to predict its location.

From D-Day onwards, the area of the landings and far inland was saturated with Allied fighters. For three months this intense pressure was kept up. Between 6 June and 5 September—by which time the German army was in headlong retreat—an incredible 203,357 Allied fighter sorties were flown; an average of more than 1,600 each day. After a slow start, the *Luftwaffe* put up 31,833 sorties during the same period. Outnumbered by more than six to one, 3,521 German aircraft were lost; an unsustainable 11%. Allied losses were a mere 516; one quarter of one percent.

At this stage of the war new fighter aces were very rare birds indeed. For the Allies, opportunities were lacking. In the period under discussion, it took nearly 58 Allied fighter sorties for each German fighter brought down. Under these circumstances, even experienced flyers had difficulty in adding to their scores.

186

As the tidal waves of Allied troops and armour rolled across France and up through the Low Countries, the *Luftwaffe* sought vainly to stem the advance in the face of overwhelming air superiority. Consequently they were generally to be found at medium and low altitudes, and this was where most combats took place. Many Allied fighter squadrons were also heavily committed to close air support and interdiction, to the disgust of many who now found their sleek Spitfires laden with bombs. However, this brought its own reward. 'Johnnie' Johnson's 144 Wing discovered that bomb shackles could be adapted to carry beer barrels, and a service was laid on to keep the wing supplied.

Even at high altitudes, wing formations had been difficult to lead effectively. Lower down, in the tactical flying that now took place, they were far too cumbersome, and in addition were all too easy to spot from a distance. Most wing leaders now reverted to using single squadrons, albeit often with two or more in the same general area to give mutual assistance if the going got tough. The *Luftwaffe* also reverted to smaller formations than of yore, flying in *Staffel* strength and only rarely in *Gruppen*.

The ever-lengthening lines of communication made the problems of keeping such massive armies supplied too great until such time as the port of Antwerp could be opened. This was not done until early November, and the Allied offensive ground to a halt. This, coupled with worsening weather, gave the *Luftwaffe* a breathing space, in which the fighter arm was expanded using pilots from disbanded bomber units and re-equipped with new aircraft. At this stage the *Jagdflieger* was of very mixed worth; undertrained and inexperienced pilots, leavened with old stagers who were very dangerous but too few in number, equipped with fighters that were basically good, and in some cases excellent, but were only effective in the right hands. From October 1944, they were increasingly handicapped by a shortage of fuel.

Allied fighter units advanced to bases near the German border, which enabled them to range deep into Germany. From this point on, fighter operations became inextricably linked with the American long-range escort missions, even though they were not an integral part of them.

187

What amounted to the last throw of the *Luftwaffe* came at dawn on 1 January 1945, with *Operation Bodenplatte*. This was an all-out assault on Allied airfields on the continent by 800 or more fighters. While this destroyed almost 300 Allied aircraft, *Jagdflieger* losses were horrendous; many irreplaceable fighter leaders went down during this operation. The attack caused a hiatus in Allied fighter operations, the brunt of the air fighting for the next week or so being borne by the Tempests of 122 Wing, which had escaped the onslaught. The *Jagdflieger* never recovered. From this moment on they were encountered in the air only infrequently, though the fuel shortages meant that those met with were more than likely to be *Experten*. In spite of this, a handful of Allied fighter pilots managed to build up respectable scores, even though opportunities were few.

The Fighters

During this period the US 9th Air Force operated the P-38 Lighting, the P-47D Thunderbolt, and the P-51B and D Mustang. 2nd TAF flew mainly the Spitfire IX (and the almost identical Packard-Merlin engined Spitfire XVI), the Griffon-engined Spitfire XIV, and the Hawker Tempest V. Performance details of the American fighters have already been given, as have most of those of the Spitfire IX.

At this stage of the war, the rifle calibre machine-gun had been recognised as almost useless against heavily armoured and protected aircraft. While the Spitfire IX retained its basic armament of two 20mm cannon, the four .303 Brownings were largely supplanted by two .50 calibre machine-guns, which while giving equal hitting power had a much longer effective range.

Late in 1943, the gyro gun-sight entered service. Whereas the standard reflector sight, by now used by all nations, relied on natural marksmanship to score against a manoeuvring target, the gyro gun-sight was to a degree able to compensate for angle off deflection shooting. The pilot had to track his target for a short period, during which he had to set the wing span of the enemy aircraft on the graticule. The sight computer then adjusted the amount of 'aim-off' for the range and speed to give the exact value of the deflection needed. For the average squadron pilot, this doubled his effectiveness.

Fig. 25. The Gyro Gunsight

With the sight set to match the wingspan of the target, and the diamonds adjusted to enclose it, the gyro gunsight computed the deflection needed. While a boon to poor shots, the better marksmen felt that it made little difference to their results.

> *I always felt that I spent too much time with my head in the office ...*
> 'Johnnie' Johnson (34 victories)

For the ace, able instinctively to calculate the amount of aim-off needed, and reluctant to spend a second or so tracking a target when they could have opened fire, it was less useful, and some retained the old-fashioned fixed graticule.

The Spitfire IX remained in the front line until the end; in fact, of the six RAF pilots to amass double figures in the final months of the war, five of them flew this model.

As the war progressed, performance took ever greater priority over manoeuvrability. This in turn demanded ever more powerful engines, and by now the Rolls-Royce Merlin had reached the limits of its potential. But this had long been foreseen, and the company had produced the far more potent Griffon, which powered the final Spitfire variant to see widespread service in the Second World War, the Mark XIV.

Tremendously fast, and with a sparkling rate of climb, the Spitfire XIV was not nearly so nice to handle as previous variants. In part this was due to increased weight, while diving speed was restricted by 'aileron float', which was never entirely cured. Nor did it have quite the same fine lines. Nose contours were revised to suit the lines of the new engine; fin and rudder area was increased, with a more pointed shape; the fuselage was lengthened; and the wing shape revised. However, in terms of sheer performance it outclassed both the FW 190A and the Bf 109G.

As a successor to the Hurricane, Hawkers had designed the Typhoon around the massive 24-cylinder Napier Sabre engine. The new fighter had a troubled gestation; engine and structural failures were all too frequent events. Although designed as a high-speed fighter, it lacked manoeuvrability, performance fell off with altitude, and at high speeds it became nose-heavy. In consequence, it was relegated to the close air support role.

The fighter requirement remained, and the Typhoon was extensively redesigned to fill this. The fuselage was cleaned up aerodynamically and lengthened, a much thinner wing with an elliptical plan form was adopted, giving increased area, and the fin and rudder were redesigned. Four 20mm cannon in the wings gave more than adequate hitting power. The result was the Tempest V, a superb fighter at low and medium altitudes, which entered service shortly before the invasion of Normandy.

The Allied tactical fighters of the immediate post-invasion period were opposed mainly by the Messerschmitt Bf 109G and Focke-Wulf FW 190A. The final variant of the former was the Bf 109K, but this barely began to enter service before the war ended; the latter began to be replaced by the FW 190D from the autumn of 1944. Known to the *Jagdflieger* as the Dora, and to the Allies as the 'long-nose', the FW 190D was powered by a liquid-cooled Junkers Jumo 213A, the annular radiator of which gave the appearance of a radial engine. Slightly larger overall, it was faster, and climbed and dived better, than its predecessor. Turn rate was about the same, although roll rate was slower, and it was comparatively sluggish in pitch. This aside, it was treated with great respect by Allied fighter pilots. A high-altitude variant, the Ta 152, entered service during the last few weeks of the war, but had little impact on events.

The Aces
Notwithstanding the superb performance of the Spitfire XIV and the

---

Table 18. Tactical Fighters, June 1944–May 1945

	Supermarine Spitfire XIV	Hawker Tempest V	Focke-Wulf FW 190D-9
Wingspan	36ft 10in	41ft 0in	34ft 5$\frac{1}{2}$in
Length	32ft 8in	33ft 8in	33ft 5in
Height	12ft 8in	16ft 1in	11ft 0in
Wing area	242 sq ft	302 sq ft	197 sq ft
Engine	Rolls-Royce Griffon 65 rated at 2,050hp	Napier Sabre II rated at 2,420hp	Junkers Jumo 213A rated at 2,240hp
Loaded weight	8,500lb	11,500lb	9,480lb
Wing loading	35lb/sq ft	38lb/sq ft	48lb/sq ft
Maximum speed	448mph	435mph	426mph
Service ceiling	44,500ft	36,000ft	39,372ft
Rate of climb	4,580ft/min	4,700ft/min	c.4,200ft/min
Range	460 miles	740 miles	520 miles

Tempest V, the vast majority of aces of this period flew the Spitfire IX. This reflects two major factors; opportunity, and the respective quantities of each type in service. Even then, there were not so many opportunities that high scores could be amassed. Canadian Don Laubman emerged top with 14 and one shared, all 109s and 190s, before being shot down by flak in April 1945 and taken prisoner. He was closely followed by fellow-countryman Bill Klersy with 13 and one shared. Only five others got into double figures, including American 'Foob' Fairbanks with 12, 11 of them with the Tempest, the other with a Spitfire V. 'Johnnie' Johnson notched up 10 of his total of 34 during this period, as did Canadians Dick Audet and John MacKay (the latter going on to shoot down a MiG-15 in Korea). The top-scoring Spitfire XIV pilot was Harry Walmsley with nine, eight of which came between 13 March and 25 April 1945. New Zealander Warren Schrader did even better flying a Tempest. In 22 days between 10 April and 1 May 1945, he claimed nine victories, all 109s and 190s; then, flying a Meteor jet, he destroyed three aircraft on the ground on 3 May.

JAMES EDGAR 'JOHNNIE' JOHNSON 'Johnnie' Johnson commenced flying training pre-war with the RAF Volunteer Reserve. He joined No 616 Squadron at Coltishall in September 1940, but his combat debut was delayed until the following year by surgery to correct an old rugger injury. In the spring of 1941, the squadron went south to Tangmere. Here the future ace served his apprenticeship, flying in the section led by the already legendary Douglas Bader. He recalled:

Table 19. Leading RAF Fighter Aces, June 1944–May 1945

Name	Nationality	Score in Period	War Total	Types Used
Don Laubman	Canadian	14	14 + 2sh	Spitfire IX
Bill Klersy	Canadian	13 + 1sh	14 + 1sh	Spitfire IX
'Foob' Fairbanks	American	12 + 1sh	12 + 1sh	TempestV/Spitfire IX
'Johnnie' Johnson	British	10	34 + 7sh	Spitfire IX
Dick Audet	Canadian	10 + 1sh	10 + 1sh	Spitfire IX
John MacKay	Canadian	10 + 2sh	10 + 2sh	Spitfire IX
Harry Walmsley	British	9 + 1sh	11 + 1sh	Spitfire XIV
'Smokey' Schrader	New Zealander	9 + 1sh	11 + 2sh	Tempest V
Wilfred Banks	Canadian	9	9	Spitfire IX

For me it was a period of acute frustration. My job as a wingman in Bader's finger four was to guard the remainder of the section from a flank or stern attack, whilst Smith did likewise from his position on the port side. So my head was usually turned to the left or strained right round so that I could watch our rear. We had little idea what lay ahead, but knew from the radio chatter and our own manoeuvres when Bader was working his way into a bunch of 109s. Then suddenly we were in the middle of a fight.

As experience grew, 'Johnnie' started leading a pair, and his first victory, a Bf 109E, came on 26 June. Gradually his score mounted, and by 21 September had reached six, all 109s. A spell in the Midlands followed, first with No 616 Squadron, then from July 1942 in command of No 610 Squadron. Only one victory came while he led this unit, an FW 190 over Dieppe in August of that year. The squadron returned to the south in January 1943, and much inconclusive fighting followed. Then in March he became Wing Leader at Kenley—later 127 Wing 2nd TAF—which flew the much more potent Spitfire IX.

Against the formidable FW 190A this made all the difference. Over the next five months 14 German fighters went down before the guns of the Wing Leader, plus another six shared. Johnson had become an accomplished hunter, his speciality being the careful stalk, followed by the swift surprise bounce.

Rested in September, he was appointed to lead 144 Wing in March 1944. Three more victories followed prior to Operation Overlord, then, as already recounted, he scored a further 10 by 27 September to bring his total to 34 with another seven shared, three and two shared probables, and 10 and three shared damaged. He retired from the RAF in 1966 with the rank of Air Vice Marshal.

DAVID CHARLES 'FOOB' FAIRBANKS An American who joined the RCAF in 1941, Fairbanks' early service is obscure, but by June 1944 he was a flight commander with No 501 Squadron. His first victory came over Deauville on 8 June, when, flying a Spitfire V, he shot down a Bf 109 and damaged another. August saw 'Foob' transfer to No 274 Squadron, equipped with Tempest Vs. At first defensive sorties were flown against Doodlebugs (as the V-1 flying bombs were known), and 'Foob' accounted for one of these on 29 August.

Late in September No 274 Squadron moved to the continent, but it was a while before young Fairbanks reopened his account. This was at least partly due to the number of strafing missions undertaken at this time. He had a close shave on 19 November, when the fuel tank in his port wing was set on fire by flak. Fortunately the fire went out, but not before it had badly damaged the tail on that side.

On 17 December 1944 he led eight Tempests into battle against superior numbers of Bf 109s of *III/JG 3* near Munster. In the lengthy action which followed, three 109s were shot down and one damaged. 'Foob' claimed two Bf 109s—one without firing a shot—and one damaged. An FW 190 on 4 January 1945 then two more German fighters on 14 January made him the first Tempest ace.

Fairbanks, sometimes referred to as 'The Terror of Rheine', has been depicted as a slayer of the German jets. While it is certain that whenever opportunity offered, he patrolled the vicinity of the German jet airfield at Rheine, looking for trade, all he ever claimed were an Arado Ar 234 shot down on 11 February (misidentified as an Me 262), and an Me 262 damaged three days later. In the last days of the month he added four more victories to his tally, but finally over-reached himself. On 28 February he led his flight of six Tempests against an estimated 40 FW 190s north of Osnabrück. Only four returned. Fairbanks was last heard calling that he had five on his tail. He baled out, to survive the war as a prisoner.

RICHARD (DICK) JOSEPH AUDET A Canadian from Alberta, Dick Audet was commissioned in the RCAF in October 1942. Although initially posted to No 421 Squadron in England, for reasons which are obscure he spent the next 20 months with non-operational units, flying, among other things, target tugs. Not until September 1944 did he manage to reach a fighter unit, when he transferred to No 411 'Grizzly Bear' Squadron, based on the continent, to fly Spitfire IXEs fitted with the gyro gun-sight.

In terms of flying hours he was now a very experienced pilot, which stood him in good stead. But as we have seen before, opportunities are needed, and at first these were lacking. Not until 29 December, on his 53rd sortie, did he engage the enemy in the air. Below were four Bf 109s and eight FW 190s, flying in an unusual line

> *I now went around in a defensive circle until I spotted an FW 190. I attacked from 250 yards down to 100 yards and from 30 degrees to line astern. I saw strikes over the cockpit and to the rear of the fuselage. It burst into flames.*
>
> Dick Audet, combat report

astern formation. Audet led his Yellow section down to attack the trailing aircraft, a 109, and a quick burst from a range of 600ft set it on fire.

Whether it was impetuosity, or simply frustration after his years of waiting, he tore into the enemy in a classic dogfight. When it was over, he had shot down no less than five, the only Spitfire pilot ever to do so. His claims were confirmed by film from his camera gun.

Over the next 25 days Audet accounted for another five, including a Me 262 jet, but from then on air combat eluded him. With a score of 10 victories and one shared, and another Me 262 damaged, he was shot down by flak and killed on 3 March 1945.

EPILOGUE

Nations have always needed heroes, leaders, men who can inspire others. In the 20th century, this mantle has largely fallen on the fighter pilot, whose deeds, in an element alien to man, have a glamour surpassing those of other warriors. The motives of many were mixed. Some fought for liberty, some for love of country, a few for revenge, and a minority for excitement.

Fighter pilots have generally been judged by results — the number of enemy aircraft they have shot down. But as is widely known, this measure is frequently inaccurate.

Overclaiming

The vexed issue of overclaiming has bedevilled the question of fighter pilot scores since air combat began. In theory it should be simple; to use the modern expression, the body count should give exact answers. But it doesn't. Rarely does the number of bodies match the number of claims. There are many reasons for this, most of which arise from the confusion of a fast-moving three-dimensional combat. Possibly three or four fighters attacked a stricken aircraft simultaneously, or in quick succession. The pilot of a damaged aircraft might 'play dead', leading to a mistaken claim. If the action took place over water, there might be no bodies to count. And even the most careful reconstruction often failed to reveal who did what with any degree of certainty.

If we are to avoid a nonsense on the subject of scores, we must avoid the expression 'kill', and substitute 'victory', defining a victory as an event which occurs when an enemy aircraft is defeated in combat in circumstances where the victor believes that it will be a total loss. Only then are we on surer ground.

196

Relative Scores

The question has often been raised as to how German fighter aces in the Second World War were able to out-score their Allied counterparts by margins of between 7:1 and 10:1. Several factors were involved. Firstly, the quality of the opposition. This is largely a matter of pilot quality. The best aeroplanes achieve little if flown by mediocre pilots. Another factor was opportunity. Most top-scoring German aces gained the vast majority of their victories against the Russians who, in the early years, fielded inferior aircraft flown by poorly-trained pilots, thus creating a target-rich environment. Another factor is the number of sorties flown. German Erich Hartmann flew 1,352 sorties, in which he encountered the enemy on 825 occasions. By contrast, few Allied pilots flew 400 or more sorties, and the sortie/encounter ratio was much lower.

The one thing that the enormous number of sorties flown did was to allow a few successful *Jagdflieger* to develop individual and very effective methods. These, outlined in the companion volume *Luftwaffe Fighter Aces*, were only rarely paralleled by the Allies, due to lack of time and opportunity. An Allied 'old hand' returning to the fray usually spent several missions in 'catching up' with the latest developments. There was little opportunity for individuals to undergo a continuous learning process. This situation arose because Allied pilots were pulled out of combat and rested at frequent intervals, whereas the only extended rest most *Jagdflieger* got was in hospital.

While Allied fighter pilots saw much less action than their German counterparts, plenty of examples exist which show that the top Allied aces were the equal of their foes. Pull up a sandbag, and we'll take a look.

In the annals of mass destruction we have David McCampbell's nine victories in a single sortie. Also in the Pacific, Marine Corsair pilot Bob Hanson destroyed 20 Zeros over Rabaul in six sorties in January 1944. He was shot down by ground fire and killed on 3 February, with his score standing at 25.

Then there is marksmanship. At the height of his powers, *Experte* Hans-Joachim Marseille is said to have needed an average of 15 rounds per victory. In Burma, Jim Lacey shot down a Hayabusa with a mere five rounds, while in Europe, Canadian Wally McLeod shot down two FW 190As with a total expenditure of 26 rounds.

In terms of strike rates, Lacey's 28 victims were amassed in little over 80 encounters with the enemy, while P-47 ace Bob Johnson flew 91 sorties for a similar score. This sortie/victory ratio would have ensured them a ranking in the *Jagdflieger* list far above Erich Hartmann, or Adolf Galland.

It has been postulated, purely on Second World War results, that Germans are naturally better fighter pilots. This can be refuted by taking a glance at the relative scores for World War One; in this conflict there was no basic difference. The only conclusion is that British, American and Commonwealth pilots in the second conflict were at least the equal of their opponents, and given identical circumstances, would have matched anything the *Jagdflieger* achieved.

Mirror, Mirror, on the Wall...

Who was the greatest ace of all? To attempt to answer this is invidious, as the operational circumstances of the far-flung theatres in which the Allies fought differed so widely as to make fair comparisons impossible.

Both the Germans and the Japanese were formidable opponents in the first years of the war, but became less so towards the end. Were victories in the Battle of Britain harder to come by than those in the Pacific in 1942? Against fighters this is extremely doubtful; the main difference was that most carrier bombers and torpedo planes were single-engined, and therefore more vulnerable than their twin-engined German counterparts.

What of the top scorers? 'Pat' Pattle headed the Allied list, but more than half of his victories were over Italian opposition. On the other hand, some 15 of these were scored while flying the Gladiator biplane. In the Pacific, Dick Bong scored 40 while flying fighters which were generally outclassed over Europe. He was closely followed by Tommy McGuire of the same unit (38 victories). 'Johnnie' Johnson fought over Western Europe from 1941 to the end of 1944, ending as the most successful wing leader of them all. His aircraft was only once hit by an enemy fighter.

'Screwball' Beurling has his supporters. His record over Malta was unsurpassed, and he was widely recognised as one of the best shots in the RAF. But he was not a team player, and on his return to Europe he achieved little. His clashes with authority were such that he was allowed to retire in October 1944, just as Canadian fighter squadrons were sweeping across Europe.

Australian 'Killer' Caldwell's record was remarkable. His 19 victories over the desert, mainly against German opposition while flying the inferior P-40, was a tremendous feat, especially when one considers that three German *Experten* were among his victims. In 1943 he flew Spitfire Vs against the Japanese and gained another eight victories.

Then there is leadership. Douglas Bader was undoubtedly the most inspirational fighter leader of all, and his occasional wrong-headed lapses should not be allowed to obscure this. Four decades after the Battle of Britain he was quoted as saying: 'I don't say I was as good a shot as Bob Tuck, but then I was a better pilot. I wish he could hear that. I have told him several times, actually.' The only possible description of this impossible man was indomitable. He simply never gave up.

One other leader springs to mind, to whom the word legendary is often attached, though his personal score was not great: 14 and one shared, plus three probables, and nine and one shared damaged. This was American Don Blakeslee who, as a volunteer in the RCAF, joined No 401 Squadron in England in May 1941. By the time of the Dieppe operation in August 1942, he was with No 133 'Eagle' Squadron. When in the following month the three 'Eagle' squadrons were transferred to the USAAF to become the 4th Fighter Group, he had flown about 120 sorties and had been credited with three confirmed victories.

When the 4th FG traded its Spitfire Vs for Thunderbolts, Don was not entirely happy. After his first flight in it, he commented to 'Johnnie' Johnson that the Thunderbolt seemed very reluctant to leave the ground and very anxious to get back on it. He downed three FW 190s with the Jug, but was twice badly shot up. This notwithstanding, the shape of things to come was revealed on 12 August 1943, when

199

4th FG claimed 18 German fighters for the loss of just one Thunderbolt. Although Blakeslee himself failed to score, much of this success was credited to his skilful direction of the Group.

Attached to the newly-arrived 354th FG to introduce them to operations, he flew the P-51B Mustang for the first time. When on his return to the 4th in January 1944 he was promoted to command the group, he pressed for re-equipment with Mustangs. Asked about the time needed to convert, he replied that as the majority of his pilots had flown Spitfires with the 'Eagles', only 24 hours was needed. He kept his word.

On 6 March, the 8th AF mounted the first big daylight raid on Berlin. Leading the escort was Don Blakeslee at the head of the 4th FG, which claimed 15 victories for four losses. Over the next three months, in what 'Johnnie' Johnson has described as 'the toughest air fighting of the Second War', another seven fighters fell to the guns of Blakeslee's Mustang. Then on 21 June he led a force of more than 60 Mustangs on the first shuttle raid via Russia. He rendezvoused with the bombers near the Polish border, fought off a force of '109s near Warsaw, and arrived over the assigned Russian airfield almost exactly on time after eight hours in the air, having navigated from 16 different maps.

From Russia the 4th flew to Italy, from where they carried out two operations in support of 15th Air Force. During one of these Don shot down a Bf 109G over Budapest for his final recorded victory. He led the Group home on 5 July.

'Johnnie' Johnson has described Blakeslee as 'one of the best leaders ever to fight over Germany' — no mean tribute from such a man. So high did Blakeslee's standing become that on one Berlin raid he was assigned to direct the entire force of escort fighters. But for one man in the cockpit of a Mustang, with inadequate communications, the task of directing fighters spread out over a hundred miles or so was simply impossible.

At the end of October 1944, Blakeslee returned to the USA for a long overdue rest. He had been almost continuously in action for three years, in which time he had flown about 500 sorties and amassed more than 1,000 hours' flying time. It is believed that, like *Luftwaffe*

Experte Adolf Galland, he doctored his records in the last year to avoid being grounded.

Who was in fact the greatest Allied fighter ace depends on the criteria adopted. In this instance the reader must judge.

APPENDICES

Appendix 1. Leading Aces of the British and Commonwealth Air Forces

This appendix contains brief details of those aces credited with at least 10 confirmed victories, plus a handful of others whose records are in some way exceptional or of outstanding interest. For more details, the reader is referred to the superb 1994 edition of *Aces High* by Christopher Shores and Clive Thomas.

The following abbreviations have been used:

Score

CD	confirmed destroyed
Dam	damaged (shared damaged are not differentiated)
FV	first victory; i.e. the first claim made, whether just a damaged or a confirmed kill.
P	probable
SD	shared destroyed
SP	shared probable
UD	unconfirmed destroyed

Units

AFDU	Air Fighting Development Unit
BSDU	Bomber Support Development Unit
FIU	Fighter Interception Unit
OTU	Operational Training Unit
Sq	squadrons or other units
WL	Wing Leader

Theatres of Operations

ADGB	air defence of Great Britain (covers all daylight defensive actions from September 1939 to Spring 1941, including the Battle of Britain)

CF	Channel Front 1941 to 5 June 1944 (offensive operations over occupied Europe)
F	France 1939/40 and Dunkirk
FE	Malaya, Indonesia, India, Burma
Gr	Greece
I	Italy
M	Malta (defensive operations)
Med	Mediterranean area
N	night operations
NDGB	night defence of Great Britain
NI	night intruder and bomber support operations over Western Europe and Germany
Pac	Pacific/Indian Ocean
T	Tunisia
Th	theatres
WF	Western Front, 6 June 1944 to May 1945
WD	Western Desert

Aircraft

s/e	single engined
2/e	twin-engined
TF	fighter types flown

Casualties

KAS	killed on active service
KIA	killed in action
KIFA	killed in flying accident
MIA	missing in action
PoW	prisoner of war

Aircrew

G	gunner
RO	radar operator

Decorations

DFC	Distinguished Flying Cross
DFM	Distinguished Flying Medal
DSO	Distinguished Service Order
*	denotes bar to decoration

British Aces

J.E. 'Johnnie' Johnson DSO**, DFC*. Score 34 CD, 7 SD, 3 P, 2 SP, 13 Dam. FV 15.1.41. Sq 616, 610, WL Kenley, 127 Wing, 144 Wing. Th CF, WF. TF Spitfire. Almost all victims s/e fighters. Only once hit by enemy fire.

B. 'Cherry' Vale DFC*. Score 30 CD, 3 SD, 7 Dam. FV 1.7.40. Sq 33, 80. Th WD, Gr, Syria. TF Gladiator, Hurricane. Victims include no less than 13 different types: Italian, German and Vichy French. Died in car accident Nov. 81.

J.R.D. 'Bob' Braham DSO***, DFC***. Score 29 CD, 2 P, 5 Dam. FV 24/25.8.40. Sq 29, 510 OTU, 141, 613, 305, 21, 107. Th NDGB, NI, WF. TF Blenheim, Beaufighter, Mosquito. Several ROs, of whom 'Sticks' Gregory DFC, DFM, and Henry 'Jacko' Jacobs DFC were the most notable. Victims known to include high scoring German night fighter pilots Heinz Vinke (54 victories), August Geiger (53 victories), and Georg Kraft (14 victories), all of whom were killed. PoW 25.6.44 when shot down by FW 190 of *Luftwaffe Experte* Robert Spreckels. Died Feb. 74.

J.H. 'Ginger' Lacey DFM*. Score 28 CD, 5 P, 9 Dam. FV 13.5.40. Sq 501, 602, 155, 17. Th F, ADGB, CF, FE. TF Hurricane, Spitfire. Victories mainly F and ADGB; one Japanese. Died May 89.

R.R.S. 'Bob' or 'Tommy' Tuck DSO, DFC**. Score 27 CD, 2 SD, 1 UD, 1 SUD, 6 P, 7 Dam. FV 23.5.40. Sq 65, 92, 257, WL Duxford, Biggin Hill. Th F, ADGB, CF. Shot down by ground fire, France, 28.1.42 and PoW. Died May 87.

Neville F. Duke DSO, DFC**. Score 26 CD, 2 SD, 1 P, 6 Dam. FV 26.4.41. Sq 92, 112, 145. Th CF, WD, T, I. TF Spitfire, Tomahawk, Kittyhawk. Top-scorer in the Mediterranean theatre. Total 486 sorties.

E.S. 'Sawn-Off' Lock DSO, DFC*. Score 26 CD, 8 P. FV 15.8.40. Sq 41, 611. Th ADGB, CF. TF Spitfire. 15 CD in 16 days. MIA while strafing near Calais 3.8.41.

Frank R. Carey DFC**, DFM. Score 25 CD, 3 SD, 4 UD, 3 P, 9 Dam. FV 30.1.40. Sq 43, 3, 135, WL 267 Wing. Th F, ADGB, FE. TF Hurricane. 13 CD in France, all except one bombers. 5 CD in Burma.

D.E. 'Don' Kingaby DSO, DFM**. Score 21 CD, 2 SD, 6 P, 11 Dam. FV 12.8.40. Sq 266, 92, 64, 122, 501, WL Hornchurch. Th ADGB, CF, WF. TF Spitfire. 13 victories WF. Died Dec. 92.

Branse A. Burbridge DSO*, DFC*. Score 21 CD, 2 P, 1 Dam, plus 3 V-1s CD. FV 3.6.42. Sq 141, 157, 85. Th NDGB, NI. TF Havoc, Mosquito. RO Bill Skelton DSO*, DFC*. All CD between 22.2.44 and 2/3.1.45. 14 intruder/bomber support victories.

Douglas R.S. Bader DSO* DFC*. Score 20 CD, 4 SD, 6 P, 1 SP, 11 Dam. FV 1.6.40. Sq 222, 242, WL Tangmere. Th F, ADGB, CF. TF Spitfire, Hurricane. PoW 9.8.41. Died 5.9.82.

Michael N. Crossley DSO, DFC. Score 20 CD, 2 SD, 1 UD, 1 Dam. FV 19.5.40. Sq 32. Th F, ADGB. TF Hurricane. Shot down twice. No further victories after 25.8.40. Died Sept. 87.

John Cunningham DSO*, DFC*. Score 20 CD, 3 P, 7 Dam. FV 19/20.11.40. Sq 604, 85. Th NDGB. TF Blenheim, Beaufighter, Mosquito. Top-scoring night ace in ADGB, mainly with RO Jimmy Rawnsley DSO, DFC, DFM*.

G. 'Sammy' Allard DFC, DFM*. Score 19 CD, 5 SD, 2 P. FV 10.5.40. Sq 85. Th F, ADGB, NDGB. TF Hurricane. KAS in Havoc, Lincolnshire 13.3.41.

Billy Drake DSO, DFC*. Score 18 CD, 2 SD, 2 UD, 4 P, 2 SP, 6 Dam. FV 20.4.40. Sq 1, 421 Flight, 128, 112, WL Halfar Wing, 20 Wing. Th F, CF, WD, M. TF Hurricane, Spitfire, Kittyhawk, Typhoon. No victories on the latter. It is possible that Drake's score may be higher than listed.

D.A.P. 'Des' McMullen DFC**. Score 17 CD, 5 SD, 4 UD, 1 SUD, 6 P, 1 SP, 12 Dam. FV 24.5.40. Sq 54, 222, 151, 266, 602, 124, 64, 65. Th F, ADGB, NDGB, CF. TF Spitfire, Hurricane, Defiant. Three night victories with latter. Died July 85.

James Rankin DSO*, DFC*. Score 17 CD, 5 SD, 3 P, 2 SP, 19 Dam. FV 22.1.41. Sq 64, 92, WL Biggin Hill, 15 Wing, 125 Wing. Th CF, WF. TF Spitfire. Virtually all victims s/e fighters. Died post-war.

A.A. 'Killer' McKellar DSO, DFC*. Score 17 CD, 3 SD, 5 P, 3 Dam. FV 16.10.39. Sq 602, 605. Th ADGB. TF Spitfire, Hurricane. All CD with Hurricane, 605 Sq. Sobriquet of 'Killer' bestowed by the press. KIA near Maidstone 1.11.40.

Wilfred G.G. Duncan-Smith DSO*, DFC. Score 17 CD, 2 SD, 6 P, 2 SP, 8 Dam. FV 29.12.40. Sq 611, 603, 411, 64, WL North Weald, Luqa, 244 Wing. Th CF, M, I. TF Spitfire.

H.J.L. 'Jim' Hallowes DFC, DFM*. Score 17 CD, 2 SD, 4 P, 8 Dam. FV 3.2.40. Sq 43, 65, 122, 222, 165, 504. Th F, ADGB, CF. TF Hurricane, Spitfire. Score possibly one higher, as Bf 109 pilot Julius Neumann believes that he was shot down by Hallowes on 18.8.40. Died Oct. 87.

W.T.E. 'Bill' Rolls, DFC, DFM. Score 17 CD, 1 SD, 3 P, 2 Dam. FV 2.9.40. Sq 72, 122, 126. Th ADGB, CF, M. TF Spitfire. Died July 88.

N. 'Fanny' Orton DFC*. Score 17 CD, 8 P, 4 Dam. FV 23.11.39. Sq 73, 242, 54. Th F, CF. TF Hurricane, Spitfire. 15 CD France, although details lacking. Shot down and badly burned 15.5.40. KIA 17.9.41.

A.D.J. 'Tony' Lovell DSO*, DFC*. Score 16 CD, 6 SD, 2 P, 13 Dam. FV 31.5.40. Sq 41, 145, 1435, WL Safi, 322 Wing, 244 Wing. Th F, ADGB, CF, M, I. TF Spitfire. Shot down 28.7.40 by *Luftwaffe Experte* Werner Molders, with slight wounds. KIFA 17.8.45.

Alfred E. Marshall DFC, DFM. Score 16 CD, 2 SD, 2 P, 1 Dam, 1 V-1. FV 19.5.40. Sq 73, 250, 25. Th F, ADGB, WD, NDGB. TF Hurricane, Kittyhawk, Mosquito. 14 CD WD. KAS Coltishall 27.11.44.

A.C. 'Sandy' Rabagliati DFC*. Score 16 CD, 1 SD, 4 P, 7 Dam. FV 18.8.40. Sq 46, 126, WL Takali, Coltishall. Th ADGB, M, CF. TF Hurricane, Spitfire, Typhoon. All victories in Hurricane. KIA 6.7.43, shot down over North Sea by flak.

S.W. 'Dan' Daniel DSO, DFC*. Score 16 CD, 1 SD, 2 P, 12 Dam. FV 27.4.42. Sq 72, 601, 145. Th CF, T, I. 9 CD Tunisia. TF Spitfire. Korea, 1 MiG-15 damaged 10.4.51. Died Mar. 82.

James A.F. MacLachlan DSO, DFC**. Score 16 CD, 1 SD, 4 Dam. FV 9.1.41. Sq 261, 1, AFDU. Th M, NI, CF. TF Hurricane, Mustang. Shot down over Malta 16.2.41 and left arm amputated. Flew Hurricanes on night intruder sorties with artificial arm from Nov. 41. KIA Dieppe 18.7.43.

M.L. 'Mike' Robinson DSO, DFC. Score 16 CD, 4 P, 1 SP, 9 Dam. FV 31.8.40. Sq 87, 601, 238, 609, WL Tangmere. Th F, ADGB, CF. TF Hurricane, Spitfire. 10 CD CF. KIA 10.4.42, shot down by FW 190 of *JG 26*.

E.W.F. 'Ted' Hewett DFM. Score 16 CD, 2 P. FV 4.12.40. Sq 80. Th WD, Gr. TF Gladiator, Hurricane. All victories Gr. Believed to have flown Spitfires and Typhoons later in the war.

Peter M. Brothers DSO, DFC*. Score 16 CD, 1 P, 3 Dam. FV 18.5.40. Sq 32, 257, 457, 602, WL Tangmere, Culmhead. Th F, ADGB, CF, WF. TF Hurricane, Spitfire.

Adrian H. 'Ginger' Boyd DSO, DFC*. Score 15 CD, 3 SD, 6 P, 4 Dam. FV 22.5.40. Sq 145, 501, WL Middle Wallop. Th F, ADGB, CF. TF Hurricane, Spitfire. Died Jan. 75.

R.H. 'Ray' Harries DSO*, DFC**. Score 15 CD, 3 SD, 2 P, 6 Dam. FV 12.3.42. Sq 43, 131, 91, WL Westhampnett, 135 Wing. Th CF, WF. TF Spitfire. All CD s/e fighters. KIFA 14.5.50, in Meteor.

W. Dennis David DFC*. Score 15 CD, 2 SD, 5 UD, 4 Dam. FV 2.11.39. Sq 87, 213, 152, 89. Th F, ADGB. TF Hurricane. 8 CD and 5 UD France. All victories except one with 87 Sq.

M.M. 'Mike' Stephens DSO, DFC**. Score 15 CD, 3 SD, 3 UD, 1 P, 5 Dam. FV 12.5.40. Sq 3, 232, 274, 80, 249. Th F, ADGB, WD, M. TF

Hurricane, Spitfire. Score does not include two Italian S-84s shot down over Turkey in 41 while flying Turkish AF Hurricanes as advisor.

E.M. 'Imshi' Mason DFC. Score 15 CD, 2 SD, 6 Dam. FV 9.12.40. Sq 80, 274, 261, 94. Th WD, M, Iran. TF Hurricane, Kittyhawk. All victories with Hurricane, including one in Iran. KIA WD 15.2.42, shot down by Bf 109 of *Luftwaffe Experte* Otto Schulz.

J.R. Baldwin DSO* DFC*. Score 15 CD, 1 SD, 4 Dam. FV 15.12.42. Sq 609, 198, WL 146 and 123 Wings. Th CF, WF. TF Typhoon. Top-scoring Typhoon pilot. MIA Korea in F-86 Sabre 15.3.52.

John E. Scoular DFC. Score 15 CD, 1 SD, 1 UD, 4 Dam. FV 23.11.39. Sq 73, K Flt, 250. Th F, East Africa, WD. TF Hurricane, Gladiator, Tomahawk. 12 CD in France.

A.J. 'Ginger' Owen DFC, DFM. Score 15 CD, 1 P, 3 Dam, 1 V-1. FV 21/22.12.42. Sq 600, 85. Th T, Med, NDGB, NI. TF Beaufighter, Mosquito. RO Vic McAllister DSO, DFC.

Ronald 'Ras' Berry DSO, DFC*. Score 14 CD, 10 SD, 9 P, 17 Dam. FV 7.12.39. Sq 603, 81, WL 322 Wing. Th ADGB, CF, T. TF Spitfires. Died 91.

G.K. 'Sheep' Gilroy DSO, DFC*. Score 14 CD, 10 SD, 2 SP, 9 Dam. FV 28.10.39. Sq 603, 609, WL 324 Wing. Th ADGB, CF, T, Med. TF Spitfire.

R. Finlay Boyd DSO, DFC*. Score 14 CD, 7 SD, 3 P, 7 Dam. FV 7.7.40. Sq 602, 54, WL Kenley. Th ADGB, CF. TF Spitfire. Died Apr. 75.

Thomas F. Dalton-Morgan DSO, DFC*. Score 14 CD, 3 SD, 1 P, 4 Dam. FV 12.7.40. Sq 43, WL Middle Wallop/Ibsley. Th ADGB, CF. TF Hurricane, Spitfire.

Peter G. Wykeham-Barnes DSO*, DFC*. Score 14 CD, 3 SD, 1 P, 4 Dam. FV 19.6.40. Sq 80, 274, 73, 257, 23. Th WD, I. TF Hurricane, Gladiator, Mosquito.

R.F.T. 'Bob' Doe DFC*. Score 14 CD, 2 SD, 5 Dam. FV 15.8.40. Sq 234, 238, 66. 130. Th ADGB, CF. TF Spitfire, Hurricane.

J.W.M. 'Max' Aitken DSO, DFC. Score 14 CD, 1 SD, 1 P, 3 Dam. FV 18.5.40. Sq 601, 68. Th F, ADGB, WF, ND, Med. TF Hurricane, Spitfire, Beaufighter. Three victories in 'borrowed' aircraft; a Bf 109 over France in June 41 in a 610 Sq Spitfire; two Ju 52 transports over the Aegean on 5/6.3.44 in a Beaufighter X of 46 Sq. Died 1.5.85.

J. 'Hamish' Dodds DFM. Score 14 CD, 6 P, 7 Dam. FV 1.12.41. Sq 274. Th WD. TF Hurricane. Top-scoring Hurricane pilot in North Africa.

D.A.S. 'Don' McKay DFM*. Score 14 CD, 2 UD, 1 SUD, 4 Dam. FV 12.5.40. Sq 501, 421 Flt, 91, 130, 213, 33, 274. Th F, ADGB, WF, WD. TF Hurricane, Spitfire. No victories WD. Record is confused, score may well be higher. Died Sept. 59.

R.M. 'Dickie' Milne DFC*. Score 14 CD, 1 SD, 1 UD, 1 P, 11 Dam. FV 17.5.40. Sq 151, 92, 222, WL Biggin Hill. Th F, ADGB, CF. TF Hurricane, Spitfire. 7 CD CF. PoW 14.3.43.

Richard P. Stevens DSO, DFC*. Score 14 CD, 1 SD, 2 P, 1 Dam. FV 15/16.1.41. Sq 151, 253. Th NDGB, NI. TF Hurricane. Most successful 'catseye' night fighter. All victories NDGB with 151 Sq. KIA Holland on intruder mission 15/16.12.41.

Nevil E. Reeves DSO, DFC*. Score 14 CD, 2 Dam. FV 2/3.7.42. Sq 89, 239, BSDU. Th WD, M, NI. TF Beaufighter, Mosquito. RO A. O'Leary DFC*. KIFA 27.1.49 in Meteor jet.

W. Peter Green DSO, DFC. Score 14 CD, 13 V-1s. FV 14/15.4.43. Sq 85, 410, 96, 219. Th NDGB, NI. TF Mosquito. Former air-sea rescue pilot. Nine victories over Europe with top-scoring RO Douglas Oxby DSO, DFC (21 victories). KIFA Amiens 1.3.45.

John W. Allan DSO, DFC. Score 14 CD. FV 12/13.7.43. Sq 256. Th M. TF Mosquito. Originally a Spitfire pilot, converted to night fighters in 42. During Allied invasion of Sicily, he and RO H. Davidson accounted for nine Ju 88s and four Cant Z1007s in 18 days, including five in one night. His final victory, another Cant, came at the end of Aug. 42. During the following year he flew night ranger sorties over Europe, with no further success. Died July 88.

Roy G. Dutton DSO, DFC*. Score 13 CD, 6 SD, 2 P, 9 Dam. FV 13.1.40. Sq 111, 145, 19, 141, 452. Th F, ADGB, CF, NI. TF Hurricane, Spitfire. No success as night fighter with 141 Sq. Led 512 Sq (Dakotas) on Rhine crossing Mar. 45. Died Sept. 88.

Count Manfred B. Czernin DSO, DFC. Score 13 CD, 5 SD, 2 UD, 3 P, 1 SP, 5 Dam. FV 19.5.40. Sq 85, 17, 65, 222, 41. Th F, ADGB. TF Hurricane. Anglo-Austrian parentage, born in Berlin. No victories after 17.11.40, but awarded MC for partisan activities in Italy. Died Oct. 62.

J.W. 'Pancho' Villa DFC*. Score 13 CD, 4 SD, 4 P, 4 Dam. FV 2.6.40. Sq 72, 92, 65, 501, 198. Th F, ADGB, CF. TF Spitfire, Typhoon. All CD 40. Died 83.

I.R. 'Widge' Gleed DSO, DFC. Score 13 CD, 3 SD, 4 P, 3 SP, 4 Dam. FV 18.5.40. Sq 87, WL Middle Wallop/Ibsley, 244 Wing. Th F, ADGB, CF. TF Hurricane, Spitfire. KIA 16.4.43, probably shot down by *Luftwaffe Experte* Ernst-Wilhelm Reinert.

William H. Franklin DFM*. Score 13 CD, 3 SD, 3 Dam. FV 22.5.40. Sq 65. Th F, ADGB. TF Spitfire. 11 Bf 109 CD. KIA 12.12.40 when shot down by return fire from Ju 88.

G.C. 'Grumpy' Unwin DFM*. Score 13 CD, 2 SD, 2 UD, 2 P, 1 Dam. FV 27.5.40. Sq 19. Th F, ADGB. TF Spitfire. Final victory 28.11.40.

John S. Taylor DFC*. Score 13 CD, 2 SD, 2 P, 12 Dam. FV 11.7.42. Sq 145, 601. Th WD, T, Med. TF Spitfire. KIA Sicily 12.7.43.

James G. Sanders DFC. Score 13 CD, 1 SD, 2 UD, 1 P, 6 Dam. FV 29.12.39. Sq 615, 422 Flt, 96, 257, 255, WL Llandow, Rednal. Th F, ADGB, NDGB. TF Gladiator, Hurricane, Defiant, Mustang. No known victories on the last. Records incomplete.

R.W. 'Bobby' Oxspring DFC**. Score 13 CD, 1 SD, 2 P, 13 Dam, 4 V-1s. FV 29.7.40. Sq 66, 616, 41, 91, 72, 222, WL 24 Wing, 141 Wing, Detling. Th ADGB, CF, T, WF. TF Spitfire. Died 89.

John Ellis DFC*. Score 13 CD, 1 SD, 2 P, 2 Dam. FV 27.5.40. Sq 610, WL Krendi. Th F, ADGB, CF, M. TF Spitfire. PoW 13.6.43, shot down in Sicily by *Luftwaffe Experte* Gerhard Michalski.

C.E. 'Cas' Casbolt DFM. Score 13 CD, 1 SD, 1 P, 4 Dam. FV 19.11.40. Sq 80, 250. Th WD, Gr. TF Gladiator, Hurricane, Kittyhawk. All but two victories Gr.

Harry Broadhurst DSO*, DFC*. Score 13 CD, 7 P, 10 Dam. FV 29.11.39. Sq 111, 60 Wing, Hornchurch Wing. Th F, ADGB, CF. TF Hurricane, Spitfire. All victims except two s/e fighters.

R.T. 'Reg' Llewellyn DFM. Score 13 CD, 1 SD, 1 UD, 1 P, 2 Dam. FV 29.5.40. Sq 263, 41, 213. Th F, ADGB. TF Gladiator, Spitfire, Hurricane. All victories with Hurricane of 213 Sq. Shot down and wounded 15.9.40; no further operational flying.

P.P. 'Prosser' Hanks DSO, DFC. Score 13 CD, 1 P, 1 SP, 6 Dam. FV 1.4.40. Sq 1, 5 OTU, 257, 56, WL Duxford, Coltishall, Luqa. Th F, ADGB (1 CD with 5 OTU only) CF, M. TF Hurricane, Spitfire.

John G. Topham DSO, DFC*. Score 13 CD, 1 P, 1 Dam. FV 15/16.8.40. Sq 219, 125. Th NDGB, NI. TF Blenheim, Beaufighter, Mosquito. RO 'Wilbur' Berridge DSO, DFC*. Died 87.

John C. Dundas DFC*. Score 12 CD, 4 SD, 2 P, 5 Dam. FV 3.7.40. Sq 609. Th ADGB. TF Spitfire. All victims except one were bombers or Bf 110s. KIA 28.11.40, shot down by *Luftwaffe Experte* Rudi Pflanz, seconds after destroying the Bf 109E of leading German *Experte* Helmut Wick.

T.F. 'Ginger' Neil DFC*. Score 12 CD, 4 SD, 2 P, 1 Dam. FV 7.9.40. Sq 249. Th ADGB, M. TF Hurricane. 11 CD between 7.9 and 7.11.40.

J.E. 'Jas' Storrar DFC*. Score 12 CD, 2 SD, 1 UD, 2 P, 1 SP, 3 Dam. FV 23.5.40. Sq 145, 421 Flt, 73, 274, 65, 64, 165, 234, WL Hunsdon, Digby,

Molesworth. Th F, ADGB, WD, CF, WF. TF Hurricane, Spitfire, Mustang. Majority of victories Hurricane 145 Sq.

A.C. 'Tony' Bartley DFC*. Score 12 CD, 1 SD, 4 P, 8 Dam. FV 23.5.40. Sq 92, 74, 65, 111. Th Dunkirk, ADGB, CF, T. TF Spitfire.

E.R. 'Ted' Thorn DFC*, DFM*. Score 12 CD, 1 SD, 2 Dam. FV 28.5.40. Sq 264, 32, 169. Th F, ADGB, NDGB, CF, NI. TF Defiant, Hurricane, Mosquito. All victories in Defiant. With G Fred Barker top-scoring Defiant team of the war. KIFA in Meteor jet 12.2.46.

Stanley D.P. Connors DFC. Score 12 CD, 2 UD, 4 Dam. FV 18.5.40. Sq 111. Th F, ADGB. TF Hurricane. KIA Kenley 18.8.40, by 'friendly' ground fire.

G.H. 'Cyclops' Bennions DFC. Score 12 CD, 5 P, 5 Dam. FV 28.7.40. Sq 41. Th ADGB. TF Spitfire. All victories ADGB. Shot down by Bf 109s 1.10.40 and blinded in one eye, hence his nickname.

J.A.A. 'Johnny' Gibson DFC. Score 12 CD, 1 SD, 2 UD, 1 P, 11 Dam. FV 27.5.40. Sq 501, 15 RNZAF, 80. Th F, ADGB, Pac, WF. TF Hurricane, Warhawk, Corsair, Tempest. All victories except one France and ADGB. Shot down five times, but survived the war.

Edward D. Crew DSO, DFC*. Score 12 CD, 1 SD, 5 Dam, 21 V-1s. FV 11.8.40. Sq 604, 85, 96. Th ADGB, NDGB. TF Blenheim, Beaufighter, Mosquito.

P.A. 'Paddy' Schade DFM. Score 12 CD, 3 P, 1 SP, 2 Dam, 2 V-1s. FV 9.4.42. Sq 54, 126, 91. Th CF, M, WF. TF Spitfire. KIA 31.7.44, collided with Tempest while chasing V-1.

Arthur J. Hodgkinson DSO, DFC*. Score 12 CD, 1 P, 5 Dam. FV 21/22.7.40. Sq 219, 264, 23. Th NDGB, Med. TF Blenheim, Beaufighter, Mosquito. KIA Sicily 10.7.43.

F.W. 'Taffy' Higginson DFC, DFM. Score 12 CD, 1 P, 2 Dam. FV 17.5.40. Sq 56. Th F, ADGB, CF. TF Hurricane, Typhoon. All victories on Hurricane before 30.9.40.

H.E. 'Harry' White DFC**. Score 12 CD, 4 Dam. FV 3/4.7.43. Sq 141, BSDU. Th NI. TF Beaufighter, Mosquito. RO Mike Allan. Died Mar. 90.

Michael M. Davison DFC*. Score 12 CD, 1 P, 1 Dam, 1 V-1. FV 3.9.42. Sq 46, 108, 264. Th WD, I, WF. TF Beaufighter, Mosquito. RO A. Willmott. KIFA post-war.

Alwyn B. Downing DFC, DFM. Score 12 CD. FV 30.4.43, instant ace when he shot down five Ju 52 transports in 10 minutes. Sq 600, 169. Th Med, I, NI. TF Beaufighter. RO John Lyons DFC, DFM.

Allan R. Wright DFC*. Score 11 CD, 3 SD, 7 P, 7 Dam. FV 23.5.40. Sq 92,

29. Th F, ADGB, CF, NDGB. TF Spitfire, Beaufighter.

John C. Freeborn DFC*. Score 11 CD, 2 SD, 3 UD, 1 SUD, 1 P, 4 Dam. FV 21.5.40. Sq 74, 602, 118, WL 286 Wing. Th F, ADGB, CF, I. TF Spitfire.

John T. Webster DFC. Score 11 CD, 2 SD, 2 UD, 3 Dam. FV 17.12.39. Sq 41. Th F, ADGB. TF Spitfire. Often credited with shooting down *Luftwaffe Experte* Werner Mölders 28.7.40. KIA 5.9.40, collision with Spitfire.

J.J. 'Orange' O'Meara DSO, DFC*. Score 11 CD, 2 SD, 1 UD, 4 P, 12 Dam. FV 21.5.40. Sq 64, 72, 421 Flt, 91, 164, 234, 131. Th F, ADGB, CF. TF Spitfire, Hurricane.

John C. Mungo-Park DFC*. Score 11 CD, 2 SD, 5 P, 4 Dam. FV 24.5.40. Sq 74. Th F, ADGB, CF. TF Spitfire. 9 CD ADGB. KIA 27.6.41.

A. 'Andy' McDowell DFM*. Score 11 CD, 2 SD, 2 P. FV 23/24.7.40. Sq 602, 245, 232, 616. Th ADGB, WF. TF Spitfire, Meteor. All victories in ADGB with 602 Sq Spitfire. One destroyed on ground with Meteor jet 24.4.45. Died Nov. 81.

Peter A. Nash DFC. Score 11 CD, 1 SD, 5 P, 1 SP, 5 Dam. FV 7.8.41. Sq 65, 609, 249. Th CF, M. TF Spitfire. KIA Malta 17.5.42.

H.N. 'Harry' Howes DFM. Score 11 CD, 1 SD, 2 P, 5 Dam. FV 20.5.40. Sq 85, 605. Th F, ADGB. TF Hurricane. KIFA 22.12.40.

Leonard Cottingham DFC. Score 11 CD, 1 SD, 1 P, 2 SP. FV 4.7.40. Sq 33. Th WD, Gr. TF Gladiator, Hurricane. Shot down and wounded over Piraeus 20.4.41. No further operational flying.

F.N. 'Fred' Robertson DFM. Score 11 CD, 1 SD, 3 P, 7 Dam. FV 2.6.40. Sq 66, 261, 219, 153, 96. Th F, M, NI. TF Spitfire, Hurricane, Defiant, Beaufighter, Mosquito. No claims as night fighter. KIFA 31.8.43, night collision with B-17.

H.E. 'Harry' Walmsley DFC*. Score 11 CD, 1 SD, 1 P, 4 Dam. FV 9.1.43. Sq 611, 132, 130, 350. Th CF, WF. TF Spitfire.

Desmond Ibbotson DFC*. Score 11 CD, 4 P, 4 Dam. FV 27.9.41. Sq 54, 112, 601. Th CF, WD, I. TF Spitfire, Kittyhawk.

C.P. 'Paddy' Green DSO, DFC. Score 11 CD, 3 P, 1 SP, 1 Dam. FV 23.5.40. Sq 92, 421 Flt, 600, 125. Th F, ADGB, CF, T, I. TF Spitfire, Beaufighter. Four Ju 88s in one sortie 14/15.7.43.

John H. Lapsley DFC. Score 11 CD. FV 17.8.40. Sq 80, 274. Th WD. TF Hurricane. All victims Italian. Operational flying ceased due to wounds 19.4.41, when shot down by Bf 109s and strafed on ground.

W.F. 'Andy' Miller DFC*. Score 11 CD. FV 12/13.6.43. Sq 219, 125, 169. Th NDGB, NI. TF Beaufighter, Mosquito. RO F.C. Bone DFC. PoW 12/13.8.44 when damaged by debris from He 219 victim.

George E. Goodman DFC. Score 10 CD, 6 SD, 3 Dam. FV 13.5.40. Sq 1, 73. Th F, ADGB, WD. TF Hurricane. KIA by flak, Libya 14.6.41.

C.F. 'Bunny' Currant DSO, DFC*. Score 10 CD, 5 SD, 2 P, 12 Dam. FV 15.8.40. Sq 605, 501, WL 122 Wing. Th F, ADGB, WF. All CD ADGB.

A. Geoffrey Page DSO, DFC*. Score 10 CD, 5 SD, 3 Dam. FV 13.7.40. Sq 56, 132, AFDU, 122, WL 125 Wing. Th ADGB, WD, CF, WF. TF Hurricane, Mustang, Spitfire. Shot down 12.8.40 and badly burned. Shot down Bf 110 of *Luftwaffe Experte* Hans-Joachim Jabs 29.4.44.

Francis J. Soper DFC, DFM. Score 10 CD, 4 SD, 1 SUD, 3 Dam. FV 23.11.39. Sq 1, 257. Th F, CF. TF Hurricane. Most victories France. MIA 5.10.41 after engaging a bomber over North Sea.

Jack R.H. Hussey DFC, DFM. Score 10 CD, 4 SD, 1 P, 5 Dam. FV 26.11.42. Sq 72, 19. Th T, I. TF Spitfire, Mustang. All victories with 72 Sq Spitfires. KAS England Feb. 45.

P.P. 'Pat' Woods-Scawen DFC. Score 10 CD, 3 SD, 2 UD, 1 P. FV 10.5.40. Sq 85. Th F, ADGB. TF Hurricane. KIA Kent 1.9.40.

John K. Buchanan DSO, DFC*. Score 10 CD, 3 SD, 7 Dam. Originally a bomber pilot. FV 21.11.42. Sq 272, 227. Th M, Med. TF Beaufighter. Top-scoring Beaufighter strike pilot of the war. Shot down by flak into the Aegean 16.2.44 and died of exposure.

Kenneth W. Mackenzie DFC. Score 10 CD, 3 SD, 3 Dam. FV 4.10.40. Sq 501, 247. Th ADGB, CF. TF Hurricane. Shot down by flak Brittany 29.9.41 and PoW.

E.N. 'Timber' Woods DFC*. Score 10 CD, 2 SD, 4 P, 9 Dam. FV 23.3.42. Sq 124, 72, 249, WL 286 Wing. Th CF, M, I. TF Spitfire. KIA Yugoslavia 16.12.43.

Osgood V. Hanbury DSO, DFC*. Score 10 CD, 2 SD, 2 P, 5 Dam. FV 7.9.40. Sq 602, 260. Th ADGB, WD. TF Spitfire, Hurricane, Kittyhawk. Originally an Army Co-operation pilot. KIA over Biscay as passenger in Hudson 3.6.43.

R.D. 'Dolly' Doleman DSO, DFC. Score 10 CD, 2 SD, 1 P, 1 Dam, 3 V-1s. FV 12.2.44. Sq 157. Th CF, NI. TF Mosquito. RO 'Bunny' Bunch DFC. All CD NI missions.

Paul H.M. Richey DFC*. Score 10 CD, 1 SD, 1 UD, 1 P, 1 SP, 6 Dam. FV 29.3.40. Sq 1, 609, 56. Th F, CF. TF Hurricane, Spitfire, Typhoon. No victories on the last. Died Feb. 89.

M.C.B. 'Bod' Boddington DFC, DFM. Score 10 CD, 1 SD, 1 P, 1 Dam. FV 12.8.40. Sq 234, 242. Th ADGB, M, I. TF Spitfire I and V. Died 77.

W.L. 'Bill' Dymond DFM. Score 10 CD, 1 SD, 1 P, 6 Dam. FV 10.4.40. Sq

111. Th F, ADGB. TF Hurricane. Most victories bombers. KIA Thames Estuary 2.9.40.

Ronald F. Hamlyn DFM. Score 10 CD, 1 SD, 1 P, 1 Dam. FV 3.7.40. Sq 610, 242. Th ADGB, CF. TF Spitfire, Hurricane. Five CD in one day 24.8.40; eight during that week. Later air-sea rescue. Died early 90s.

C.J. 'Sammy' Samouelle DFC. Score 10 CD, 4 P, 9 Dam. FV 17.7.42. Sq 92, 41, 130. Th WD, WF. TF Spitfire.

John E. Willson DFC*. Score 10 CD, 1 P, 1 Dam. FV 6/7.7.42. Sq 219, 153. Th NDGB, NMed, NT. TF Beaufighter. KIA Algiers 26/27.8.43.

J.A.A. 'Jasper' Read DFC*. Score 10 CD, 1 P. FV 28/29.4.42. Sq 604, 89, 46, 108. Th NDGB, WD, Med. TF Beaufighter. Started war as a light bomber pilot. Seven victories in a week, Sicily, July 42.

J.H. 'Jeff' Wedgwood DFC*. Score 10 CD, 12 Dam. FV 1.9.40. Sq 253, 80, 92. Th ADGB, WD. TF Hurricane, Spitfire. KAS by 'friendly fire' while passenger in Halifax 17.12.42.

James G. Benson DSO DFC. Score 10 CD, 4 Dam, 6 V-1s. FV 22/23.12.40. Sq 141, 157. Th ADGB, ND, NI. TF Defiant, Beaufighter, Mosquito. Usual RO Lewis Brandon. Last victory He 219 5/6.1.45. Died 87.

Gordon L. Sinclair DFC. Score 10 CD, 1 Dam. FV 26.5.40. Sq 19, 310, 313, 56. Th F, ADGB, CF. TF Spitfire, Hurricane, Typhoon. No victories on last.

A.D.McN. 'Archie' Boyd DSO, DFC. Score 10 CD. FV 16/17.5.41. Sq 600, 219. Th NDGB, Med. TF Beaufighter. RO Alexander Glegg DFC.

Leslie Stephenson DFC*. Score 10 CD. FV 17.4.43. Sq 141, 153, 219. Th NDGB, T, NI. TF Beaufighter, Mosquito. RO G.A. Hall DFC*.

N.G. 'Lanky' Cooke DFC. Score 9 CD, 3 SD. FV 12.5.40. Sq 264. Th F. TF Defiant, G Albert Lippett DFM. Eight CD on one day over Dunkirk 29.5.40. Both shot down and killed over Dunkirk 31.5.40.

R.A. 'Bob' Cross DFM. Score 9 CD, 1 P, 9 Dam. FV 23.1.43. Sq 136. Th FE. TF Hurricane, Spitfire. All victims Japanese. Died early 70s.

R.A. 'Rory' Chisholm DSO, DFC. Score 9 CD, 1 P, 1 Dam. FV 13/14.3.41. Sq 604, FIU. Th NDGB, NI. TF Beaufighter, Mosquito.

Charles H. Dyson DFC*. Score 9 CD. FV 11.12.40. Sq 33. Th WD, Gr. TF Hurricane. Seven victories (6 CR 42s, 1 S-79) claimed in one mission 11.12.40. Twice shot down in Greece, but no further successes.

James A.S. 'Sandy' Allen DFM. Score 7 CD, 3 P, 6 Dam. FV 8.2.42. Sq 232. Th Singapore, Java, Sumatra. TF Hurricane IIb. Allen's confirmed victories were all over the Japanese Zero.

Joseph Berry DFC*. Score 1 CD, 59 V-1s CD. FV 9.9.43. Sq 255, FIU,

501. Th Med, CF. TF Beaufighter, Tempest. Top scorer against the V-1 'Doodlebug' with the latter. KIA by flak, Holland 2.10.44.

American Aces

NB: Americans who achieved their first victories with the RAF but went on to achieve high scores with the USAAF are listed in Appendix 2.

L.C. 'Wildcat' Wade DSO, DFC**. Score 22 CD, 2 SD, 1 P, 13 Dam. FV 18.11.41. Sq 33, 145. Th WD, T, I. TF Hurricane, Spitfire. KAS Foggia, Italy, Jan. 44, in Auster light aircraft. Top-scoring American in RAF.

Claude Weaver DFC, DFM*. Score 12 CD, 1 SD, 3 P. FV 17.7.42. Sq 412, 185, 403. Th M, Med, CF. Shot down by *Luftwaffe Experte* Gerhard Michalski on Malta; then by MC 202 over Sicily; one year as PoW. Escaped and returned to action. KIA France 28.1.44, believed shot down by FW 190 of *Luftwaffe Experte* Gerhard Vogt.

D.C. 'Foob' Fairbanks DFC**. Score 12 CD, 1 SD, 3 Dam, 1 V-1. FV 8.6.44. Sq 501, 274, 3. Th WF. TF Spitfire, Tempest. Score includes one Ar 234 jet. Top-scoring Tempest pilot. PoW 28.2.45, shot down by FW 190. Died post-war.

John J. Lynch DFC*. Score 10 CD, 7 SD, 1 P, 2 Dam. FV 17.4.42. Sq 71 'Eagle', 249. Th CF, Med. TF Spitfire. KIFA in F-84 Thunderjet 9.3.56.

R.F. 'Tiger' Tilley DFC. Score 7 CD, 3 P, 6 Dam. FV 24.3.42. Sq 121 'Eagle', 601, 126. Th CF, M. TF Spitfire. All CD Malta. Sobriquet of Tiger from character in *Playbox* comic, Tiger Tilly.

John F. 'Tex' Barrick DFM. Score 5 CD, 2 Dam. FV 7.2.42. Sq 17. TF Hurricane IIb. Th FE, China. Top scorer during the retreat. All victims Ki 27s and Ki 43s.

Australian Aces

C.R. 'Killer' Caldwell DSO, DFC. Score 27 CD, 3 SD, 6 P, 15 Dam. FV 26.6.41. Sq 250, 112, WL 1 RAAF, 80 RAAF. Th Syria, WD, CF, Pac. TF Tomahawk, Kittyhawk, Spitfire. Victories known to include three *Luftwaffe Experten*, Wolfgang Lippert, Erbo von Kageneck and 'Fifi' Stahlschmidt, plus eight Japanese aircraft.

A.P. 'Tim' Goldsmith DFC, DFM. Score 16 CD, 1 SD, 2 P, 7 Dam. FV 26.3.42. Sq 126, 242, 452. Th M, Pac. TF Hurricane, Spitfire.

John L. Waddy DFC. Score 15 CD, 1 SD, 7 P, 6 Dam. FV 2.12.41. Sq 250, 260, 4 SAAF, 92, 80 RAAF. Th WD, Pac. TF Tomahawk, Kittyhawk, Spitfire. All victories WD. Died Sept. 87.

R.N. 'Ape' Cullen DFC. Score 15 CD, 2 P, 1 Dam. FV 9.10.40. Sq 80. Th

WD, Gr. TF Gladiator, Hurricane. All victims Italian. KIA 4.3.41.

P.C. 'Pat' Hughes DFC. Score 14 CD, 3 SD, 1 SUD, 1 P. FV 8.7.40. Sq 234. Th ADGB. TF Spitfire. 12 CD Bf 109s. KIA 7.9.40.

K.W. 'Bluey' Truscott DFC*. Score 14 CD, 3 P, 3 Dam. FV 9.8.41. Sq 452, 76 RAAF. Th CF, Pac. TF Spitfire, Kittyhawk. All victories except one CF with 452 Sq. KAS near Darwin 28.3.43.

C.C. 'Charlie' Scherf DSO, DFC*. Score 13 CD, 1 SD, 1 forced down and destroyed on the ground. Sq 418 RCAF. Th CF. TF Mosquito. All victories on daylight intruder missions. Killed in car accident 13.7.49.

Mervyn C. Shipard DFC*. Score 13 CD, 2 P, 2 Dam. FV 1/2.11.41. Sq 68, 89. Th NDGB, M, WD. TF Beaufighter. All victories with RO Doug Oxby DFC* who later flew with night ace Peter Green DSO DFC.

J.W. 'Slim' Yarra DFM. Score 12 CD, 2 P, 6 Dam. FV 1.5.42. Sq 232, 64, 249, 185, 453. Th M, CF. TF Hurricane, Spitfire. KIA 10.12.42, shot down by flak off Dutch coast.

Peter St.G.B. Turnbull DFC. Score 12 CD, 1 P, 2 Dam. FV 26.12.40. Sq 3 RAAF, 75 RAAF, 76 RAAF. Th WD, Syria, Pac. TF Gauntlet, Gladiator, Hurricane, Tomahawk, Kittyhawk. Victims include German, Italian, Vichy French and Japanese aircraft. KIA New Guinea 27.8.42.

F.A.O. 'Tony' Gaze DFC**. Score 11 CD, 3 SD, 4 P, 5 Dam, 1 V-1. FV 26.6.41. Sq 610, 616, 64, 453, 129, 66, 610, 41. Th CF, WF. TF Spitfire. Victories include 1 Me 262 jet and 1 Ar 234 jet (shared).

Howard C. Mayers DSO, DFC*. Score 11 CD, 1 SD, 3 P, 1 SP, 6 Dam. FV 8.8.40. Sq 601, 94, WL 239 Wing. Th ADGB, WD. TF Hurricane, Kittyhawk. Eight CD ADGB. Shot down and PoW 20.7.42, believed killed when ship carrying prisoners to Italy was sunk.

A.W. 'Nicky' Barr DFC*. Score 11 CD, 3 P, 8 Dam. FV 12.12.41. Sq 3 RAAF. Th WD. TF Tomahawk, Kittyhawk. Flew 84 sorties, shot down three times. PoW 26.6.42.

Charles A. Crombie DSO, DFC. Score 11 CD, 3 P, 1 Dam. FV 19/20.6.42. Sq 89, 176. Th Med, FE. TF Beaufighter. RO R.C. Moss. KIFA Aug. 45.

R.J.C. 'Bob' Whittle DFM. Score 10 CD, 3 SD, 2 P, 2 Dam. FV 30.6.41. Sq 250, 86 RAAF. Th WD, Pac. TF Tomahawk, Kittyhawk. Majority of victories WD.

R.H.M. 'Bobby' Gibbes DFC*. Score 10 CD, 2 SD, 5 P, 16 Dam. FV 13.6.41. Sq 3 RAAF, WL 80 Wing RAAF. Th WD, Syria, Pac. TF Tomahawk, Kittyhawk, Spitfire. No victories in the Pacific with Spitfire.

Hugo T. Armstrong DFC*. Score 10 CD, 1 SD, 3 P, 2 Dam. FV 21.9.41. Sq 129, 72, 611. Th WF. TF Spitfire. All victims s/e fighters. KIA 5.2.43, shot down into the Channel by FW 190 flown by Heinz Gomann.

John R. Cock DFC. Score 10 CD, 1 SD, 1 UD, 4 P, 1 Dam. FV 10.4.40. Sq 87. Th F, ADGB. TF Hurricane, Spitfire, Tempest. All victories scored with 87 Sq before 10.10.40, despite further operational postings to 453, 93rd USAAF, 222, 24 RAAF, 54 (in Australia), 3 (with Tempests). Died Aug. 88.

V. Paul Brennan DFC, DFM. Score 10 CD, 1 P, 6 Dam. FV 17.3.42. Sq 64, 249. Th WF, M. TF Spitfire V. All victories Malta between 17.3 and 7.7.42. KIFA Australia June 43.

W.J. 'Jack' Storey DFC. Score 8 CD, 2 P. FV 29.1.42. Sq 135. Th FE. TF Hurricane. All victories Japanese s/e fighters.

Canadian Aces

G.F. 'Screwball' or 'Buzz' Beurling DFC, DFM*. Score 31 CD, 1 SD, 9 Dam. FV 1.5.42. Sq 41, 249, 403, 412. Th CF, M, WF. TF Spitfires. All except four victories scored in Malta, almost all s/e fighters. Outstanding marksman. KIFA Rome 20.5.48.

H.W. 'Wally' McLeod DSO, DFC*. Score 21 CD, 3 P, 13 Dam. FV 27.9.41. Sq 132, 485, 602, 411, 603, 1435, 443. Th CF, M, WF. TF Spitfire. 13 CD Malta. KIA Wesel, Germany, 27.9.44.

V.C. 'Woody' Woodward DFC*. Score 18 CD, 4 SD, 2 UD, 3 P, 11 Dam. FV 14.6.40. Sq 33, 213. Th WD, Gr. TF Gladiator, Hurricane.

W.L. 'Willie' McKnight DFC*. Score 17 CD, 1 SD, 3 UD. FV 19.5.40. Sq 615, 242. Th F, ADGB, CF. TF Hurricane. 11 CD France. KIA France 12.1.41.

R.W. 'Buck' McNair DSO, DFC*. Score 16 CD, 5 P, 14 Dam. FV 27.9.41. Sq 411, 249, 133, 403, 416, 421. Th CF, M. TF Spitfire. Died Jan. 71.

M.H. 'Hilly' Brown DFC*. Score 15 CD, 4 SD, 1 P, 2 Dam. FV 23.11.39. Sq 1. Th F, ADGB, M. TF Hurricane. Majority of victories in France. KIA by flak, Sicily 12.11.42.

J.F. 'Eddie' Edwards DFC*, DFM. Score 15 CD, 3 SD, 8 P, 1 SP, 13 Dam. FV 2.3.42. Sq 94, 260. 92, 274, WL 127 Wing. Th WD, T, I. TF Kittyhawk, Spitfire. 12 CD while flying Kittyhawks WD, mainly Bf 109F.

E.F.J. 'Jack' Charles DSO, DFC*. Score 15 CD, 1 SD, 6 P, 1 SP, 5 Dam. Originally Army Co-operation pilot. FV 17.4.41. Sq 54, 64, 611, WL Middle Wallop, Portreath. Th ADGB, CF. All victories CF.

D.C. 'Don' Laubman DFC*. Score 14 CD, 2 SD, 3 Dam. FV 30.12.43. Sq 412, 402. Th CF, WF. TF Spitfire. CD 8 FW 190, 6 Bf 109. PoW 14.4.45 when shot down by flak over Germany.

W.T. 'Bill' Klersy DSO, DFC*. Score 14 CD, 1 SD, 3 P. FV 7.3.44. Sq 401.

Th CF, WF. TF Spitfire. KIFA 22.5.45.

R.C. 'Moose' Fumerton DFC*. Score 14 CD, 1 Dam. FV 1/2.9.41. Sq 406, 89. Th NDGB, WD, M. TF Beaufighter, Mosquito. RO L. Bing DFC. Top-scoring Canadian night fighter pilot.

R.I.A. 'Rod' Smith DFC*. Score 13 CD, 1 SD, 1 SP, 1 Dam. FV 18.7.42. Sq 126, 401, 412. Th M, WF. TF Spitfire. SD was an Me 262.

R.A. 'Butch' Barton DFC*. Score 12 CD, 5 SD, 2 P, 5 Dam. FV 15.8.40. Sq 249. Th ADGB, M. TF Hurricane. Last op Dec. 41.

John H. Turnbull DFC*. Score 12 CD, 1 SD. FV 4.10.42. Sq 125, 600. Th NDGB, I. TF Beaufighter. RO Cecil Fowler DFM*.

J.A. 'Johnnie' Kent DFC*. Score 12 CD, 3 P, 2 Dam. FV 9.9.40. Sq 303, 92, WL Northolt, Kenley. Th ADGB, CF, Med. TF Hurricane, Spitfire. Died Oct. 85.

George C. Keefer DSO*, DFC*. Score 12 CD, 2 P, 9 Dam. FV 7.12.41. Sq 274, 416, 412, WL 126 Wing, 125 Wing. Th WD, CF, WF. TF Hurricane, Spitfire.

A.U. 'Bert' Houle DFC*. Score 11 CD, 1 SD, 1 P, 7 Dam. FV 1.9.42. Sq 213, 145, 417. Th WD, FE. TF Hurricane, Spitfire.

George U. Hill DFC**. Score 10 CD, 8 SD, 3 P, 10 Dam. FV 19.8.42. Sq 421, 453, 403, 111, 442. Th CF, T, Med. TF Spitfire. All CD T/Med. Died Nov. 69.

I.F. 'Hap' Kennedy DFC*. Score 10 CD, 5 SD, 1 P. FV 7.2.43. Sq 240, 185, 111, 93, 401. Th Med, FE, WF. TF Spitfire.

John MacKay DFC*. Score 10 CD, 2 SD, 4 Dam. FV 25.9.44. Sq 401. Th WF. TF Spitfire. One MiG-15 shot down in Korea 53 flying F-86.

John D. Mitchner DFC*. Score 10 CD, 1 SD, 1 P, 2 SP, 3 Dam. FV 17.1.43. Sq 263, 247, 116, 402, 421, 416. Th CF, WF. TF Whirlwind, Spitfire. All victories Spitfire, all victims s/e fighters. Died Dec. 64.

P.S. 'Stan' Turner DSO, DFC*. Score 10 CD, 1 SD, 3 UD, 1 P, 8 Dam. FV 25.5.40. Sq 242, 145, 411, 249, 134, 417, WL 244 Wing. Th F, ADGB, CF, M, I. TF Hurricane, Spitfire. Died July 85.

R.A. 'Bob' Kipp DSO, DFC. Score 10 CD, 1 SD, 1 SP, 1 Dam. FV 12.12.43. Sq 418, Fighter Experimental Flight. Th NI. TF Mosquito. KIFA in Vampire July 49.

Hamilton C. Upton DFC. Score 10 CD, 1 SD, 1 P. FV 12.7.40. Sq 43, 607. Th ADGB. TF Hurricane. Fate uncertain.

Richard J. Audet DFC*. Score 10 CD, 1 SD, 1 Dam. FV 29.12.44. Sq 411. Th WF. TF Spitfire IXE. Only Spitfire pilot to claim five victories in one sortie, 29.12.44. All victims s/e fighters. KIA by flak, Germany 3.3.45.

Czech Aces

K.M. 'Kuttel' Kuttelwascher DFC*. Score 18 CD, 2 SD, 2 P, 5 Dam. FV 19.5.40. Sq GCIII/6, 1, 23. Th F, CF, NDGB, NI. TF MS 406, D 520, Hurricane, Mosquito. No CD with *L'Armée de l'Air* or with Mosquito. 15 CD as night intruder in 42. Died Aug. 59.

Josef Frantisek DFM*. Score 17 CD, 1 P. FV 2.9.40. Sq 303. Th ADGB. TF Hurricane. All victories scored during Sept. 40. KAS Northolt 8.10.40.

Danish Aces

Kaj Birksted DSO, DFC. Score 10 CD, 1 SD, 5 Dam. FV 19.6.42. Sq 331, WL 132 Wing. Th CF. TF Spitfire. One of the great fighter leaders. Died 96.

French Aces

J-F 'Moses Morlaix' Demozay DSO, DFC*. Score 18 CD, 2 P, 4 Dam. FV 8.11.40. Sq 1, 242, 91. Th CF. TF Hurricane, Spitfire. 13 CD with 91 Sq. KIFA Dec. 45.

Pierre H. Clostermann DFC. Score 11 CD (possibly 7 more), 2 or 5 P, 9 Dam. FV 17.6.43. Sq 341, 602, 274, 56, 3. Th CF, WF. TF Spitfire, Tempest. Much confusion exists as to Closterman's exact score, exacerbated by his semi-autobiographical book *Le Grand Cirque*, but there is no doubt that his record is distinguished.

Irish Aces

F. Desmond Hughes DSO, DFC**. Score 18 CD, 1 SD, 1 P, 1 Dam. FV 26.8.40. Sq 264, 125, 600, 604. Th NDGB, T, Med, NI. TF Defiant, Beaufighter, Mosquito. Former Army Co-operation pilot. Five CD with Defiant, G Fred Gash DFM. 15 night victories, last 13/14.1.45. Died Jan. 92.

J.I. 'Killy' Kilmartin DFC. Score 12 CD, 2 SD, 1 SUD, 4 P, 2 Dam. FV 23.11.39. Sq 1, 43, 602, 313, 128, 504, WL Hornchurch, 136 Wing, 910 Wing. Th F, ADGB, WF, FE. TF Hurricane, Typhoon, Thunderbolt. All victories with Hurricane by 7.9.40.

F. Victor Beamish DSO* DFC. Score 10 CD, 11 P, 1 SP, 5 Dam. FV 30.6.40. Station Commander North Weald. Th ADGB, CF. TF Hurricane, Spitfire. MIA Calais 28.3.42.

New Zealand Aces

Colin F. Gray DFC**. Score 27 CD, 2 SD, 6 P, 4 SP, 12 Dam. FV 24.5.40. Sq 54, 43, 1, 403, 616, 485, 64, 81, WL 322 Wing. Th F, ADGB, CF, T, I.

TF Spitfire, Hurricane. ADGB score 15 CD. Died 97.

E.D. 'Rosie' Mackie DSO, DFC*. Score 20 CD, 3 SD, 2 P, 11 Dam. FV 26.3.42. Sq 485, 243, 92, 274, 80, WL 122 Wing. Th CF, T, Med, I, WF. TF Spitfire, Tempest. Died 80s.

W.V. 'Bill' Crawford-Compton DSO*, DFC*. Score 20 CD, 1 SD, 3 P, 1 SP, 13 Dam. FV 21.9.41. Sq 485, 611, 64, 122, WL Hornchurch, 145 Wing. Th CF, WF. TF Spitfire. All victims s/e fighters. High-scoring CF ace. Died Jan. 88.

R.B. 'Ray' Hesselyn DFC, DFM*. Score 18 CD, 1 SD, 2 P, 7 Dam. FV 1.4.42. Sq 249, 277, 222. Th M, CF. TF Spitfire. 12 CD Malta, remainder CF. PoW 3.10.43, shot down by Bf 109s over France. Died Nov. 63.

A.C. 'Al' Deere DSO, DFC*. Score 17 CD, 1 SD, 2 UD, 1 SUD, 4 P, 8 Dam. FV 23.5.40. Sq 54, 602, 611, WL Biggin Hill. Th F, ADGB, WF. TF Spitfire. Noted for legendary escapes in action. Died 95.

E.J. 'Cobber' Kain DFC. Score 16 CD, 1 Dam. FV 8.11.39. Sq 73. Th F. TF Hurricane. First Allied ace of the war. KIFA France 6.6.40.

Brian J.G. Carbury DFC*. Score 15 CD, 2 SD, 2 P, 5 Dam. FV 7.12.39. Sq 603. Th ADGB. TF Spitfire. All CD Bf 109s between 29.8 and 10.10.40. Died July 62.

Gray Stenborg DFC. Score 14 CD, 1 SD, 3 Dam. FV 26.4.42. Sq 111, 185, 91. Th CF, M. TF Spitfire. All CD s/e fighters. KIA near Poix, France, 24.9.43.

John M. Checketts DSO, DFC. Score 14 CD, 3 P, 8 Dam, 2 V-1s. FV 13.1.43. Sq 611, 485, WL 142 Wing. Th CF, WF. TF Spitfire. All victims s/e fighters. Shot down over France by FW 190s 6.9.43 but evaded capture.

E.P. 'Hawkeye' Wells DSO, DFC*. Score 12 CD, 4 P, 7 Dam. FV 17.10.40. Sq 266, 41, 485, WL Kenley, Tangmere, West Malling. Th ADGB, CF. TF Spitfire. All CD s/e fighters. Majority of victims CF. Outstanding marksman.

J.D. 'Jack' Rae DFC*. Score 11 CD, 2 SD, 8 P, 1 SP, 6 Dam. FV 12.8.41. Sq 485, 603, 249. Th CF, M. TF Spitfire. PoW France after engine failure 22.8.43. Should not be confused with post-war TV personality and Canadian fighter pilot Jackie Rae.

W.E. 'Smoky' Schrader DFC*. Score 11 CD, 2 SD. FV 12.11.43. Sq 165, 1435, 486, 616. Th CF, M, Med, WF. TF Spitfire, Tempest, Meteor. Nine CD with Tempest, three destroyed on ground with Meteor.

Geoffrey B. Fisken DFC. Score 11 CD, 1 P, 1 Dam. FV 12.1.42. Sq 67, 243, 21 RAAF, 453 RAAF, 14 RNZAF. Th EF (Singapore), Pac. TF Buffalo, Kittyhawk. Six victories with Buffalo. Leading Commonwealth ace against

Japanese. Invalided from AF Dec. 43.

G.E. 'Jamie' Jameson DSO, DFC. Score 11 CD, 2 Dam. FV 27/28.7.42. Sq 125, 488. Th NDGB, NI. TF Beaufighter, Mosquito. Top-scoring NZ night fighter pilot.

M.V. 'Mindy' Blake DSO DFC. Score 10 CD, 3 SD, 1 Dam. FV 21.8.40. Sq 238, 234. WL Polish, Portreath. Th ADGB, CF. TF Hurricane, Spitfire. Shot down into Channel off Dieppe 19.8.42 and PoW. Died 30.11.81.

Nigel M. Park DFM. Score 10 CD, 1 SD, 1 Dam. FV 28.7.42. Sq 126. Th M. TF Spitfire. KIA 18.11.42. Nephew of Sir Keith Park.

R.L. 'Spud' Spurdle DFC*. Score 10 CD, 2 P, 1 SP, 11 Dam. FV 14.9.40. Sq 74, 91, 16 RNZAF, 130, 80. Th ADGB, CF, Pac, WF. TF Spitfire, Kittyhawk, Tempest. No victories on last type.

Norwegian Aces

Svein Heglund DSO, DFC*. Score 14 CD, 1 SD, 5 P, 7 Dam. FV 19.6.42. Sq 331, 85. Th CF, NI. TF Spitfire, Mosquito. Last three victims Bf 110s at night; remainder all s/e fighters.

Helner G.E. Grundt-Spang DFC*. Score 10 CD, 1 SD, 2 P, 3 Dam. FV 1.6.42. Sq 331. Th CF, WF. TF Spitfire. All victims s/e fighters.

Polish Aces

Stanislaw Skalski DSO, DFC**. Score 21 CD, 3 UD, 1 P, 5 Dam. FV 1.9.39. Sq 142 Esk, 302, 501, 306, 316, 317, 145, 601, WL 131, 133. Th Poland, ADGB, CF, T, WF. TF PZL P.11c, Hurricane, Spitfire, Mustang. Six CD in Polish Campaign. Russian-born.

B.M. 'Mike' Gladych DFC. Score 18 CD, 1 P, 1 Dam. FV 23.6.41. Sq 303, 302, 56th FG (USAAF). Th CF, WF. TF Spitfire, P-47. 10 victories claimed with P-47. Possible victories with the Polish and French air forces in 39/40, but these cannot be verified.

Witold Urbanowicz DFC. Score 17 CD, 1 P. FV 8.8.40. Sq 145, 303, 75th USAAF. Th ADGB, China. TF Hurricane, Warhawk. Russian reconnaissance aircraft shot down over Eastern Poland in 36 not included in score. Two Japanese in China in 43 with USAAF.

Eugeniusz Horbaczewski DSO, DFC*. Score 16 CD, 1 SD, 1 P, 1 Dam, 4 V-1s. FV 6.11.41. Sq 303, 145, 601, 43, 315. Th CF, T, I, WF. TF Spitfire, Mustang. KIA Beauvais 18.8.44, after accounting for three FW 190s.

Jan E.L. Zumbach DFC*. Score 12 CD, 2 SD, 5 P, 1 Dam. FV 10.6.40. Sq 303, WL 133 Wing. Th F, ADGB, CF. TF Morane MS 406, Hurricane, Spitfire, Mustang. One SD with *L'Armée de l'Air*. Post-war flew as a mercenary for Katanga and Biafra. Died 86.

Michal M. Maciejowski DFC, DFM. Score 11 CD, 1 SD, 3 P, 1 Dam. FV 29.10.40. Sq 111, 249, 317, 316. Th ADGB, CF. TF Hurricane, Spitfire. Shot down Montreuil 9.8.43 and PoW.

Marion Pisarek DFC. Score 11 CD, 1 SD, 1 P, 1 Dam. FV 2.9.39. Sq 141 Esk, 303, 315, 308, WL Polish Wing. Th Poland, ADGB, CF. TF PZL P.11c, Hurricane, Spitfire. KIA Hardelot 29.4.42.

Rhodesian Aces

John A. Plagis DSO, DFC*. Score 15 CD, 2 SD, 2 P, 2 SP, 7 Dam. FV 10.3.42. Sq 65, 266, 249, 185, 64, 126, WL Bentwaters. Th CF, M, WF. TF Spitfire, Mustang. 10 CD Malta. All victories with Spitfire. Died post-war.

William I.H. Maguire DFC*. Score 13 CD, 1 P, 2 Dam. FV 28/29.4.42. Sq 253, 81, 154. Th NDGB, T, Med. TF Hurricane, Spitfire.

South African Aces

M.T.St.J. 'Pat' Pattle DFC*. Score 50 CD, 2 SD, 7 P, 1 SP, 6 Dam. FV 4.8.40. Sq 80, 33. Th WD, Gr. TF Gladiator, Hurricane. 15 CD with Gladiator, remainder with Hurricane. 23 CD German, 27 CD Italian. Final 25 CD (mainly German) in 15 days. KIA Eleusis Bay 20.4.41. The loss of records means that Pattle's score is approximate only, but there can be no doubt that he was the top scorer of the RAF in WW2.

A.G. 'Sailor' Malan DSO*, DFC*. Score 27 CD, 7 SD, 2 UD, 1 SUD, 3 P, 16 Dam. FV 21.5.40. Sq 74, WL Biggin Hill. Th F, ADGB, CF. TF Spitfire. Died Sept. 63.

Albert G. Lewis DFC*. Score 18 CD, 2 P, 1 SP, 1 Dam. FV 12.5.40. Sq 85, 249, 261. Th F, ADGB, FE. TF Hurricane. Six victories in one day 27.9.40. No operational flying after 9.4.42 when shot down and wounded over Ceylon (Sri Lanka).

J.J. 'Chris' Le Roux DFC**. Score 18 CD, 2 P, 8 Dam. FV 16.5.41. Sq 91, 111, 602. Th CF, T, WF. TF Spitfire. Former light bomber pilot. All victims s/e fighters. MIA over Channel 29.8.44.

P.H. 'Dutch' Hugo DSO, DFC**. Score 17 CD, 3 SD, 2 UD, 3 P, 7 Dam. FV 20.5.40. Sq 615, 41, WL Tangmere, Hornchurch, 322 Wing. Th F, ADGB, CF, T, I. TF Hurricane, Spitfire. Died 86.

J.E. 'Jack' Frost DFC*. Score 14 CD, 2 SD, 3 P, 2 SP, 3 Dam. FV 3.2.41. Sq 3 SAAF, 5 SAAF. Th Somalia, WD. TF Hurricane, Tomahawk. Destroyed 23 enemy aircraft on the ground. Virtually all victims Italian. SAAF top-scorer. KIA 16.6.42, shot down by Bf 109F.

Kenneth W. Driver DFC. Score 10 CD, 1 Dam. FV 16.12.40. Sq 1 SAAF. Th Eritrea, Med, WD. TF Hurricane. Almost all victims Italian. PoW 14.6.41 when shot down by *Luftwaffe Experte* Ludwig Franzisket.

Fleet Air Arm and Royal Marines

British naval aviation failed to produce any high-scoring fighter aces. In the main this was due to lack of opportunity; in those rare cases where targets abounded, they were often handicapped by low-performing fighters.

R.J. 'Dickie' Cork DSO, DSC. Score 9 CD, 2 SD, 1 P, 4 Dam. FV 30.8.40. Sq 242 (RAF), 880, WL 15 Wing. Th ADGB, Madagascar, Med. TF Hurricane, Sea Hurricane, Corsair. Seconded to RAF during ADGB and often flew as Bader's wingman. 5 CD with RAF. KIFA in Corsair, Ceylon 14.4.44.

R.E. 'Jimmie' Gardner DSC. Score 6 CD, 4 SD, 1 P. FV 10.7.40. Sq 242 (RAF), 807. Th ADGB, Med. TF Hurricane, Fulmar. Four CD with RAF.

A.J. 'Jackie' Sewell DSC. Score 5 CD, 7 SD, 1 SP, 5 Dam. FV 2.9.40. Sq 806, 804. Th Med, T. TF Fulmar, Sea Gladiator, Sea Hurricane. Almost all victories with Fulmar. KIFA in Corsair, USA Sept. 43.

Rupert A. Brabner Score 5 CD, 1 SD, 1 P, 1 Dam. FV 4.5.41. Sq 805, 801. Th Med. TF Buffalo, Fulmar, Sea Hurricane.

Graham A. Hogg DSC*. Score 4 CD, 8 SD. FV 29.9.40. Sq 806. Th F, Med, Syria. TF Skua, Fulmar, Hurricane. All victories in Med with Fulmar. KAS Scotland as passenger in Anson, 18.3.42.

J.M. 'Bill' Bruen DSO, DSC. Score 4 CD, 4 SD, 4 Dam. FV 3.7.40. Sq 803, 800, 836. Th Med. TF Skua, Fulmar, Sea Hurricane. Irish national.

R.C. 'Ronnie' Hay DSO, DSC*. Score 3 CD, 1 UD, c.9 SD, 3 Dam. FV 27.4.40. Sq 801, 808, WL 47 Wing. Th Norway, Med, Pac. TF Skua, Fulmar, Corsair. One of the few to record victories over German, Vichy French, Italian and Japanese aircraft. 2 CD and 2 SD with Corsair.

Edward T. Wilson DSC. Score 3 CD, 4 SD. FV 19.10.44. Sq 1844. Th FE, Pac. TF Hellcat. South African. Top-scoring Hellcat pilot.

C. Le G. 'Crash' Evans DSO, DSC. Score 2 CD, 8 SD, 1 P, 1 SP. FV 26.9.39. Sq 803, 806. Th Norway, F, Med. TF Skua, Fulmar. Most victims Italian. Died Dec. 81.

Richard H. Reynolds DSC. Score 2 CD, 3 SD, 1 Dam. FV 22.8.44. Sq 894, 899. Th Murmansk convoys, Pac. TF Seafire. Top-scoring Seafire pilot.

William P. Lucy DSO. Score 7 SD, 1 P, 3 Dam. FV 20.3.40. Sq 803. Th Norway. TF Skua. Most successful Skua pilot. KIA 14.5.40 while attacking He 111s off Norway.

Lightning.

Robert M. DeHaven Score 14 D. 49th FG. TF Curtiss P-40, P-38 Lightning.

D.T. 'Danny' Roberts Score 14 D. 475th FG. TF Curtiss P-40, P-38 Lightning. KIA 9.11.43, mid-air collision with wingman.

Kenneth G. Ladd Score 12 D. 8th FG. TF P-38 Lightning.

James A. Watkins Score 12 D. 49th FG. TF Curtiss P-40, P-38 Lightning.

Richard L. West Score 12 D. 8th FG. TF P-38 Lightning.

Francis J. Lent Score 11 D. 475th FG. TF P-38 Lightning.

John S. Loisel Score 11 D. 475th FG. TF P-38 Lightning.

Cornelius M. Smith Score 11 D. 8th FG. TF P-38 Lightning.

Kenneth C. Sparks Score 11 D. 35th FG. TF P-38 Lightning. KIFA 44.

Robert W. Aschenbrenner Score 10 D. 49th FG. TF P-38 Lightning.

W. Kenny Giroux Score 10 D. 8th FG. TF P-38 Lightning.

E.A. 'Bill' Harris Score 10 D. 49th FG. TF Curtiss P-40, P-38 Lightning. Died 49.

Andrew J. Reynolds Score 10 D. 17th FS, 49th FG. TF Curtiss P-40.

Paul M. Stanch Score 10 D. 35th FG. TF Curtiss P-40, P-38 Lightning.

Elliot Summer Score 10 D. 475th FG. TF P-38 Lightning.

8th and 9th Air Forces, Western Europe

F.S. 'Gabby' Gabreski DSC, SS. Score 28 D, plus 6 D and 1 SD in Korea. 45th FS, 315 Sqn RAF, 56th FG. TF Curtiss P-40 (Hawaii Dec. 41), Spitfire (43), P-47 Thunderbolt. All victories with 56th FG. FV 24.8.43. PoW 20.7.44, after hitting ground near Coblenz while strafing.

R.S. 'Bob' Johnson DSC, SS. Score 28 D. 56th FG. FV 13.6.43. TF P-47 Thunderbolt. CM 91.

G.E. 'Ratsy' Preddy DSC, SS*. Score 25 D, 5 SD. 49th FG (defence of Australia—2 Dam), 352nd FG. FV 1.12.43. TF Curtiss P-40, P-47 Thunderbolt, P-51 Mustang. CM 143 in Europe. KIA 25.12.44, shot down over Ardennes by 'friendly' ground fire.

John C. Meyer DSC**, SS*. Score 23 D, 2 SD. Two further victories in Korea. 33rd FS (convoy patrols Iceland), 352nd FG. FV 26.11.43. TF Curtiss P-40, P-47 Thunderbolt, P-51 Mustang. Injured in car crash, Belgium 9.1.45; returned to USA.

W.H. 'Bud' Mahurin DSC, SS. Score 22 D (one Japanese), plus 3 D and 1 SD in Korea. 56th FG, 3rd AC in SW Pacific. TF P-47 Thunderbolt, P-51 Mustang. CM 85 in Europe.

R.S. 'Ray' Wetmore DSC*, SS*. Score 22.59 D. 359th FG. TF P-47

Thunderbolt, P-51 Mustang. Final victory Me 163 rocket fighter. CM 142. KIFA 14.2.51.

D.C. 'Dave' Schilling DSC*, SS**. Score 22 D, 1 SD. 56th FG. FV 2.10.43. Five victories on 23.12.44, all s/e fighters. TF P-47 Thunderbolt. CM 132. Died in car accident, England, 14.8.56.

D.S. 'Don' Gentile DSC, SS. Score 21 CD, 2 SD, 5 P, 16 Dam. 133 'Eagle' Sq RAF, 4th FG. FV 19.8.42, 2 D with RAF. 12 CD and 1 SD in one month, Mar. 44. TF Spitfire, P-47 Thunderbolt, P-51 Mustang. KIFA in T-33 jet trainer 28.1.51.

F.J. 'Rat-Top' Christensen DSC, SS. Score 21 D, 1 SD. 56th FG. TF P-47 Thunderbolt. Six victories 7.7.44.

Glenn T. Eagleston Score 19.5 D, plus two victories in Korea. 354th FG. TF P-51 Mustang. Top-scorer 9th AF.

Duane W. Beeson Score 19.33 D. 73 'Eagle' Sq RAF, 4th FG. TF Spitfire, P-47 Thunderbolt, P-51 Mustang. 12 victories with P-47. Shot down by flak near Berlin 5.4.44 and PoW. Died 13.2.47.

Glenn E. Duncan Score 19 D. 353rd FG. TF P-47 Thunderbolt, P-51 Mustang. All victories P-47. Shot down by flak over Holland 7.7.44, but evaded capture and returned to command unit in Apr. 45.

L.K. 'Kit' Carson Score 18.5 D. 357th FG. TF P-51 Mustang. FV 8.4.44. Five FW 190s 27.11.44.

John F. Thornell Score 18.5 D. 352nd FG. TF P-47 Thunderbolt, P-51 Mustang.

Walter C. Beckham DSC. Score 18 D. 353rd FG. TF P-47 Thunderbolt, P-51 Mustang. CM 57. All victories with P-47. Shot down by ground fire near Bonn 22.2.44 and PoW.

John T. Godfrey SS*. Score 18 D. 4th FG. TF P-47 Thunderbolt, P-51 Mustang. Shot down by flak 24.8.44 and PoW. Canadian-born. Died 6.12.58.

Gerald W. Johnson DSC. Score 18 D. 56th FG. TF P-47 Thunderbolt. CM 88. Shot down by ground fire 27.3.44 and PoW.

H.A. 'Hub' Zemke DSC. Score 17.75 D. 56th FG, 479 FG. TF P-47 Thunderbolt, P-51 Mustang. Majority of victories in P-47. PoW 30.10.44 when Mustang suffered structural failure in a storm.

Henry W. Brown DSC, SS. Score 17.5 D. 355th FG. TF P-47 Thunderbolt, P-51 Mustang. Shot down by ground fire 3.10.44 and PoW.

John B. England Score 17.5 D. 357th FG. TF P-51 Mustang. Four victories 27.11.44. KIFA France 17.11.54.

Robert W. Foy Score 17 D. 357th FG. FV 6.3.44. TF P-51 Mustang. KIFA post-war.

R.K. 'Kid' Hofer Score 16.5 D. 4th FG. FV 8.10.43. TF P-47 Thunderbolt, P-51 Mustang. KIA Mostar, Yugoslavia, 2.7.44.

C.E. 'Bud' Anderson Score 16.25 D. 357th FG. TF P-51 Mustang. CM 116.

William T. Whisner DSC*. Score 15.5 D, plus 5.5 victories in Korea. 352nd FG. TF P-47 Thunderbolt, P-51 Mustang. CM 137. Five victories 21.11.44.

Donald M. Beerbower Score 15.5 D. 354th FG. TF P-51 Mustang. KIA by flak 9.8.44.

Richard A. Petersen Score 15.5 D. 357th FG. TF P-51 Mustang.

Jack T. Bradley Score 15 D. 354th FG. TF P-51 Mustang.

J.A. 'Jimmy' Goodson DSC. Score 15 D. 133 'Eagle' Sq RAF, 4th FG. TF Spitfire, P-47 Thunderbolt, P-51 Mustang. One victory with RAF. Shot down by flak 20.6.44 and PoW.

D.H. 'Don' Bochkay Score 14.84 D. 357th FG. TF P-51 Mustang. CM 123. Victories include two Me 262 jets.

D.J.M. 'Don' Blakeslee DSC. Score 14 CD, 1 SD, 3 P, 10 Dam. 133 'Eagle' Sq RAF, 4th FG, 357th FG. TF Spitfire, P-47 Thunderbolt, P-51 Mustang. Three victories with RAF. CM 400 plus. One of the greatest fighter leaders of the war.

Joseph H. Powers Score 14.5 D. 56th FG. TF P-47 Thunderbolt. KIFA 18.1.51.

John D. Landers SS**. Score 14.5 D. 49th FG (5th AF), 55th FG, 357th FG, 78th FG. TF Curtiss P-40, P-38 Lightning, P-47 Thunderbolt, P-51 Mustang. Six victories Pacific with 49th FG. Strafing ace Europe.

Robin Olds Score 14 D, plus 4 D in Vietnam. 479th FG. TF P-38 Lightning, P-51 Mustang. Nine victories with P-38.

Bruce Carr Score 14 D. 354th FG. TF Mustang. Five victories 2.4.45.

K.H. 'Ken' Dahlberg Score 14 D. 354th FG. TF P-51 Mustang. Four victories 12.12.44.

Wallace N. Emmer Score 14 D. 354 FG. TF P-51 Mustang. Died of wounds 44 as PoW.

Arthur F. Jeffrey Score 14 D. 479th FG. TF P-38 Lightning, P-51 Mustang. First American pilot to encounter Me 163 rocket fighter.

Donald J. Strait Score 13.5 D. 356th FG. TF P-47 Thunderbolt, P-51 Mustang.

Donald S. Bryan Score 13.34 D. 352nd FG. TF P-51 Mustang. Five victories 2.11.44. Victories include one Arado Ar 234 jet bomber.

George W. Carpenter Score 13.3 D. 133 Sqn RAF, 4th FG. TF Spitfire, P-

47 Thunderbolt, P-51 Mustang. Shot down over Germany 18.4.44 and PoW.

W.W. 'Millie' Millikan Score 13 D. 4th FG. TF P-47 Thunderbolt, P-51 Mustang.

Glennon T. Moran Score 13 D. 352nd FG. TF P-47 Thunderbolt, P-51 Mustang.

Robert W. Stephens Score 13 D. 354th FG. TF P-51 Mustang. KIFA date unknown.

Felix D. Williamson Score 13 D. 56th FG. TF P-47 Thunderbolt. Five victories 14.1.45.

Lowell K. Brueland Score 12.5 D, plus 2 D in Korea. 354th FG. TF P-51 Mustang.

James C. Stewart Score 12.5 D. 56th FG. TF P-47 Thunderbolt.

Quince L. Brown Score 12.33 D. 78th FG. TF P-47 Thunderbolt, P-51 Mustang. All victories wih P-47.

James H. Howard CMH. Score 12.33 D. AVG, 354th FG. TF Curtiss P-40, P-51 Mustang. 6.33 victories with AVG.

Clyde B. East Score 12 D. 10th TRW. TF P-51 Mustang.

George W. Gleason Score 12 D. 479th FG. TF P-38 Lightning, P-51 Mustang.

H.D. 'Deacon' Hively Score 12 D. 4th FG. TF P-51 Mustang.

P.W. 'Mac' McKennon Score 12 D. RAF, 4th FG. TF Spitfire, P-47 Thunderbolt, P-51 Mustang. 10.5 victories with P-47. Shot down over France 28.8.44, evaded capture, and returned to unit. Shot down by flak near Prenzlau Mar. 45; rescued by George Green, who landed his Mustang beside McKennon.

Michael G. Quirk Score 12 D. 56th FG. TF P-47 Thunderbolt.

Leroy A. Schreiber Score 12 D. 56th FG. TF P-47 Thunderbolt.

N. 'Cowboy' Megura Score 11.84 D. 4th FG. TF P-51 Mustang.

James A. Clark Score 11.5 D. 'Eagle' Sqn RAF, 4th FG. TF Spitfire, P-47 Thunderbolt, P-51 Mustang.

Paul A. Conger Score 11.5 D. 56th FG. TF P-47 Thunderbolt.

W.T. 'Bill' Halton Score 11.5 D. 352nd FG. TF P-47 Thunderbolt, P-51 Mustang.

John A. Kirla Score 11.5 D. 357th FG. TF P-51 Mustang.

C.E. 'Chuck' Yeager Score 11.5 D. 357th FG. TF P-51 Mustang. Shot down over France 5.3.44, but evaded capture and returned to unit. Five victories 22.10.44. Later famous as first man to exceed speed of sound.

L.H. 'Red Dog' Norley Score 11.33 D. 4th FG. TF P-51 Mustang. Score includes one Me 163 rocket fighter 2.11.44.

Richard E. Turner Score 11 D, 2 V-1s. 354th FG. TF P-51 Mustang.

Carl M. Frantz Score 11 D. 354th FG. TF P-51 Mustang.

Frank Q. O'Connor Score 10.75 D. 354th FG. TF P-51 Mustang.

William J. Hovde Score 10.5 D, plus 1 in Korea. 355th FG. TF P-51 Mustang.

Charles F. Anderson Score 10.5 D. 4th FG. TF P-47 Thunderbolt, P-51 Mustang. Shot down near Kassel 19.4.44, PoW.

George F. Cuellers Score 10.5 D. 364th FG. TF P-51 Mustang. Score includes one Me 262 jet.

George A. Doersch Score 10.5 D. 359th FG. TF P-51 Mustang.

Raymond H. Littge DSC. Score 10.5 D. 352nd FG. TF P-51 Mustang. KIFA 48.

John H. Storch Score 10.5 D. 357th FG. TF P-51 Mustang.

F.W. 'Fred' Glover Score 10.33 D. 4th FG. TF P-51 Mustang.

Wayne K. Blickenstaff Score 10 D. 353rd FG. TF P-51 Mustang. Five victories 24.3.45.

Joseph Broadhead Score 10 D. 357th FG. TF P-51 Mustang.

Aldwin M. Jucheim Score 10 D. 78th FG. TF P-47 Thunderbolt, P-51 Mustang. All victories with P-47.

E.E. 'Ted' Lines Score 10 D. 4th FG. TF P-47 Thunderbolt, P-51 Mustang.

Robert J. Rankin Score 10 D. 56th FG. TF P-47 Thunderbolt. Five victories 12.5.44.

Sydney S. Woods Score 10 D. 49th FW (5th AF), 479th FG, 4th FG. TF Curtiss P-40, P-38 Lightning, P-51 Mustang. Five victories with last 22.3.45. Shot down by ground fire 13.4.45 but evaded capture.

12th Air Force

William J. Sloan Score 12 D. 82nd FG. TF P-38 Lightning.

William L. Leverette Score 11 D. 14th FG. Later with 15th AF. TF P-38 Lightning. Seven victories (Ju 87s) 9.10.43.

Charles M. McCorkle Score 11 D. 31st FG. Later with 15th AF. TF Spitfire, P-51 Mustang.

Norman L. McDonald Score 11 D. 52nd FG, 325th FG (15th AF). TF Curtiss P-40.

Levi R. Chase Score 10 D. 33rd FG. TF Curtiss P-40.

13th Air Force, Pacific

Robert B. Westbrook Score 20 D. 347th FG, 18th FG. TF Curtiss P-40, P-38 Lightning. KIA 22.11.44, shot down by ground fire.

Bill Harris Score 16 D. 18th FG. TF P-38 Lightning.
Coatsworth B. Head Score 12 D. 18th FG. TF P-38 Lightning. KIA 19.1.45.
John W. Mitchell Score 11 D, plus 4 D in Korea. 339th FS, 15th FG, 51st FG (20th AF). TF P-38 Lightning, P-51 Mustang.
Murray J. Shubin Score 11 D. 347th FG. TF P-38 Lightning. Five victories (Zeros) 16.6.43. Died 23.7.56.

14th Air Force, Far East/China
Charles H. Older Score 18.5 D. AVG, 23rd FG. 10.5 victories with AVG. TF Curtiss P-40, P-51 Mustang.
D.L. 'Tex' Hill Score 18.25 D. AVG, 23rd FG. 12.25 victories with AVG. TF Curtiss P-40, P-51 Mustang.
J.C. 'Pappy' Herbst Score 18 D. 23rd FG. TF Curtiss P-40, P-51 Mustang. Rumoured to have flown with an RCAF sqn in England and shot down a Bf 109 (not included in score). KIFA in P-80 Shooting Star jet 4.7.46.
William N. Reed Score 17.5 D. AVG, 3rd CACW. 10.5 victories with AVG. TF Curtiss P-40. KIA 19.12.43.
Robert H. Neale Score 16 D. AVG. TF Curtiss P-40.
John F. Hampshire Score 14 D. 23rd FG. TF Curtiss P-40. KIA 2.5.43.
Edward O. McComas Score 14 D. 23rd FG. TF Curtiss P-40, P-51 Mustang. Died June 54.
Robert L. Scott Score 13 D. 23rd FG. TF P-43 Lancer, Curtiss P-40, P-51 Mustang.
George T. Burgard Score 10.75 D. AVG. TF Curtiss P-40.
Kenneth A. Jernstadt Score 10.5 D. AVG. TF Curtiss P-40.
Robert L. Little Score 10.5 D. AVG. TF Curtiss P-40. KIA 22.5.42.
J.V.K. 'Jack' Newkirk Score 10.5 D. AVG. TF Curtiss P-40. KIA 24.3.42.
Edward E. Rector Score 10.5 D. AVG, 23rd FG. TF Curtiss P-40. 6.5 victories with AVG.
William L. Turner Score 10.5 D. 3rd CACW. TF Curtiss P-40.
William D. McGarry Score 10.25 D. AVG. TF Curtiss P-40. PoW 42.
James J. England Score 10 D. 311th FG, also 10th AF. TF P-51 Mustang.
Bruce K. Holloway Score 10 D. 23rd FG. TF Curtiss P-40.

15th Air Force, Southern Europe, Italy
John J. Voll Score 21 D. 31st FG. TF Spitfire, P-51 Mustang.
Herschel H. Green Score 18 D. 325th FG. TF Curtiss P-40, P-47 Thunderbolt. Six victories in latter 30.1.44. FV May 43.

James S. Varnell Score 17 D. 52nd FG. TF P-47 Thunderbolt. KIFA 9.4.45.
S.J. 'Sam' Brown Score 15 D. 31st FG. TF P-51 Mustang. Four victories 26.6.44.
Robert C. Curtis Score 14 D. 52nd FG. TF P-47 Thunderbolt.
J.L. 'Jim' Brooks Score 13 D. 31st FG. TF P-51 Mustang. Four victories 26.6.44.
Harry A. Parker Score 13 D. 325th FG. TF P-51 Mustang. KIA Apr. 45.
Michael Brezas Score 12 D. 14th FG. TF P-38 Lightning. KIFA 5.2.54.
Norman C. Skogstad Score 12 D. 31st FG. TF P-51 Mustang.
Robert J. Goebel Score 11 D. 31st FG. TF P-51 Mustang.
John B. Lawler Score 11 D. 52nd FG. TF P-47 Thunderbolt.
Wayne L. Lowry Score 11 D. 325th FG. TF P-51 Mustang.
Leland P. Molland Score 11 D. 31st FG. TF P-51 Mustang.
Robert H. Riddle Score 11 D. 31st FG. TF P-51 Mustang.
Walter J. Goehausen Score 10 D. 31st FG. TF P-51 Mustang.

United States Navy
David McCampbell CMH. Score 34 D. CAG 15. TF F6F Hellcat. FV 11.6.44. Nine victories 24.10.44, seven victories 19.6.44.
Cecil E. Harris Score 24 D. VF-18, VF-27. TF F4F Wildcat, F6F Hellcat. Four victories in one day on three occasions.
E.A. 'Gene' Valencia Score 23 D. VF-9. TF F6F Hellcat. Six victories 17.4.45.
Patrick D. Fleming Score 19 D. VF-80. TF F6F Hellcat. Five victories 16.2.45. KIFA 16.2.56.
A. 'Alex' Vraciu Score 19 D. VF-6, VF-16, VF-20. TF F6F Hellcat. Six victories 19.6.44.
Cornelius N. Nooy Score 18 D. VF-31. TF F6F Hellcat. Five victories 21.12.44. Died 12.3.58.
Ira C. Kepford Score 17 D. VF-17. TF F4U Corsair. Four victories 11.11.43.
Charles R. Stimpson Score 17 D. VF-11. TF F4F Wildcat, F6F Hellcat.
Douglas Baker Score 16 D. VF-20. TF F6F Hellcat. KIA 14.12.44.
Arthur R. Hawkins Score 14 D. VF-31. TF F6F Hellcat. Five victories 13.12.44.
E. Scott McCuskey Score 14 D. VF-42, VF-3, VF-6, VF-8. TF F4F Wildcat, F6F Hellcat. Five victories 4.6.42 (Midway).
John L. Wirth Score 14 D. VF-31. TF F6F Hellcat. KIFA 45.
George C. Duncan Score 13.5 D. VF-15. TF F6F Hellcat.

Roger W. Mehle Score 13.33 D. VF-6, VF-28. TF F4F Wildcat. FV Wake Is. 1.2.42.

Roy W. Rushing Score 13 D. VF-15. TF F6F Hellcat. Six victories 24.10.44 as McCampbell's wingman.

John R. Strane Score 13 D. VF-15. TF F6F Hellcat. Four victories 25.10.44.

Wendell V. Twelves Score 13 D. VF-15. TF F6F Hellcat.

Daniel A. Carmichael Score 12 D. VF-2, VBF-12. TF F6F Hellcat.

Clement M. Craig Score 12 D. VF-22. TF F6F Hellcat. Five victories 21.1.45.

Roger R. Hedrick Score 12 D. VF-17, VF-84. TF F4U Corsair.

W.E. 'Bill' Henry Score 12 D. VF(N)-79, NAG-41. TF F6F Hellcat. FV 12.12.44. Top-scoring Navy night ace.

William J. Masoner Score 12 D. VF-19. TF F6F Hellcat. Six victories 24.10.44.

Hamilton McWhorter Score 12 D. VF-9, VF-12. TF F4F Wildcat.

E.H. 'Butch' O'Hare CMH. Score 12 D. VF-3, VF-2. TF F4F Wildcat, F6F Hellcat. Five victories 20.2.42. KIA 27.11.43.

James A. Shirley Score 12 D. VF-27, VF-22. TF F6F Hellcat. Five victories 24.10.44.

George R. Carr Score 11.5 D. VF-15. TF F6F Hellcat. Five victories 19.6.44.

Frederick E. Bakutis Score 11 D. VF-20. TF F6F Hellcat.

J.T. 'Tommy' Blackburn Score 11 D. VF-17. TF F4U Corsair. Four victories 6.2.44.

William A. Dean Score 11 D. VF-2. TF F6F Hellcat. Four victories 11.6.44.

James E. French Score 11 D. VF-9. TF F6F Hellcat.

Phillip L. Kirkwood Score 11 D. VF-10. TF F6F Hellcat. Six victories 16.4.45.

Charles M. Mallory Score 11 D. VF-18. TF F6F Hellcat.

James V. Reber Score 11 D. VF-30. TF F6F Hellcat. Four victories 6.4.45.

James E. Rigg Score 11D. VF-15. TF F6F Hellcat. Five victories 12.12.44.

Donald E. Runyon Score 11 D. VF-6, VF-18. TF F4F Wildcat, F6F Hellcat. Top-scoring USN Wildcat pilot with eight victories.

Richard E. Stambrook Score 11 D. VF-27. TF F6F Hellcat. Four victories 19.6.44.

S.W. 'Swede' Vejtasa Score 11 D. VSB-5, VF-10. TF SBD Dauntless (three victories 8.5.42) and F4F Wildcat (seven victories 26.10.42).

Marshall U. Beebe Score 10.5 D. VF-17. TF F4U Corsair. Five victories

18.3.45.

Russell L. Reiserer Score 10.5 D. VF-10, VF(N)-76. TF F6F Hellcat. Five victories 19.6.44.

Armistead B. Smith Score 10.5 D. VF-9. TF F6F Hellcat.

John C.C. Symmes Score 10.5 D. VF-21. TF F4F Wildcat.

Albert O. Vorse Score 10.5 D. VF-3, VF-2, VF-6, VF-80. TF F4F Wildcat, F6F Hellcat. Four victories 16.2.45.

Robert E. Murray Score 10.33 D. VF-29. TF F6F Hellcat. Four victories 16.10.44.

R.H. Anderson Score 10 D. VF-80. TF F6F Hellcat. Five victories 14.12.44.

Carl A. Brown Score 10 D. VF-27. TF F6F Hellcat. Five victories 24.10.44.

Thaddeus T. Coleman Score 10 D. VF-6, VF-23, VF-83. TF F6F Hellcat. Four victories 3.4.45.

Harris E. Mitchell Score 10 D. VF-9. TF F6F Hellcat.

T. Hamil Reidy Score 10 D. VF-83. TF F6F Hellcat. Scored last USN victory of war.

Arthur Singer Score 10 D. VF-15. TF F6F Hellcat.

J. Malcolm Smith Score 10 D. VF-17, VF-84. TF F4U Corsair, F6F Hellcat.

James S. Swope Score 10 D. VF-11. TF F4F Wildcat, F6F Hellcat.

United States Marine Corps

G. 'Pappy' Boyington CMH. Score 28 D. AVG, VMF-214. TF Curtiss P-40, F4U Corsair. Six victories with AVG. Shot down near Rabaul and PoW 3.1.44.

J.J. 'Joe' Foss CMH. Score 26 D. VMF-121. TF F4F Wildcat, F4U Corsair. All victories with Wildcat; top-scoring Wildcat pilot of the war.

R.W. 'Bob' Hanson CMH. Score 25 D. VMF-214, VMF-215. TF F4U Corsair. KIA by ground fire 3.2.44.

Kenneth A. Walsh CMH. Score 21 D. VMF-124, VMF-223. TF F4U Corsair, F4F Wildcat.

Donald N. Aldrich Score 20 D. VMF-215. TF F4U Corsair. KIFA 47.

John L. Smith CMH. Score 19 D. VMF-223. TF F4F Wildcat.

Marion E. Carl Score 18.5 D. VMF-221, VMF-223. TF F4F Wildcat, F4U Corsair. Two victories with latter.

Wilbur J. Thomas Score 18.5 D. VMF-213. TF F4F Wildcat.

J.E. 'Zeke' Swett CMH. Score 16.5 D. VMF-213. TF F4F Wildcat. Seven victories 7.4.43.

Harold L. Spears Score 15 D. VMF-215. TF F4U Corsair. KIFA 44.

Archie G. Donahue Score 14 D. VMF-112, VMF-451. TF F4F Wildcat. Five victories 11.4.45.

K.D. Frazier Score 12 D. VMF-223. TF F4F Wildcat.

James N. Cupp Score 13 D. VMF-213. TF F4U Corsair.

Robert E. Galer CMH. Score 13 D. VMF-224. TF F4F Wildcat.

W.P. 'Guts' Marontate Score 13 D. VMF-121. TF F4F Wildcat. KIA 15.1.43 in mid-air collision with Japanese fighter.

Edward Shaw Score 13 D. VMF-213. TF F4U Corsair. KIA, details not known.

Kenneth D. Frazier Score 12.5 D. VMF-223. TF F4F Wildcat.

Loren D. Everton Score 12 D. VMF-223, VMF-212, VMF-113. TF F4F Wildcat, F4U Corsair.

Harold E. Segal Score 12 D. VMF-221. TF F4U Corsair.

Eugene A. Trowbridge Score 12 D. VMF-224. TF F4F Wildcat.

William N. Snider Score 12 D. VMF-221. TF F4U Corsair.

Philip C. Delong Score 11.17 D. VMF-212. TF F4U Corsair.

H.W. 'Indian Joe' Bauer CMH. Score 11 D. VMF-212. TF F4F Wildcat. KIA 14.11.42.

H. Stapp Donald Score 11 D. VMF-222. TF F4F Wildcat. Noted for post-war deceleration trials.

Jack E. Conger Score 10.5 D. VMF-212. TF F4F Wildcat.

Frank B. Baldwin Score 10 D. VMF-221. TF F4U Corsair.

Herbert H. Long Score 10 D. VMF-121, VMF-122, VMF-451. TF F4F Wildcat.

Thomas H. Mann Score 10 D. VMF-224, VMF-121. TF F4F Wildcat, F4U Corsair.

BIBLIOGRAPHY

A Fighter Pilot (Tim Johnston), *Tattered Battlements, a Malta Diary*, Peter Davies, London, 1943.

Beurling, George, and Roberts, Leslie, *Malta Spitfire*, Arms & Armour Press, London, 1971.

Bickers, Richard T., *Ginger Lacey, Fighter Pilot*, Robert Hale Ltd, London, 1962.

—— and others, *The Battle of Britain*, Salamander Books, London, 1990.

Bowyer, Chaz, *Hurricane at War*, Ian Allan, Shepperton, 1974.

Braham, J.R.D., *Scramble!*, Frederick Muller, London, 1961.

Brennan, Paul; Hesselyn, Ray; and Bateson, Henry, *Spitfires over Malta*, Jarrolds, London, 1943.

Brown, David, *Carrier Fighters*, Macdonald and Jane's, London, 1975.

Chisholm, Roderick, *Cover of Darkness*, Chatto & Windus, London, 1953.

Clarke, R. Wallace, *British Aircraft Armament, Vol. 2*, Patrick Stephens Ltd, Sparkford, Somerset, 1994.

Clostermann, Pierre, *Flames in the Sky*, Chatto & Windus, London, 1952.

Collier, Richard, *Eagle Day*, Hodder & Stoughton, London, 1966.

Cunningham, Robert E., *Aces High*, General Dynamics, Fort Worth, Texas, 1989.

—— *Tumult in the Clouds*, General Dynamics, Fort Worth, Texas, 1990.

Duke, Neville, *Test Pilot*, Allan Wingate, London, 1953.

Franks, Norman, *The Greatest Air Battle*, William Kimber, London, 1979.

—— *Sky Tiger*, William Kimber, London, 1980.

Freeman, Roger A., *The Mighty Eighth*, McDonald & Janes, London, 1970.

—— *Mustang at War*, Ian Allan, Shepperton, 1974.

Gelb, Norman, *Scramble, a Narrative History of the Battle of Britain*, Michael Joseph, London, 1986.

Gentile, Don, and Wolfert, Ira, *One-Man Air Force*, L.B.Fischer, New York, 1944.

Godfrey, John T. *The Look of Eagles*, Random House, New York, 1958.

Green, William, *Famous Fighters of the Second World War*, McDonald and Jane's, London, 1975.

Hall, Roger, *Clouds of Fear*, Bailey Bros & Swinfen Ltd, London, 1975.

Hess, William N., *The American Aces of World War II and Korea*, Arco Publishing, New York, 1968.

Johnson, Johnnie, *Wing Leader*, Chatto & Windus, London, 1956.

—— *The Story of Air Fighting*, Hutchinson, London, 1985.

Johnson, Robert S., with Caidin, Martin, *Thunderbolt!*, Rinehart, New York, 1958.

Jones, Ira, *Tiger Squadron*, W.H. Allen, London, 1954.

Mason, Francis, *Battle over Britain*, Alban Books, Norfolk, 1969.

O'Leary, Michael, *United States Naval Fighters of World War II*, Blandford Press, Poole, 1980.

Price, Alfred, *The Last Year of the Luftwaffe, May 1944 to May 1945*, Arms and Armour Press, London, 1991.

—— *Late Marque Spitfire Aces 1942–45*, Osprey, London, 1995.

—— *Early War Spitfires and Aces*, Osprey, London, 1996.

Rawnsley, C.F., and Wright, Robert, *Night Fighter*, Collins, London, 1957.

Richey, Paul, *Fighter Pilot*, Arrow Books, 1955.

Sakai, Saburo. *Samurai*, NEL, London, 1969.

Shores, Christopher, *Regia Aeronautica*, Squadron/Signal Publications, Michigan, 1976.

—— *Duel for the Sky*, Blandford Press, Poole, Dorset, 1985.

—— and Williams, Clive, *Aces High*, Grub Street, London, 1994.

—— Ring, Hans, and Hess, William, *Fighters over Tunisia*, Neville Spearman, London, 1975.

Sims, Edward H., *American Aces of World War II*, McDonald, London, 1958.

—— *The Fighter Pilots*, Cassell & Co, London, 1967.

—— *Fighter Tactics and Strategy 1914–1970*, Cassell & Co, London, 1972.

Spick, Mike, *Fighter Pilot Tactics*, Patrick Stephens Ltd, Sparkford, Somerset, 1983.

—— *The Ace Factor*, Airlife, Shrewsbury, 1988.

—— *All-Weather Warriors*, Arms & Armour Press, London, 1994.

—— *Luftwaffe Fighter Aces*, Greenhill Books, London, 1996.

Tillman, Barrett, *Wildcat Aces of World War 2*, Osprey, London, 1995.

Walton, Frank E., *Once They Were Eagles*, University Press of Kentucky, 1986.

Winton, John, *Air Power at Sea 1939–45*, Sidgewick and Jackson, London, 1976.

Wood, Derek, and Dempster, Derek, *The Narrow Margin*, Arrow Books, London, 1969.

Other Sources

AAHS Journal, Summer 1970, 'Anatomy of an Air Battle' by Thomas G. Miller.

Aeroplane Monthly, September 1996, article by John Alcorn.

Air Enthusiast (various issues).

Air International (various issues).

Feasibility Study, Fighter Pilot Effectiveness, McDonnell Douglas Astronautics, St Louis, April 1977.

Naval Aviation News, May–June 1986.

RAF Flying Review and *Flying Review International* (various issues).

Top Gun Magazine, 1982, 'Fire, Movement and Tactics' by Major (since Colonel) Barry D. Watts USAF.

INDEX